FLOW OF GRACE:

THE LIFE OF WILLIAM M. CARRIGAN, PADRE PIO'S BEST AMERICAN FRIEND

AVA R. MONTES

ISBN: 979-8-9913383-0-1 (Paperback)

Front cover image by Makena Duffy and Ava R. Montes.
Book design by Kwame Fenyi Aidoo (deekay_1 on fiverr).

Printed by IngramSpark, Inc., in Tennessee, USA

First printing edition 2024.

IngramSpark
One Ingram Blvd.,
La Vergne, TN 37086

https://www.avamonteswriter.com/

In loving memory of Chuck Furr, whose great desire was to see his beloved uncle's life story preserved and passed on. May this biography be a perpetual reminder of Padre Pio's special connection to the Furr family history and a challenge to seek ever greater virtue.

Scan the QR code to access a full color chapter-by-chapter digital photo gallery for Flow of Grace.

There is also a feature documentary about William Carrigan, The Finger of God: The Life and Times of Bill Carrigan, directed by Makena Duffy.

More information is available at:

https://www.williamcarriganfilm.com/

CONTENTS

Foreword

By Chuck Furr

The first time I encountered William "Bill" Carrigan was at the funeral of my mother, Loretta Marie Carrigan Furr, in August of 1948.

We did not have electricity on our rented farm in Southern Minnesota, so we needed our 30-gallon kerosene barrel filled. The delivery man who brought gasoline to the previous farmer failed to empty the delivery hose. By an unintentional error, he pumped 8 gallons of gasoline along with 22 gallons of kerosene into our barrel. Unfortunately, this mixture was explosive and killed my mother.

In 1997, I became the legal guardian of my uncle Bill. My wife Marilyn and I went through over five hundred thousand pieces of paper—since my uncle wrote on many of them—to determine what was important enough to be saved. A very important communication was sent to my uncle from Padre Pio describing how devastated he was when he learned of the tragic death of my mother. Padre Pio assured my uncle that he was praying for him, my dad, and we the children!

Twenty-two years later, I determined I should write a book, using the valuable papers we had saved that provide the story recorded in this biography.

∞

My uncle Bill was the American Red Cross Field Director in Italy. After the German Nazis were defeated in San Giovanni Rotondo, an area near Foggia, two American GIs asked my uncle if he would take them to that location so they could attend the Catholic Mass celebrated by Padre Pio. My uncle had never heard of this priest who bore the stigmata—the wounds of Christ—on his hands, feet, and side. At the time of the consecration, Padre Pio went into spiritual ecstasy and this moment changed my uncle's life! He said, "I knew we had a destiny together."

Bill set a good example in many ways. For one thing, although he was a wealthy man, he never thought of himself in that way nor displayed himself as such; in other words, he was a very humble person in that respect.

He was very family oriented, so his patriotic Fourth of July events at Avon Hall in Washington, Virginia, were attended by thousands of families. Uncle Bill and his wife Ramona loved children, so they intentionally designed this annual event to include games for the children. Family picnicking was encouraged as well.

He could be very opinionated on certain subjects and was not hesitant to make a forceful expression of his position on such issues. An example of this was his uncompromising pro-life position. He was very proud that Christendom College always had busloads of students marching in the pro-life Roe vs. Wade demonstrations in Washington, D.C.

As far as making an impression that affected my life, actions, or position on issues, I recall one occasion when, in a serious discussion, he shared four words that changed my life. Those words were: "Just make yourself available." As a result, I found myself becoming much more willing to give of my time, talents, and treasure. I would never be able to match his financial giving, but I do consider him as an individual who illustrated his stewardship by his actions; by doing so, he caused me to desire to be like him in these regards.

The following story describes what these two spiritual men—St. Pio of Pietrelcina and William M. Carrigan—accomplished together on behalf of mankind.

Chuck Furr,
Nephew of William M. Carrigan

INTRODUCTION

The Most Important Mass Of His Life

oggia, Italy, is known today for its watermelons and tomatoes and wheat; it is an industrial hub for Southern Italy and a pleasant spot for a vacation. Home to the gorgeous, Romanesque Cathedral of Foggia, the rugged *Parco Nazionale del Gargano*, and miles of olive groves and fields, this beautiful niche in the Italian countryside has gained attention in recent times. Visitors enjoy historic sites and walk the idyllic cobbled streets. They indulge in traditional Apulian cuisine. Some travelers even laud it as an authentically Italian experience, unsullied by the tourist traps and oppressive busyness of other, more famous destinations like Rome or Naples.

In late 1943, however, it was a bomb-scarred battleground. For five months during World War II—May to September of 1943—the Allies pummeled Nazi bases in the Foggia region. Thousands of pounds of explosives detonated on fields and farms, cities and homes. Eventually, the Nazis were driven away from the area, but liberation was not without its pyrrhic price. The greater region of Foggia lost over twenty thousand civilians to Allied air raids. Those who did not abandon their homes were forced to scavenge scraps from the ruins, competing with desperate robbers and even some of the occupying soldiers for any food and valuables that had not burned in the bombings. What buildings still stood were freckled with bullet holes and missing chunks from mortars. Amid this bleak environment, Foggia and more than twenty surrounding airfields became vital bases for Allied aircraft during World War II. From landing strips in Tortorella, Amendola, Celone, and Lucera, the Allies strategically attacked Axis targets across the European continent.

Late in 1943, only a couple weeks before Christmas Eve, William "Bill" Carrigan arrived in Foggia. As an assistant field director with the American Red Cross, his job was to provide logistical and personal support for the Allied soldiers stationed in Foggia.

The forty-one-year-old Catholic layman was getting his bearings in the region when two soldiers approached him with an unusual request. They explained to Bill that some of their pals heard stories about a mystic in the region. Supposedly, this priest was marked by the stigmata, the five wounds of Christ. The troops wanted to verify these curious tales for themselves, but the Army did not lend cars out for extra-military pleasure trips. They appealed to Bill for Red Cross transportation instead.[1]

The story piqued Bill Carrigan's interest. He arranged to personally drive the twenty-five-and-a-half-mile route to San Giovanni Rotondo. Gusts of wind blew millions of snowflakes into the windshield as they took the slippery, winding roads up Monte Calvo—the mountain named "bald-headed" for its barren, rocky terrain.[2] Winter soon smoothed over the Italian countryside with ten inches of pure white. Less than an hour later, Carrigan and his soldiers arrived in San Giovanni Rotondo. They hurried through the barren courtyard to the Old Church of *Santa Maria delle Grazie.* The church and attached monastery were plain: a simple white facade with an arched main door and a small, ceramic image of the Blessed Virgin holding the child Christ. It seemed difficult to imagine an extraordinarily holy man living here.

Bill and the soldiers entered the monastery quietly. A Capuchin Franciscan friar, dressed in a dark habit with a knotted rope cincture, noticed them and ushered them into the chapel. The little church contained a main altar and three smaller side altars. Though it could hold about eighty people, fewer than ten locals sat among the resident friars.

Mass had already begun, so the American visitors quietly knelt on the cold tile floor. Bill found himself in a spot where he had a full view of the priest facing the altar.[3] This priest was short—only five foot, five inches tall—with a large nose, a gray beard, and splotches of dark red blood on both his palms. His serious eyebrows sat heavily over his deep brown eyes, which were cast down to his paten and chalice, to the Holy Eucharist. All his movements were slow and deliberate, imbued with a special reverence that revealed his high esteem for the Sacrament. Yet every motion seemed to cause him great physical pain.

The Capuchin friar celebrating Mass was St. Pio of Pietrelcina. In that Mass, his incredible miracles and his closeness to Christ were yet unknown to Bill Carrigan, but it did not take long for the assistant field director to notice a true holiness which he had never before witnessed. He related the moment which changed his life forever:

> In that hour, in that cold sanctuary, I saw a priest at the altar who touched me as no other priest had ever impressed me. As I watched him carry out the consecration of the bread and wine, I felt a deep sense of the sacredness of this central act of the Mass. I felt drawn to the altar...in a way I never had before. As I watched him, I felt he was truly bringing the body and blood of Christ to the altar. I felt that Padre Pio was with Christ as he rested his pain-ridden body against the altar... I wanted to bring my family, friends, soldiers, all, to him that he may at the same time petition our Lord for their safety and needs. In that hour, there was little doubt in my mind that I was experiencing the most important Mass of my life. I came into that sanctuary without the slightest knowledge of who or what Padre Pio was. I arrived at my own conclusion completely on my own.[4]

As deeply impactful as that moment was for Bill Carrigan, he did not yet know how far that impact would go. Nor did he know how many graces would flow from Padre Pio's communion with God to his own soul and the souls of those he encountered later on. Yet, before the final prayers of that Mass offered in the midst of a bitter, world-shaking war, Bill knew without a doubt that "we had a destiny together."[5]

OVERVIEW

"The Gospel tells us to give to everyone who begs from you. As much as any man I ever knew, Bill Carrigan seems to have done exactly that."[6]

W. Shepherdson Abell, a proficient lawyer and now-retired adjunct professor at the Georgetown University Law Center, spoke these words on November 30, 2000, at the funeral service for William Maurice Carrigan. Dozens of people—unrelated strangers of different backgrounds, faiths, ages, and vocations—attended the funeral to pay their respects to a man they knew as a benevolent donor and a good friend. Yet more than anyone else, Shep Abell was privy to the impressive breadth and depth of Bill's philanthropy. He had known Bill in life and had helped manage Bill's estate in death.

Just by looking at him, William "Bill" Carrigan seemed like an ordinary man. The Iowa-born farm boy lived most of his life in Maryland and Washington, D.C. He wore round spectacles and plaid shirts. His voice had a pitch and cadence that lends itself often to the Irish and to the Transatlantic. His eyes seemed to sparkle with youthfulness, even as he aged. He possessed a witty, dry sense of humor: At ninety-six years old, he told a judge that he had just taken out an eight-year lease on a car, much to the amusement of the court.[7] In his adult years, he held a lucrative career as a businessman and property developer in the D.C.-Virginia area. He enjoyed strawberries and birdwatching and daily Mass. A Catholic layman, a prolific yet humble philanthropist, a loving husband, an amateur poet, an intellectual, a patriot, a "stern old Irishman" who led by example and who challenged people to be of service to others without compromising their beliefs—this was Bill Carrigan.[8]

After scratching the surface of who he was in the public eye, a rich spiritual life comes to light. One might even go so far as to say his Catholicism was extraordinary in its ordinariness. His marriage—a rich and satisfying spiritual union—and his devotion to the Eucharist were paramount. From his young adulthood to his death, his faith informed his life as a layman working in both religious and secular realms. Though many remembered his charity, most talked about Bill's intense devotion to St. Pio of Pietrelcina, whom he met while serving as an American Red Cross field director during World War II. In addition to being the first uniformed American to meet Padre Pio, Bill also was the great mystic's "best American friend."[9]

"His story will always be my best," Bill once wrote, "for he has made a profound impression on me which I will never be able to erase from my mind. In him there is something which proves the spiritual quality of man and proves the fact that the soul can rise to God in a very real way...You can count on him! He is credible because he is truth."[10]

In the years following World War II, when Padre Pio was almost completely unknown in America, Bill "[beat] the drums for Padre Pio's canonization," and spread word of the man he knew from the first moment to be a living saint.[11] That mission met with great success. Through Padre Pio's influence and the graces that flowed from heaven through him, any natural inclination to virtue that Bill possessed seemed to increase.

Even with such successes, Bill considered himself a conduit, not a final destination, of God's grace. He understood the weight of this responsibility and felt keenly his own incapabilities, yet he knew his duty was to take what God gave him and pass it on to others. The light is not meant to be kept under a basket, after all. Faith and works intersected for Bill, as his philanthropy found its source in a deep well of God's truth. Shep Abell attested that Bill was a "tremendously generous person" in both public and private causes, giving to schools and healthcare institutions, as well as providing "personal loans and gifts" which were too numerous to name specifically.[12] Indeed, *generous* is one word that sums up Bill's character, if a human person could be reduced to just one adjective.

Of those who received his unsparing charity, Catholic institutes of education and benevolent secular hospitals ranked high on the list. Bill "lived a vocation...that was Catholic education."[13] He delivered Mount de Sales Academy from threatening financial burdens and helped Christendom College expand into the excellent university it is today; he established trusts with the International Eye Foundation so that Latin American countries could receive eye care; he supported religious orders whose missions were to teach; he provided ways for new parishes to be built, especially in places where the Catholic Church had no establishment yet; he personally presented hundreds of talks on Padre Pio, education, and virtue.

In sum, Bill was a man of great generosity, devotion, and service. His life, compiled as fully as possible in this book, is a challenge and an inspiration to future generations. It is a record of the doings of a self-starting, married, Catholic layman who confidently lived his faith in a disturbed and increasingly secular world. And most importantly, it is a story about the flow of grace and what is possible through obedience to the guiding Finger of God.

CHAPTER ONE

A Family History and Bill's Early Life
1902–1916

∽

FAMILY HISTORY

Bill Carrigan's story starts in the midst of a great human crisis, fifty-seven years before he was born. Between 1845 and 1852, the Potato Famine, also called the Great Hunger, swept across Ireland. In the wake of this fungus-like microorganism that infected potato plants and rotted the edible part, Irish farming communities were devastated. Historians suggest that the loss of the cheapest and most accessible staple food caused the slow starvation of between one and three million Irish, many of whom were poor tenant farmers. Those who were able and lucky enough to escape Ireland numbered around one million. Among those immigrants were four individuals: Peter Carrigan, Sarah Kelley, Patrick Maguire, and Mary O'Regan.

Peter Carrigan and Sarah Kelley, Bill's paternal grandparents, immigrated to America in the mid-1840s. They found each other while in the States and married in 1854. Soon after, their growing family moved west with the wagon trains. The American West had, by this time, earned a reputation for being a promised land of abundance and prosperity, a haven for seg-regated and despised immigrants. Banking on that reputation, Peter bought a prairie schooner—a large, horse-drawn cart with tall wooden wheels and a white canvas top—which soon carried him and his family through the Mississippi Valley and over the Mississippi River to the wide prairie expanses of the western United States. After a brief stay in Wisconsin, they settled finally in Allamakee, Iowa, to farm. Here, on July 17, 1864, Micheal Patrick Carrigan was born. He was the ninth child out of twelve and the second-youngest son.

Patrick Maguire and Mary O'Regan, Bill's maternal grand-parents, followed a similar route. They immigrated, met, then married in 1851; shortly after the wedding, the Maguire couple joined thousands of others on the wagon trains and ended up in Iowa as well, most likely in Allamakee. Over a decade later, on October 29th, 1866, their ninth child and second-youngest daughter, Mary Hanora[1] Maguire, was born.

By the time Micheal Carrigan and Mary Maguire were twen-ty-five and twenty-three, respectively, they had met and become engaged. Their wedding took place on January 13, 1890, in Palo Alto County, Iowa, where they settled down. In Silver Lake township, specifically, the young couple began their homestead. Micheal was a farmer, like his father before him, and he owned land in the neighboring township–Ayrshire–where he worked.[2] Not long after marrying, Micheal and Mary Carrigan welcomed their first child, Francis. Three years later came Sarah Theresa, who was called by her second name. John, Bernard, Micheal Leo (also called by his second name), and James followed.

Only a month after his birth, in December 1900, James passed away.

The long, cold winter months were made even longer and even colder by the touch of death upon the Carrigans. The new year showed no kindness either, for an awful wave of typhoid fever struck the family in January 1901. Less than two months after the infant James' death, the Carrigan family lost six-year-old John to typhoid.

The hardworking Irish-American farming family tasted suffering in that year before William Maurice Carrigan was born. He entered the world on June 10, 1902. Nineteen days later, Micheal and Mary baptized young Bill at Sacred Heart Catholic Church, the oldest Catholic parish in Ayrshire, Iowa. For two years, Bill was the youngest child, until Loretta came along; she was followed three years later by the baby of the family, Margaret. The seven surviving Carrigan children grew up on Midwestern prairies and farmlands.

❦

GROWING UP ON THE PRAIRIE

Though much of Bill's early childhood belongs to God's memory alone, several stories remain. These brief vignettes, recalled either by Bill himself or by those who heard his tales later on, paint a vivid picture of life on the prairie and the impactful lessons he learned as a youngster. Little is said about his faith as a child, but his Irish heritage and prompt baptism point toward Christianity being at least present in his upbringing.

Ayrshire, the nearest neighboring township where the schools and hospital resided, was a community split approximately half Catholic and half Protestant, "where people celebrated their own religion and respected their neighbor's" —a sufficient backdrop for learning about God.[3] One's environment shapes the heart and mind, especially between birth and eighteen years old; so it was with Bill.

∽

His earliest memory, a tender moment and one that influenced him long into his life, was of his father Micheal. On a bright, spring morning—a Sunday—Micheal carried Bill in his arms as they meandered "along the wood line where hundreds of black-birds were singing a great heavenly song of praise to the day."[4] Every once in a while, Micheal Carrigan stopped to point out to his little boy the birds raising their voices to the clear blue sky. "I think that day," Bill noted, "I learned to love the woods and singing birds. I became enveloped in all of nature... I soon learned to walk by myself along the rabbit paths in the woods."[5] The natural world captivated Bill, and Silver Lake township in Palo Alto certainly had no shortage of beauty to occupy his early years. The rippling waves of yellow grasses on the endlessly flat prairie and copses of bur oak served as his first playground. In the summers, the Carrigan children went to the rivers nearby to catch crayfish along the streambed. The settlers enjoyed swimming and fishing in Silver Lake, the 648-acre natural glacier lake from which the township takes its name. In the winter, ice skating on Silver Lake, about one mile from the Carrigan house, was a popular pastime. Children, including Bill, helped with farm tasks such as milking the cows, a chore expected of boys as young as six. The community was strong. The grown men and their older sons farmed and hunted and trapped for furs; younger children received education from their mothers and local teachers. Spirits were tempered and toughened by the cruelty and glory of the elements.

In the winter of 1905, when Bill was three years old, the Carrigan family received a visitor: Bernard Jacob Carrigan.[6] Bernard, Bill's paternal uncle, lived near Wild Horse, Colorado, at the time, working as a sheep rancher. He made the frigid journey, over seven hundred miles long, to stay with his extended family in Silver Lake. Little Bill was thrilled to meet his uncle from the Wild West. "I wanted to do something," Bill recollected, "to call his attention, I guess, to me."[7] So, he concocted a plan. Stored upstairs was a large box full of hickory nuts that had been harvested earlier that winter. That seemed like the perfect item of interest for a show-and-tell with Uncle Bernard.

Determined to execute his grand plan, Bill stole away from the excitement and family chatter. He located the box, only to find that it was far heavier than he expected it to be—so heavy, in fact, that he could hardly lift it.[8] Not to be deterred, he managed to pull the box into his lap. On the precipice of the top step he perched himself and began the careful descent, scooting down one step at a time on his backside. Then the box slipped. From the third step all the way to the bottom floor, the box and cascade of hickory nuts bounced down with "such a racket that ... everybody in the house was attracted" to Bill's activities.[9] A painstaking chore it was to pick up all the nuts—and with a wry laugh, Bill added: "I guess I was the biggest nut of all!"[10]

Of his childhood recollections of life at the Silver Lake farm, Bill considered one memory the most important of all. It happened in July or August of 1906, when he was four years old. The experience made an indelible mark on his soul.

One warm, summer morning, the Silver Lake farmers busied themselves threshing the grain fields. Bill, his mother, and his baby sister Marie were the only ones at home. From somewhere in the house, the ever-curious Bill discovered a box of matches and, late that morning, made his way to his father's barn to play with them. Bill clambered to the top of the ladder to the hay loft, which held freshly harvested hay everywhere except where he sat. In a personal note penned nearly eight decades later, he retold in great detail what happened next:

> I scratched a match and it flared up so fast I
> dropped it. One spear of hay was near it; it caught
> fire. I did not have [the] sense to pull it away. I saw
> it creep along the stem to some others and then I
> sensed it was going to burn the big pile. I decided

to crawl down. I was so scared I ran to the house—as I neared it my mother ran out shouting, "The barn is on fire."

I turned to look. Smoke was belching out of the big open door of the loft. I ran inside ... and crawled under a bed where I [stayed] the rest of the day. I never knew what happened out there but the threshers all came in from the field to fight it; however, it was doomed.

Some time shortly after dark, my father came looking for me, and when I came out from under the bed, he asked me where I had been all day ... I said, "In this room."

I don't remember that he asked me if I had anything to do with the fire. No one accused me. The next day my brother Leo and I were sent to work going through the ashes, picking up the nails and bolts to be used for the new barn. The neighbors came in from time to time during the summer and helped Dad build the new barn. The explanation I heard for years afterwards was that ... the hot sun shining through the glass started the fire. Years later, I tried to tell the family that I burned down the barn but no one believed me (a sin I have never paid for).[11]

Though Bill never outright explained why he considered the barn burning his most important childhood experience, it is not difficult to guess how that might have affected him. Perhaps he learned the value of being honest. Maybe it was his first lesson in taking responsibility for his actions right away, despite the consequences. No matter what lessons he drew from it, the incident remained in his mind for decades.

∾

On the prairie, winters were harsh. Temperatures in December and January between 1902 and 1910 ranged from a frosty 28 degrees to a bitingly frigid 6.2 degrees.[12] With wind chill from northern gusts howling across flat land, the temperatures felt even colder. Every snowstorm whited out the few landmarks rising above the prairie; keeping warm was imperative. It was, as Bill claimed, a different world.[13]

To his youngest son Micheal Carrigan charged the responsibility of stocking their house with firewood, which included cutting it, collecting it, and bringing it to the hearth.[14] On one particular evening, while a blizzard raged around the homestead, little Bill retired to bed, having forgotten to bring in the kindling wood. At some point during the night, Micheal woke Bill up. "He had a lantern in his hand," Bill said, "and he called me: '*Billy. Billy. Where's the kindling wood?*'" [15] Bill had no choice but to get up; not doing one's job was not tolerated, so into the below-freezing temperatures and howling winds he ventured. The snow drifts loomed six feet high and even with a lantern, he could barely see. "But," he continued, "I had to go out there and climb into the trees. That was the longest night I ever had in my life."[16] He quickly learned that responsibility should not be shirked; when given a job, "I don't feel like it," was not an acceptable answer.

∽

When Bill was just ten years old, another tragedy struck the Carrigan family, and this time, it was far worse than the barn fire. Rather than suffering the loss of a building and grain, they suffered the loss of their oldest daughter, Sarah Theresa Carrigan. The accident occurred on November 29, 1912, the day after Thanksgiving. As she normally did in the afternoons, Theresa climbed into her horse-drawn buggy and departed from the county schoolhouse where she taught.[17] She drove down the dirt roads between homes and supply stores. As she approached the railroad crossing that cut through Ayrshire, her horse suddenly spooked. Before she could control the animal, it bolted across the cattle guard, hauling the buggy—and her—into the vicinity of an oncoming train.[18]

The train did not stop quickly enough. Theresa was "dragged under [the] cow catcher" for a short distance.[19] When responders found her, her body was severely bruised and her back was broken in several places, as was one leg. According to the surgeon on the scene, she was lucky that no wheels had passed over her body; she was not cut or dismembered in any way. She died almost instantly.[20]

The circumstances around her tragic death were strongly contested. Who, if anyone, was at fault? Bill and Theresa's mother sued the Minneapolis and St. Louis Railroad Company for $15,000 (equivalent to approximately $465,000 in 2024) for negligence.[21] The plaintiffs and witnesses were Mary, her children who testified, a few of her neighbors, and some locals who were living and working near the railroad at the time. Bill was lucky that he did not actually see his sister's death; instead, he had watched and counted twenty-six freight cars pass by his house, which was only a half-mile from the crossing where Theresa was struck. His witness lent assistance to the claim that the train did not sufficiently stop before the crossing.[22]

After a week-long court battle, and despite railway employees vigorously claiming that they had followed proper procedure, the jury vote was eleven-to-one in favor of the Carrigan family.[23] Even though Theresa's death had occurred a year prior to the court proceedings, the pain of losing a child does not quickly fade, and the case most certainly drew out that sorrow. The grieving mother was awarded $5000 (an equivalent of around $155,000 in 2024 and only one-third of what she sued for).[24] A pittance for the loss of their beloved daughter and sister.

Sarah Theresa, the third Carrigan child to suffer an untimely death, was buried in the Calvary Cemetery in Ayrshire after her funeral. This experience of tragedy exposed Bill at a young age to the unique suffering that marks the loss of a loved one. Though nothing is known beyond the court case about the Carrigan family's reaction to the trying situation, it is not hard to imagine that the event shaped Bill's heart.

~

As he grew older, Bill began to seek new opportunities. In addition to the chores and responsibilities that he performed in the home and on the farm, he found enterprising ways to work for some pocket change—his first "real" work. One such example: Bill hung around "the train station near his hometown and [would] offer to wash the windows of the cabooses at the end of the trains. That's how he made his money." [25]

One of Iowa's foremost rail organizations, the Minneapolis and St. Louis Railroad Company, operated multiple lines of transit that connected Minnesota to grain-producing states further west and further south. One of their trains routinely traveled from Winthrop, Minnesota, to Fort Dodge, Iowa, passing through Ayrshire and Ruthven as it went. Bill likely trekked to one or both stops, since they were within a few miles of his home, to offer his washing services. As the train pulled into the station, he would raise his rag and bottle of washing liquid and "knock on the window and say, 'Hey, I'd be happy to clean your windows...'"[26] In return, he earned approximately ten cents per wash—not bad money for a kid in the early 1900s.[27]

In 1915, when he was around thirteen years old, Bill also discovered that he enjoyed tinkering with and fixing items that were considered unusable or lost causes. Around this time, people began throwing out their old, manual typewriters in favor of the new electric ones. Progress rendered the older style obsolete. But Bill, rather than see the machines go to waste even though they were only missing a key here or a button there, collected and fixed them.[28] In this experience with trying to restore unwanted but still functioning items, Bill learned a valuable lesson which he carried for the rest of his life: "It's the little things that need to get fixed to make the whole thing work again."[29]

∽

MOVING ON

For the first fifteen years of his life, Palo Alto and all the situations—good and bad—that came with prairie life in a railroad town shaped the youngest Carrigan boy. It toughened him, strengthened him, taught him. He learned resourcefulness, curiosity, enterprise, honesty, responsibility, independence, fortitude in the face of great loss. His formation in virtue began there, in the womb of Western America. As time passed, though, Bill began to outgrow his humble beginnings. Palo Alto County expanded and Bill entered high school in 1916, when he was fourteen years old, but he soon began to feel that life on the farm, working odd jobs, and studying were becoming monotonous. He longed for adventure—real adventure.

Chapter Two

Bill's Adventures as a Rancher
1917 – 1921

∽

Running Away To Become A Cowboy

In April of 1917, his sophomore year of high school when he was fifteen years old, Bill decided he was tired of his education. His grades were very poor, he was sick of attending school, and he wanted to escape the perceived boredom of his life in Palo Alto.[1] Besides, he felt confident that he knew everything an education had to offer, since he had learned algebra, a little Latin, and ancient history.[2] His faith did not seem to be a significant part of his life, either. So he concocted a plan to run away and become a cowboy.

This was not the first time Bill had tried leaving home. Once before, when he was less than ten years old, he tried to run away. He got no farther than the milk stand at the end of their farmhouse road before his mother caught on and sent Theresa after him. When she found him, he fled to the next farm over, but the neighbors threshing their crops noticed the boy and informed Micheal Carrigan. Bill was promptly returned home.

This time, though, he meant to really, truly leave. He knew he had extended family on his mother's side, the Kelleys, who owned a ranch in South Dakota only nine or ten miles outside De Smet, a humble prairie community now famous for being the hometown of *Little House on the Prairie* author Laura Ingalls Wilder. While most other ranches had converted their grazing pastures to grain fields, the Kelleys' ranch remained one of the last true cattle ranches in that area.[3]

Like many Americans who were pushing farther and farther toward the Pacific, Bill was enamored with the idea of going west. And like many American boys, he was especially enamored with the cowboy-rancher lifestyle that seemed like a ticket to freedom and adventure. Leaving home at only fifteen years old was unusual in those days. Boys—particularly farming boys—did not typically set out on their own before eighteen years old. But Bill was determined to carve his own path. To earn money, he worked odd jobs after school: "Mowing grass and fixing fences and shoveling snow [and] washing windows."[4] From most jobs, he earned twenty-five cents apiece.

Soon, he collected the necessary eight dollars to purchase a train ticket from Ruthven to Sioux Falls, South Dakota—the closest major train station to De Smet at the time.

At first, he kept his plan a secret. When he eventually confided in his older brother, Leo, he was met with uproarious laughter.[5] Leo did not believe that Bill would actually do such a thing, and neither did any of the others who heard about it. When Leo hinted to their mother that Bill intended to go west, she laughed too.[6]

The one person from whom Bill deliberately withheld information, however, was his father. As he himself said, Micheal "wouldn't laugh. He would know that when Bill Carrigan said he was going to do something, he would do it. And he would object. He would put me straight, right then and there."[7] Instead, Bill waited until he had boarded the morning train to Sioux Falls before he penned a letter to his father, stating where he was going and what type of work he intended to take up with the Kelleys. "And he didn't say anything about it," Bill mused. "I never got an answer to that letter. Neither did he send for me, which I expected he would."[8]

Bill arrived in Sioux Falls that same afternoon. Immediately upon his arrival, things seemed to go wrong. No train ran to De Smet until the next day, the cool April night was fast approaching, and he did not have a proper coat to keep him warm, so he started walking along the road, evidently thinking he would trek the nine-odd miles to the Kelleys' ranch. Mercifully, a few men in an old Model T jalopy noticed him and offered him a ride. They made it to De Smet around sunset. Bill Carrigan was officially in the Wild West.

His first real introduction to the west was a small restaurant he stopped in for dinner.[9] Called "The Owl," the diner held no more than ten stools for patrons and, oddly, no actual patrons. It was empty except for the man behind the bar top. "The very name made it kind of wild," Bill said.[10] Not to be intimidated, he struck up a conversation with the man: Did he know the Kelley family? Could he tell him about them? Before leaving home, Bill already had a vague notion of his ranching relatives: John Kelley had owned the ranch, but had died some time ago.[11] Through the man at The Owl, Bill quickly learned that his cousins, Alice and Lawrence Kelley, now worked the ranch—the biggest one around, sporting several hundred cattle. The Kelleys were also livestock auctioneers, the best in the state.[12] As the man talked, he fixed Bill an enormous T-bone steak on a platter. Upon handing it to the hungry boy, he declared, "I'm going to give you this and I'm going to charge the Kelleys for it."[13] This Bill recalled with a chuckle.

Though his meal satisfied his hunger, Bill still faced the problem of getting to the Kelleys' home. Luckily, the answer to that issue walked through the restaurant doors: "In came a fellow by the name of Ax Anderson, another name that [spoke of] the sharpness of the West," Bill recalled.[14] Ax Anderson, with whom Bill became briefly acquainted, did not look around. He simply sat down on a stool and ordered his own steak dinner without giving Bill a single glance. Only when the barman suggested that Ax take Bill up to the Kelleys' home did he take any interest in the boy. Following a momentary interrogation about who Bill was and what he wanted, Ax agreed, and they set off for the ranch. The stars, the only light besides the distant glow of Ax's house on a hill, shone brightly in the cold night.

At some point during the ride, Bill asked Ax not to mention to the Kelleys that he was a relative, or to even introduce him. He probably wanted to be seen as *only* someone looking for work, perhaps to avoid being laughed at again or sent home. Ax initially honored this desire. When they arrived at the Kelleys' farm around midnight, Ax let himself into the kitchen door of the massive stone house without knocking and joined Bill's two cousins and their Swedish foreman without mentioning his passenger at all. Bill remembered gathering his singular bag of belongings, following Ax into the house, and then "standing there like a dummy ... so I got a chair and sat down ... on the sideline, just in the dark."[15]

For half an hour, Bill listened to Ax and the Kelleys discuss ranch matters, until Ax finally decided it was time to leave. As Bill told it, Ax put his hand on the doorknob, and then turned around and said: "'Here's a lad I've brought over. I thought you might give him a job because he's out here looking for a job.' And one of my cousins said, 'Oh, gee, we just hired a couple fellows today. I don't know if we can put anybody else on.' ... Ax then said, 'I believe he's a cousin of yours from Iowa.'"[16]

Bill's cousins, who had been leaning back in their chairs with their feet up, both jumped up at the same time and shouted, "Mike Carrigan's boy?"[17]

"Mike Carrigan's boy," Bill laughed. "I tell you, I was home."[18]

The very next day, Bill began to live the life of hard work and adventure that he had desired. April marked the time of the year when the Kelley ranchers rounded up their cattle. For his first ten days on the ranch, he donned the "big leather chaps that the cowboys wore" and rode day in and day out, helping round up the cattle on the plains.[19] He helped brand the cattle and sell them in De Smet. He even helped respond to an emergency.

A storm swept through that summer, resulting in broken fences and escaped cows. Bill and the Kelley ranchers had no choice but to hunt all day for their lost livestock. The beasts ate a visible swath through "field after field of corn and grain," leaving no shortage of ruin in their path.[20] With no small difficulty, Bill and the ranchers rounded up all the cattle and brought them out of the damaged fields. With a chuckle, Bill said: "I don't know how my cousins ever settled with the neighbors regarding the loss of their crops, but [they] must have been near [law]suit, or maybe they brought out the shotguns."[21] Nevertheless, the cattle were brought under control and the damage restituted.

When he wasn't working, Bill was out enjoying another aspect of the cowboy life: breaking and training his very own wild horse, which he named "Star," after the white pattern on its nose. The man who sold it advised Bill never to let the beast loose, because it would run and never come back. Bill kept this advice; he housed Star in a double stall until it became accustomed to him.

An incident early on in Star's training gave Bill a brush with death. One day, young Bill brought his bronco a pail of oats for a normal feeding. His pail had no handle, so he held it by the sides in front of his chest. And good thing too—spooked by an accidental brush of the flank, Star kicked out at Bill with his rear hooves, punching holes in the pail and sending the teenager flying backwards into the stall wall.[22] At first, Bill was too stunned to do much, but when he regained his wits, he was angry! "My first thought was to get a switch and give him a doggone good whipping, but then I thought no, I won't do that. And I got another pail of oats and went around this time to his front ... and fed him from the front."[23]

For three weeks, Bill kept up this feeding routine, but the real test was whether Star could be untied without fleeing or kicking again. After a late night out in town with his extended family, Bill realized he had forgotten to bring Star into the barn. The horse had been out all day, tied to the fence, with no food except a little hay he could reach, and no water. Bill decided to take a chance. He untied the halter around Star's neck and allowed the horse to roam the fenced-in yard, to find his way to the water tank and the rest of the hay.[24] The next morning, Bill rose to perform his duties (including taking care of a cow that was producing brown milk).[25] Milking pail in hand, he made his way toward the fenced-in yard. To his great surprise, Star had not escaped. In fact, the black bronco—associating Bill's milking pail with food—came up behind him and nuzzled him, pushing him along with his nose. "I never had to tie him up again," Bill said proudly.[26] "We'd go riding in the evenings, sometimes after the day's work, and that horse was fantastic. It did almost anything I wanted it to do. We were great companions."[27]

Bill learned to ride his trusty steed and drove cattle like a real rancher. He also learned how to operate a car. His cousins bought a Buick and insisted that Bill learn to drive—at fifteen years old, no less! "And those old things," Bill said with distaste, "you could strip the gears with no trouble at all, and that's what I did... I didn't drive the car anymore. And I was glad of that, because I didn't want to drive the car."[28] He was not too keen on it after ruining the manual transmission. Cars just did not handle the same as wild broncos!

RANCHER LIFE DURING WORLD WAR I

In 1917, America was already three years deep into World War I. Noticeably absent from Bill's childhood recollections were mentions of the Great War; it seemed the effects of the international conflict did not reach the Kelleys in an impactful way. Nevertheless, the ranchers did have some exposure to homegrown support efforts through the American Red Cross. Around the Fourth of July—about four months after he arrived in De Smet—Bill noticed a "very interesting thing happening all through the Middle West: barn dances... Every Saturday night, there was a big barn dance someplace."[29] These community events existed primarily to raise money for relief aid going overseas, but they secondarily brought people together for an evening of patriotism and fun. One afternoon, one of Bill's relatives, Zita, returned from school without a date for the dance the following evening. She suggested that Bill go with her, which he did. Thus began his first encounters with the American Red Cross, with which he would serve approximately three decades later.

Bill experienced the dances positively. There was always music, always someone to "play the fiddle and the drum," he said.[30] The barn dance he and Zita attended on Independence

Day involved even more music. The two young ranchers were eager to go to this special event. The only trouble was, no one else was home at the time, and they had no means of transportation. Their neighbor, who was also away from home, did have a gorgeous team of horses and a carriage, however. "A driving team," Bill mentioned, "was really like a Cadillac today and, of course, there was nobody around ... and they were the only transportation we could get. So we just borrowed."[31] Bill, very comfortable with horses, readied the team and hooked them to the carriage. Soon, he and Zita were driving the forty miles (one way!) to the Independence Day barn dance. The festivities lasted all through the night.[32] By the time the intrepid Bill and Zita arrived home, the sun had risen over the horizon.

During the trip back, Bill wondered many times what punishment he would receive for taking the horses and carriage without permission. The night had been so enjoyable; the worry about the neighbors' reaction spoiled the trip home. "But," Bill recalled, "they never said a word to me... I put the horses away, and that was it. Nobody ever said a word to us."[33]

He and Zita attended several more dances over that summer, when they could break away from work. Work on the ranch hardly ever slowed. The very same day that Bill returned from the Independence Day barn dance, he was sent into the fields to plant corn without even a few minutes of sleep. The field was enormous, and he was tasked with marking straight lines with his planter. A rod extended out from the side so that, while the planter was laying one row of corn, the rod marked where the next, evenly spaced row would go. When Bill reached one end of the field, he would have to turn around and go back the other way. But exhaustion and trying to drive a team of horses with a planter behind did not mix well:

> I was about halfway across the field ... and I heard some shouting. The other two fellows were ... some distance from me. And I looked around and I realized I had fallen asleep, and we were about two rows over to the left from where we should have been! And they were trying to let me know to get back in line. Well, of course, when they started to plow the corn, they had to plow a lot of it out, because I really messed that one up![34]

Despite a few costly mistakes, Bill's help on the ranch was greatly appreciated, and he fit in well. He seemed suited to the job, set on becoming a rancher like the Kelleys. Nothing seemed to discourage him—not hardship, not accidents, not war, nothing.

On October 1, 1917, about six months after Ax Anderson introduced him to the Kelleys, a surprise came to Bill: he finally received a letter from his father. The news brought dismay to the whole ranch. Micheal Carrigan had broken an arm and had no sons left at home to help him harvest the annual corn crop. His eldest two boys had already moved out and started their own families. Bernard had been drafted into World War I, and it seemed likely that Leo would be drafted as well. Bill was his father's last resort. He needed to return home.

Bill felt conflicted about the request. For one thing, he enjoyed the ranching work. For another, the Kelleys depended on his help. He was "part of the operation" and received the opportunity to become a rancher himself.[35] The Kelleys were quite angry with Micheal for expecting Bill to return. They offered Bill every chance to stay, even telling him, "We are old timers here ... we're in the auctioneering business. Running the ranch is not our business anymore."[36]

Though the prospect of potentially owning the Kelley ranch in the future was tempting, Bill knew he had a duty to his father and to his family's livelihood more than to the ranch. He could not let all his father's corn crops go to waste in the oncoming winter, nor could he let his father struggle through harvesting alone with only one working arm. If it upset him to leave the ranch, Bill did not elaborate much on it. He told the Kelleys, "Well, what can I do? Dad wants me home," and reluctantly said goodbye.[37]

◇◇◇

RETURNING TO SCHOOL

Nine days after Micheal's letter arrived, Bill set to work in his father's fields. From October 10 to Thanksgiving Eve, Bill harvested and husked the corn crop. He pulled the last wagonload of corn into the barn just as a snowstorm darkened the evening sky and covered the fields in a sheet of white.[38] He shoveled every last ear of corn out of the wagon, which caused such soreness in his left arm—his dominant hand—that "I carried my arm in a sling from Thanksgiving Day until Christmas. 'Course, I could take it out and do some little things with it. But it was more comfortable in a sling."[39] No wild adventures for Bill during this time; his arm needed to recover. It gave the sixteen-year-old boy time to consider his future, now that he was out of ranching. Over Christmas, he thought often about what to do, and after the holidays passed, he told his father, "I think I ought to go back to school."[40]

The decision came on the heels of much contemplation and personal growth over his few months in South Dakota. Though the Kelleys taught him many lessons, the most important wisdom he obtained was from the Kelleys' Swedish foreman. As Bill told it: "The one thing I think I got mostly from the Swede was that I didn't know anything! That was the best lesson I ever got."[41] Humbled and aware of just how much knowledge and experience he lacked, Bill figured that going back to high school in Ruthven was the most logical option.

Before he could finish his secondary education, however, the Carrigan family uprooted from Iowa. In June of 1919, seeking better farmland, Micheal Carrigan bought a modest farm in Pipestone, Minnesota, a town named for the red stone quarries used by at least eleven Native American tribes for making their sacred pipes.[42] In January of 1920, the Carrigans made Pipestone their permanent home. Everyone traveled northeast to the forty-three-acre farm—everyone, that is, except Bill. Now nearly eighteen years old, he had partially completed his junior year, and he did not want to interrupt his studies again. Rather than move right away, he stayed in Ruthven to complete the year before following his family.[43]

Once settled in Pipestone, Bill enrolled in a new high school, which he considered bigger and better than the one he attended previously. Though official records of his education, including the name of the Pipestone high school, are lost to time, it is most likely that Bill graduated in 1921, at nineteen years old. But before that happened, he experienced one more formative undertaking. During his senior year, an interesting opportunity stretched Bill's abilities to lead and work. The senior class expressed interest in establishing a school paper. The principal, a man called Tibbets whom Bill described as "flat-footed as all get-out," completely opposed the idea.[44] Perhaps Principal Tibbets thought the seniors were incapable of such a venture, or maybe he disliked the amount of money it would cost the school. Either way, he made his disapproval known.

Luckily for the senior class, a teacher named Miss Winn stepped up to support the entrepreneurial students. Bill considered her a "terrific individual."[45] Miss Winn told Principal Tibbets that "the senior class would take full financial responsibility" for starting and upkeeping the school paper.[46] The school itself need not expend any funds for the project. Her intervention was enough to sway Principal Tibbets' mind and he agreed, though with reluctance. Bill was likely pleased, but Miss Winn was not through. She had something more to say:

Almost in the same breath she turned to me and said,
"You are going to be the manager of this paper." I
don't know where she got the idea that I could be
business manager of that paper. I went home that
night and I had a very bad night. I dreamed that I
went back to school, and that we had got the paper
started, and it was a complete flop. So it was not a
very happy thing when I went back to school the
next day. I went to her and told her, "I can't take
this job." She said, "You already have it."[47]

Bill had no other choice but to move forward as the business
manager of the paper, in spite of his trepidation and fear of failure.
Under his guidance, the senior students collectively named the
paper *The Winnewissa Ripple*, after the local waterfall and river
which, in 1937, received recognition as a national monument.

Before the class could give any positive report for the
endeavor, they needed a method of garnering attention, someone to print the paper, and enough subscriptions to finance
the business. Bill did everything in his power to make sure he
did not fail in his job or disappoint his classmates and Miss
Winn. He approached all the businesses in town and asked if
they would purchase ad space. With the help of a creditor, he
made a deal with the town's newspaper press to print *The Winnewissa Ripple*. "I didn't know what it would cost," Bill noted. "I
didn't know what it was worth. But evidently [the creditor and
printers] were fairly reasonable with us; they didn't try to cheat

anybody."[48] As the final phase of production, he and the rest of his classmates put on a subscription drive. They worked on the newspaper all year; Principal Tibbets did not bother them.

During the seniors' graduation ceremony, Bill, as *The Ripple*'s manager, presented a report to the entire school about the paper's success. On the auditorium stage in front of everyone, highly aware of Principal Tibbets' presence behind him, Bill gave a short speech:

> I likened the success of the paper to the planting of corn. You put the seed in, and then they grow, and then [you] fertilize it, you coach it along, cultivate it, and it grows into a big stalk, and then it has several ears of corn on it. Well, I said that we have successfully put on the paper, got the paper launched, and we had a very good subscription list... Our total cost for the year was four hundred dollars and we had about a hundred dollars left in the bank.[49]

In short—a resounding success, with significant funds remaining. Principal Tibbets then approached and placed an arm around Bill's shoulders. "This," the principal announced, "is the kind of thing we want to do at our school."[50] Forgotten was his strong opposition to the school paper. Instead, he wanted to take credit as if it had been his idea all along!

Moving Forward

Throughout his time as a rancher in South Dakota and his final years in a Minnesota high school, Bill matured into a competent young man. His youth was filled with tough lessons and hard work, but "work was a joy," he recalled.[51] Just as the wilderness formed his childhood, so his own determination and independence shaped his teenage years. What he learned in his boyhood laid the foundations for the important endeavors he later undertook as an adult. After graduating high school in 1921, many possibilities and choices awaited him. He just had to choose which path he wanted to take.

CHAPTER THREE

Discernment and Business Affairs
1921 – 1937

∾

LIFE AFTER HIGH SCHOOL

After his high school graduation, Bill's life seemed erratic in that he did not have a straight and pre-formed path to follow. Unlike many twenty-first century youths, he did not go directly to collegiate education. Instead, he took several gap years and worked. Thus began the most experimental period of his life. He did not settle for longer than one or two years in a specific job, or even a specific location, jumping from the Midwest to Arizona to California to Washington, D.C. Most of his activities during this time (about 1921 to about 1923) are unknown except for some of his young adult business exploits, his vocational discernment, and two of his earliest—and most notable—charitable works.

After high school, Bill attempted two vastly different career paths. In 1922, when he was twenty years old, he worked for a short time with the National Guard fighting forest fires in Minnesota. Then, in the summer of 1923, he gained possession of a music shop, most likely in Minnesota, which took the skills he had learned on the Kelley ranch and with *The Winnewissa Ripple* to a new and more vigorous level. As Bill retold it, the owner specialized in pianos and the store was a "one-man show," where the owner would use his shop primarily for storage and spend his workdays traversing the countryside, selling pianos.[1] To transport a purchased piano, the owner would winch the instrument into the back of his flatbed Ford jalopy, drive back out into the countryside, and help the buyers bring the piano into their homes. For two or three weeks, Bill participated in this business model. Then, unexpectedly, the owner told Bill that "he had to go to the hospital for a major operation" and would therefore be absent all summer.[2] Bill received the bank book and the vague instructions to "keep the place open and keep as much record as you can."[3] If any payment came in, Bill was to take it to the bank. If he had any questions, the owner's wife would be available to help. "He just gave me the keys and walked away," Bill said. "I hardly knew this fellow!"[4]

With the shop entirely in his possession, Bill began to form a vision. Determined to do the best job he could while the owner was away, he set about executing his plan to improve the shop's business model. He proposed a mutually beneficial deal to a nearby music college: the store would provide advertising space and refer musicians, and in return, the college would offer sheet music to the shop.[5] The deal was struck. Bill cleaned the shop's front windows, which were completely opaque with grime, and created eye-catching window displays with the new sheet music to entice customers in.

Just a few months earlier, the song "Yes, We Have No Bananas" by Frank Silver and Irving Cohn had been released. It topped the charts for five whole weeks and had become popular by the summertime. "So," Bill said, "I sent away for the whole orchestration, and I gave it to the local band to play. And Lord's sakes, I could hardly keep sheet music in the place."[6]

With Bill in charge, the shop did not stop at selling sheet music and pianos. Bill made the decision (without contacting the shop's owner!) to contract with a radio company to sell their products in the music shop. Soon, he sold phonographs and radios as well as pianos and sheet music. The owner, as Bill reported, was amazed and greatly pleased by the shop's success, so much so that he actually offered Bill full ownership. "You're doing fine," the owner said, "it's yours."[7] However, young Mr. Carrigan declined. He had another path he wanted to try.

In the fall of 1923, Bill chose to go to college. From Minnesota, he traveled to Arizona to attend the University of Arizona at Tucson (ASU) for a degree in geology. The beauty of nature, dear to him since childhood, and a "deep appreciation of the marvels of the universe and of God's plan," put him on a track to pursue further scientific knowledge.[8] Additionally, Bill stated that Arizona contained "the best school of mining engineering," indicating the career path he was intending to pursue.[9] During this time in his life, his Catholic faith became more important to him than ever.

At first, college life seemed great. He even managed to snag the best student housing possible: "A private apartment over the garage of the university president, in exchange for maintaining the president's car."[10] But the perks and interesting geology studies were soon overshadowed by a series of disappointments that caused him to reconsider his decisions.

To begin, Bill found himself repeatedly let down by his professors' faithless manner of teaching. He thought he could discover Truth in college, but instead realized that his teachers and mentors disregarded God entirely, going so far as to say that science *alone* revealed the secrets of the universe. To them, faith and reason were incompatible. A literature professor, Bill recalled, assigned the Bible as summer reading with the note, "'It is assigned for its poetry and prose—you need not pay any attention to content—it is only a figment of a rich imagination.'"[11]

As if this atheistic type of teaching was not burdensome enough to the young Catholic, the administration fought Bill's attempts to start a Newman club. Named after St. John Henry Newman, who loved Catholicism and the liberal arts, these clubs were first established at Oxford University in 1858. Existing to this day, they give Catholics a space to engage in activities together on secular university campuses.

Seeing that ASU did not provide any groups or events for the approximately 125 Catholic students, Bill wanted to start a Newman club. To his dismay, ASU's administration stalled for weeks and eventually "did not approve the club because it was religious."[12] Bill pushed back, pointedly noting that ASU "had big Masonic activities" on campus which the administration allowed.[13] Still, his appeal was turned down. This perceived prejudice put a damper on Bill's view toward the college.

He switched to studies in archeology and anthropology after a time and "spent several months in Mexico City digging around a 4000-year-old pyramid which was used for human sacrifice."[14] Once that brief stint concluded, he returned to the United States, abandoned archaeology, and reconsidered his trajectory. It seemed he could not find the purpose for which he sought. After only two years, he left ASU for the sunny coasts of San Francisco, California. He lived and worked there for a period, growing apples, but did not go immediately to another college. Instead, he changed universities and applied for seminary.

∽

STUDYING FOR PRIESTHOOD

Between 1926 and 1933, Bill began seriously discerning the priesthood—a strong testament to his growth in both the Catholic faith and his personal spiritual life. Friends and family happily claimed they knew he was cut out to be a priest. Was this his true calling?

Sources which offer details about his vocational life indicate that, alongside his seminary studies, Bill also attended the Catholic University of America (CUA). Of this length of time, he relayed precious little. What is abundantly clear, however, is that his discernment process continued the pattern of disappointments and directional changes that were common in his early adulthood. Though he came to understand that guidance from God sometimes involves painfully closed doors, it certainly was not an easy lesson to learn.

From the very first steps, Bill faced obstacles, both interior and exterior, that called into question his vocation. Since he came from a college where his religion was scorned, he needed to attend a preparatory seminary before any religious order could accept him as a student. These schools existed to give aspiring novices with no formal theological education a preliminary college-level course (or more) to prepare them for entrance into a full seminary.[15] Though not a setback in itself, a friend's letter which Bill received in late 1926 indicated that he needed to spend "another year in the preparatory department," which appears to have been atypical.[16] Furthermore, Bill struggled to grasp Latin; the friend wrote, "I realize what little Latin you had had and what a vast amount is to be acquired to fit you for higher studies," giving a reason for Bill's extended education.[17]

Eventually, Bill graduated from preparatory seminary, which was likely based in San Francisco, California. Immediately afterward, Bill chose to attend the Congregation of St. Paul seminary, formally known as the Missionary Society of St. Paul the Apostle. At once, he faced trouble. A Paulist priest with whom Bill exchanged letters wrote in August 1927 that the seminary *reconsidered* his application and would give him a trial.[18] Though the exact reasons are unclear, his initial application for the Paulist Fathers was denied, so he tried again.

In the fall of 1927, Bill moved from San Francisco to Oak Ridge, New Jersey, where the Paulist fathers had their novitiate living quarters. He had passed his trial; his Latin must have been sufficient. Now formally accepted as a novice alongside eleven other companions, he began to study for the priesthood.

For the next three years, Bill pursued his education and his vocation in relative obscurity. In 1931, he graduated from the Catholic University of America. His name, listed on the 1931 commencement ceremony handbook, reads "William Maurice Carrigan, C.S.P." under the Seminary Division of those graduating with a Bachelor of Arts degree.[19] C.S.P. are the credentials for the Congregation of St. Paul.

Desiring to continue his discernment of and path toward the priesthood, Bill took the next step in formation: graduate studies. The Catholic University of America contains within its many tracks of study a theologate—a graduate-level seminary program—offered by the Society of St. Sulpice.[20] In operation since the late 19th century, this Theological College attracted Bill's attention. He must have identified himself with their mission as the only Catholic "diocesan priests in the world with the sole responsibility of educating, guiding, and supporting fellow priests."[21] Education, especially a Catholic one, had become important to him. So, he continued on at CUA.

His trajectory seemed to finally be going smoothly, until the summer of 1933. Bill was deep in his studies when his hopes of holy orders were dealt a devastating blow that marked the beginning of the end of his priesthood discernment. On June 28, 1933, a Paulist father sent Bill a letter which read thus:

My dear Mr. Carrigan,

I write to ask you again to petition the Congregation of Religious for permission to resign from the Society. You told me when you were here that you could not honestly sign the petition made up for you by Father Cartwright. Of course, since you could not sign it honestly, we did not wish you to sign it at all. However, we do wish you to make that petition, to base it on grounds that accord with the facts, namely, on the ground that you failed to obtain a passing mark in your studies at the Sulpician Seminary, and that you failed again this year to secure approval of your scholastic standing and attainment from Fr. McVann.

After due consideration of your suggestion that we allow you to continue your Theological studies at the Catholic University, I am obliged to say that we cannot follow it, and that for us a student's failure to obtain a passing mark in the Sulpician Seminary at Washington is satisfactory and sufficient evidence that he cannot make the grade which we consider essential.

I know that you are reluctant to resign from the Community, and I sympathize with you in your predicament, but I must make it clear to you that the Community feels it must insist upon your

resignation and that in view of your past failures
we cannot send you on elsewhere for further study,
nor can we at any time propose you as a candidate
for Holy Orders. So far as the present Council is
concerned, this decision is final ... within a week
I ask your formal petition for permission to resign
from the Community.[22]

It is not hard to imagine how difficult this was for Bill to accept.
Even harder to bear was the implication in the priest's letter that
this was not the first time Bill had failed to attain passing grades.

Determined not to give up on what he thought was the
right course and despite the Council's decisions, however, Bill
fought to continue studying for priesthood. Only a few months
later, in September 1933, the same Paulist father congratulated
Bill on receiving a scholarship from the local bishop in order
to continue studying at the Sulpician seminary. In addition to
this scholarship money, the priest sent a check requested by
Bill, but emphasized that "the Council authorizes this contribution to your support during the current school year simply as
an evidence of our good-will toward you. It is something that
we have never done before for a former student of ours, and
something that we do not think other religious Communities
would be likely to do. Nor are we ourselves likely to make it a
precedent."[23] How long this scholarship lasted is now unknown,
but at some point, Bill finally discerned that the priesthood was
not the path God wanted him to take. At around thirty-one years
old, Bill reentered lay society.

～

Two Swimming Pools For Orphans

Though not called to the priesthood, Bill's time in seminary produced good fruits, not only in his own heart, but also in society. In the early 1930s, while still a seminarian, Bill commenced the first of two significant projects that garnered public attention for a while: building a pool for 140 orphans living at the St. Vincent's Home in Washington, D.C. This orphanage dreamed of having a wading pool for years.[24] Summers in America's capitol were sweltering, and a pool would provide both refreshment and fun for the children whom the Home served.

Having frequently visited the orphanage, Bill quickly became aware of the children's dream. "They had about 175 girls and no place for them to play," Bill remembered. "Nothing. No playground at all. And the sisters didn't have any money, because this was the pits of the Depression. But they said they would like to put in a wading pool, and I said I would build it during the summer if they could feed me one meal a day."[25]

For two or three years, he tried to raise support for a project of this size, but with no luck.[26] Like he said, it was the era of the Great Depression, which left American citizens starving in the wake of extreme economic crises. Money was sparse, barely enough to keep most families fed. Communities resorted to growing what fruits and vegetables they could and making creative meals out of very few, cheap ingredients. Lines outside soup kitchens stretched for blocks. A third of banks failed;

homelessness and unemployment soared. People were suffering. It seemed impossible that a luxury such as a pool could be built, especially because "all [engineering] experts' estimates for the construction of the pool averaged about $7000."[27] For reference, that estimated cost in 2024 equals just under $164,000. Who, in a time of national poverty, could scrape together that much?

Though Bill was dismayed by those outrageous costs, he did not give up. He was nothing if not stubborn in doing what he considered the right course; he would take action, even if no one else would.

In the later years of his life, Bill repeated the tale of how he managed the pool-building project several times to several different news sources. Rarely do the facts differ, though one publication may have different details than another. The following compilation of news excerpts gives the fullest story. In the summer of 1933, he got to work:

> Staggered, but not felled by this mountainous figure, Mr. Carrigan decided that the only way to get the pool was to build without money, and the only way to do that was to build it himself.[28]

> He obtained a horse, and found a retired farmer to help with the work of gouging out the earth, and gave it a go. It was a very slow go. "I called the biggest paver in the city, a man with an Irish name, and asked him to come out to the orphanage.

He came out, and there we were, and the girls were picking out rocks and putting them aside." What, the Irishman wanted to know, was going on. "We're building a garden." Would a power shovel and two trucks help? In 12 hours the hole was dug—not for a garden or a wading pool but for a 45-by-75-foot swimming pool.[29]

[Bill] then bethought himself of securing the donation of a little cement from a local company and was successful in his solicitation. And that unloosed a flood of generosity from other local concerns until practically all the supplies necessary for the pool were given gratis.[30]

Every day I called contractors and suppliers. I never asked for money. I just asked if they would come out and talk to me. In 30 days we talked to 40 businessmen, and in 30 days we had a completed swimming pool, without spending any money. People wanted to give money to help with the pool, but I told them we weren't asking for money, although they could give it to the sisters. When the job was done the sisters had collected about $700. We decided the girls ought to have showers after they got out of the pool, so we built eight shower stalls. And there was still enough money left over to buy each of the girls a new bathing suit.[31]

And all this at the cost of $750 donated instead of the $7,000 figure that nearly stunned Mr. Carrigan into despair.[32]

In that small way, that anecdote typifies the way William Carrigan gets things done. "I learned on the farm," he says, "to do whatever you can to make things better. Do it quietly. And make it stick."[33]

With the free help of contractors, equipment operators, and various businesses who loaned equipment and personnel, as well as those who raised the monetary donations, Bill oversaw the construction. Within a month, the pool was complete.[34] The orphans were thrilled. Newspapers printed photos of beaming young girls in bathing suits and swim caps, frolicking in their new pool.

∽

Just under two years later, Bill helped build *another* swimming pool, this time for the St. Joseph's Home and School. Alongside the local Calvert Club, he supervised the operation. He had done it once before, so he knew he could do it again. He executed his vision with increasingly sharp managerial skills.

On July 4, 1935, St. Joseph's Home and School officially dedicated and opened a new swimming pool for their orphaned boys with "flag-raising ceremonies" given by the Boy Scouts and a special blessing by the Monsignor and president of St. Joseph's Home and School, Charles F. Thomas.[35] Bill performed the duty of master of ceremonies. The band from St. Vincent Home and School provided the event with music. The dedication "reached its climax after the program when boys of the school, donning bathing suits, made a mass dive into the water."[36]

Bill's ability to draw people together for a charitable cause worked out to the benefit of both orphanages and the hundreds of children who lived there. The Great Depression—a time of intense hardship—could not stop Bill from inspiring the locals to do what they could to help those in need. He was immensely proud of these ventures.[37] An old adage comes to mind: where there's a will, there's a way. Indeed, when William M. Carrigan was involved, things had a way of getting accomplished.

CARROLL HOUSE

During the time that Bill attended CUA as a layman and cared for underprivileged children, he took psychology courses at the university. At the time, psychology was a relatively new branch of science. Bill was one of CUA's first psychology students ever.[38] Though he did not graduate a second time, likely by his own choosing, he did undertake another charitable project aimed at assisting the marginalized: the Carroll House, a program nestled under the Boys' Guidance Association. Started in 1937 by Bill and CUA psychology professor Dr. Edward J. Rauth (possibly spelled *Reuth*), the Carroll House served delinquent or behaviorally challenged boys aged eleven through sixteen. It soon grew—as things in Bill's hands tended to do—into a program which gained strong professional support, a board of directors, and national recognition by prominent individuals who spoke for the Association.

At the Carroll House, CUA's psychology department studied the behavior problems and Bill, serving as Director for several years, ensured that the House offered a "normal home environment" and family-like atmosphere for troubled boys.[39] It was designed to "assist generally in providing guidance and opportunities for study, work and play enjoyed by boys in normal homes."[40] In addition, the House gave behavioral counseling, which Bill personally monitored, and helped boys prepare for returning to school or working various trades. Bill practiced what he had learned in seminary and psychology classes; he became "a father figure to more than seventy-five boys in six years" and "took a personal interest in each."[41]

By taking notes on the boys' lives and behaviors, he and the psychology department were able to figure out what each boy needed in order to become a healthy member of society, then deliver those needs with firmness and compassion. The reward for the difficult work was, Bill stated, that a few boys "still visit and write."[42] Bill took special pride in one Carroll House graduate who later adopted two troubled children of his own as a way of paying forward the positive impact Bill had had on his life.[43]

Carroll House, leading this Boy's Guidance Program, also contained a women's auxiliary group, Carroll Auxiliary.[44] Under the provision of the Carroll House, the associated ladies hosted a series of seminars open to the community, in which notable local and national speakers considered the topics of "family life, social service, security, educational, legal, psychological and medical needs" for children.[45] And who provided the opening lecture? None other than the beloved Fulton J. Sheen—then monsignor, now Venerable and on the way to sainthood.[46]

SEEKING THE NEXT STEP

Though Bill initially had no straightforward direction for his life after high school and his disappointments were many, he did not let himself become paralyzed. He picked up and carried on, conducting his efforts by a principle he verbalized later in his life: "If you have a good work to do, the people who have the means will help, if it is put to them in the right way."[47] His faith in God and his love for the Catholic Church increased. His paternal care for children grew. These experiences—disappointing, painful, confusing, joyful, fulfilling, and exciting—marked the strong beginning of what Bill would later call "the flow of grace" or the "Finger of God" that guided him and provided opportunities for him to use his talents for the good of others.

After Bill accepted that priesthood was not part of God's plan for him, he turned his attention to the other state in life: marriage. In the years post-seminary, while conducting charitable endeavors that showed his reverence for the family unit and his attentiveness to the needs of children, he asked the Lord for a good wife. After nearly ten long years of waiting, he encountered the woman who would become his biggest supporter and closest confidante: Ramona.

CHAPTER FOUR

Ramona Newman: Love of Bill's Life

1903–1943

❧

RAMONA

On January 19, 1903, seven months after Bill Carrigan's birth and over a thousand miles away from his childhood home, Harry and Anne[1] Newman welcomed their first child into the world. They named her Ramona Jane Newman.

The proud parents baptized her into the Catholic Church forty-one days later at St. Malachy's Church in their hometown, Philadelphia. They moved closer to the Atlantic soon after. Whereas Bill spent his childhood in the wild prairies, Ramona grew up in Delaware and Washington, D.C., decidedly urban areas. She became a big sister twice over to a sister and a brother—Arlene Lucile in 1906 and Harry, Jr. in 1910. The family owned a cottage in Rehoboth Beach, Delaware, speaking of their probable wealth.[2]

Her father, Harry S. Newman, Sr.—a veteran of the Spanish-American war during which he served as a Naval paymaster—worked to maintain his family and their comfort. Interestingly, Harry, Sr. held a position as an audit clerk for the Panama

Canal Commission from the 1920s until his death in 1947.[3] The Panama Canal Commission assisted the federal government in keeping the famous Atlantic-Pacific passage in operation. Ramona's mother, Mrs. Anne Newman (*n.* Armstrong), was a popular socialite, a pillar in her local community even as she kept home and raised her children. Anne participated in the Excelsior book club, took on the role of president of the local Village Improvement Club[4]–the most active group associated with Delaware's State Federation of Women's Clubs–and even found time to become a prominent member of the Daughters of the American Revolution.[5] Additionally, Anne served on the local town board as the chairwoman of Ways and Means, a sub-role of Rehoboth's Social Committee, which cemented the Newman family's strong presence in their community.[6]

With her parents deeply involved in society, Ramona and her siblings grew up on the edge of the public eye. Surviving accounts of Ramona's childhood reveal a polite, sensitive, thoughtful girl who organized going-away parties for school friends, frequently attained a place on the monthly honor roll in elementary and middle school, and was even elected as secondary Vice-President for the St. Anne's parish Junior Auxiliary group.[7] That position included attending annual diocesan meetings in different counties, where Ramona acted as a delegate for her home parish. Like her mother, the young girl became accustomed to the social aspects of life in and around Washington, D.C., and Rehoboth Beach.

When World War I dominated hearts and headlines across the nation in July 1914, eleven-year-old Ramona dove right into supporting relief aid sponsored by the American Red Cross. Just six months after the official beginning of the Great War, she donned a child-sized costume of a Red Cross nurse and "sold Red Cross stamps to the audience" at a community talk in Delaware.[8] The sale of these stamps funded tuberculosis prevention and treatment for Americans at home and fighting overseas—a fundraiser which started only seven years earlier in Wilmington, Delaware, not far from the Newman family's home.[9] In her own small way, Ramona did what she could to help the war effort.

Her service to her community continued into her teen and adult years. A significant portion of her activities included music. Gifted with a charming voice, she offered her talent to many events, such as singing for men being drafted into World War I.[10] Her accomplishments as a soprano and later as a contralto featured in local newspapers and on radio stations many times. In one notable instance, she was only eighteen years old when the neighborhood Y.M.C.A. invited her to sing as a soloist soprano.[11] Her evening repertoire included "Rose in the Bud," by Dorothy Forster, "Thoughts Have Wings," by Liza Lehrmann, and "The Snowdrop," by Alexander Gretchaninov—all pieces that require a strong command of the voice.[12] Another important time, Ramona took part in a program run by the Sons of the American Revolution, who asked her to sing as a soloist on WJSV radio—a popular station in Washington, D.C.—at 8:15 pm on April 8, 1931.[13] Ramona was twenty-nine years old then.

Singing and serving, Ramona grew up. People around her, including her younger sister Arlene Lucile, married. A bridesmaid at least once, Ramona may have begun to wonder about her own vocation.[14] Unlike Bill, it does not appear that she ever considered religious life. She did, however, pursue education, both for herself and for others. Immediately after high school, Ramona attended the James Ormond Wilson Normal School and graduated from the same in 1924, having received training to become a schoolteacher.[15] She then attended the Catholic University of America. Regarding advancements in collegiate education, she was just as much a pioneer as Bill was. While he worked in the new field of psychology, Ramona became one of the first women *ever* to be included into CUA's programs. She chose to study education as her major and graduated in 1936 with a Bachelor of Arts in said field; she was one of only nine people, all women, who had earned that degree that year.[16] Furthermore, from 1924 to her retirement in 1954, Ramona taught mainly at Oyster Elementary School and partially at West School, both nearby her home in Bethesda, Maryland.[17] She loved young children and dedicated herself to their schooling for thirty years. She was also a supporter of the teachers themselves: she was an "outspoken advocate of better compensation and conditions for teachers" throughout her entire career.[18]

At the same time she was studying and teaching, she also became associated with the Daughters of the American Colonists (DAC) and the Daughters of the American Revolution (DAR), following in her mother's footsteps. Her lineage connection to both the first English settlers in America and the brave fighters for independence during the Revolutionary War built a sense of patriotism in her. She sought to teach others about America's history. As a young woman, she planned events for the organizations, and even donned costumes to partake in fundraising plays. Once, putting her good humor and willingness to be silly in the spotlight, she dressed as a hula dancer and participated in a night of amusing skits and other pleasant entertainment at the DAR's annual state officers' dinner.[19]

Then, at fifty-five years old, she became "national president of the Daughters of the American Colonists for three years beginning in 1958, and during that period she established the organization's office on Massachusetts Avenue NW."[20] She served as the chairwoman of the DAC's Headquarters Committee until 1985 and the volunteer office manager from 1960 to 1985.[21] With the DAR, Ramona was the "chairwoman of the Pages Ball at the Mayflower Hotel, the society's most important event, for nearly twenty years."[22] Long into her life, she worked with the DAC and DAR as a leading figure in their social and educational events.

Outside the field of education, Ramona's life was that of a pleasant, social woman. Despite the diversity of activity in her life, she was not yet married; by the time she obtained her university degree, she was already in her mid-to-late thirties. Whether as a first step or as a last resort, Ramona turned to prayer, asking St. Joseph specifically for his heavenly intervention in finding an upright husband.[23] Along came Bill Carrigan.

෴

Answered Prayers

Bill and Ramona most likely met at the Catholic University of America in the mid-1930s. They both participated in the same Greek life group, Pi Gamma Mu, and Ramona was a member of the Carroll Auxiliary, the women's offshoot of Bill's guidance program.[24] Despite their shared activities, it was Ramona's attire that caught Bill's eye—a particular yellow hat which he "first noticed in class."[25]

After those small first encounters which sparked mutual interest, Bill pursued a relationship with Ramona. It seemed that their courtship was serious from the beginning. Both were above the age of thirty and genuinely desired a spouse. Bill recalled that Ramona had been dependable, always showing up on time, never rescheduling dates because of other things that came up. Instead, he was the one who sometimes left her hanging![26]

Like anything in life, the small choices Bill and Ramona made during their dating relationship proved pivotal to their later paths. Of these, two decisive moments might have changed the courses of their lives entirely if decisions had been made differently. Both involved a kiss. Ramona recalled the first instance—a kiss withheld:

> I often think about the times before we were married. Remember the time you nearly kissed me when I was at the house on Randolph St.? I

am so glad you did not. Our whole life might have been different if you had. I would probably have thought you a bit fickle and been afraid to know you any better. Maybe it was fate that stopped that kiss. Well, it was a kind fate, for it saved us for so many more joys that far exceed the joy that kiss could have afforded.[27]

Indeed, physical displays of affection seemed to be minimal between them. Ramona possessed a strong sense of propriety. Bill, who probably would have redesignated *fate* as *self-control*, valued prudence. They decided to "go steady" in earnest around Christmas of 1937.[28] Then, less than a month later, came the second kiss, this one sweetly given. Ramona recollected the tender moment; it was New Year's Eve, 1937:

New Year's Eve is an anniversary for us, Sweet. I wonder if you remember? You first kissed me on the cheek as we stood on the porch ... and watched the dawning of the year 1938. It was a little kiss, dear, but it had big results. I ... scrambled eggs for us after we came in the house and from that time on, I think we both knew that our lives were destined to be spent together.[29]

Bill mentioned it as well: "I love you, dear, and now that New Year's Eve is nearing, I remember again a certain night—a lovely kiss. Yes, it was a kiss to remember a long time."[30] One confident little moment, one innocent kiss on the cheek, one plate of scrambled eggs at the home of Ramona's parents in Maryland. A simple gesture of love sealed their destinies together.

Nineteen days later, on Ramona's thirty-fifth birthday, Bill proposed. Though he did not remember exactly what he said to her when he was on one knee, he did note, with a hint of humor, that he had probably stumbled through it because he was so lovestruck. "I don't remember whether I said [I love you] or gave you a story," he mused.[31] Whatever he said—premeditated speech or simple declaration—it was enough to convey his desire to spend the rest of his life seeking heaven alongside her. With joy, Ramona accepted his proposal and the two began to prepare for holy matrimony.

∽

A Joyous Marriage

August 1938, the end of the summer, was baking hot. Temperatures in Maryland City, only a fifty-minute drive from Bethesda where Ramona resided, ranged between blazing mid-eighties and hellish high-nineties for the entire month. Cloud cover was almost nonexistent. Wedding planning was not easy to accomplish in such overpowering heat, and Ramona had to do almost all of it without Bill because, in the month or so before the wedding, he was working day and night at a boy's summer camp in Nanjemoy, Maryland. Though they kept in touch by regular phone calls and letters, Ramona was without her fiancé.

Justifiably, she felt overwhelmed. She wrote to Bill about one month before the wedding: "Honestly, lover, I don't see when I'll have time to breathe in the next few days if I do even half of what I want to do."[32] Thankfully, her family and close friends stepped in to ease her load as much as they could.

She recalled some of the things she did *sans* Bill: approving and sending for wedding invitations, making table cards, researching and planning their honeymoon destination and which hotel they would stay at, finding a caterer, deciding on flowers, choosing the parish to be married in, and of course, shopping for her wedding gown (this was stressful; with the heat and strain, she fainted while being fitted for her reception dress[33]). No, wedding planning was not easy, nor did she like making most of the decisions on her own, but she did it. Ramona had a knack for event organization; it showed clearly in the way she arranged the wedding details.

Finally, all that was left was to apply for marriage, which she and Bill did in the last week of August. They waited only a few days to meet for the last time as fiancés at St. Thomas Apostle Catholic Church to sign their application papers. Then, on the cool, clear-skied morning of September 3, 1938, in the sight of the Lord and a small but loving group of family and friends, Bill and Ramona were united in holy matrimony. Joy undoubtedly filled the hearts of the newlyweds.

Details about their wedding would be lost to time if not for a news article's brief account of the ceremony. Interestingly, a large portion of the article gave a meticulous account of the flowers Bill and Ramona used for interior decorations, the bride's bouquet, and the bridesmaids' bouquets. A seemingly insignificant part of the wedding in comparison to the sacrament itself, the flowers actually held great spiritual meaning for the ceremony and for the soon-to-be Carrigan couple. In times past, using foliage to represent certain themes was popular. Ramona made the decisions about the décor; it seems she put special thought into the meaning of each plant chosen. Her choices could not be more fitting to describe the happy union of the two Catholics.

For the decoration inside St. Thomas Apostle church, Ramona picked palms and white gladioli.[34] Palm branches typically represent victory, peace, and eternal life in the Catholic tradition—an excellent reminder of the martyrdom of selfishness that marriage requires, as well as the reality that the husband and wife have a duty to draw each other upwards to God. Gladioli flowers symbolize strength of character, moral integrity, and faithfulness. Even more than that, *white* gladioli speak of innocence and purity. All fitting for Bill and Ramona.

For her own bouquet, Ramona chose Easter lilies, representing hope and new beginnings, and lilies of the valley, representing absolute purity, discretion, and happiness.[35] For the matron of honor and bridesmaids, Ramona chose scabiosa and Joanna Hill roses.[36] The former represents true love. The latter is a yellow rose, which had specific significance to Ramona, since, to her, it stood for Bill's love in particular. For the rest of

Bill and Ramona's lives, it was the yellow rose that exclaimed the depth of their love.

As Bill and Ramona exchanged vows and received the Eucharist, even the music reflected the spiritual nature of Bill and Ramona's love. Ramona recalled, in particular, that the cantor sang *Panis Angelicus*, a 13th century hymn by St. Thomas Aquinas honoring the Eucharist—hardly a more fitting song for a devout Catholic couple receiving the Lord in Holy Communion as a union of souls. The details of the wedding Mass reflected Bill and Ramona's deep love for Christ, to which they joined their love for each other. After a joyful reception at the Newman home, the newly married Carrigan couple spent a tender honeymoon in Hershey, Pennsylvania.

∾

MARRIED LIFE

During the next five years, from 1938 to 1943, Bill and Ramona lived in and around Washington, D.C., renting a house with an older couple (the Costigans, who helped Bill and Ramona with the Carroll House) until they were able to buy their own place on North Randolph Street. Some time later, they moved to another home: 4184 Middlesex Lane, Bethesda, Maryland. Though this address no longer exists, it provided a comfortable home for the Carrigan couple for many years. Bill delved professionally into property development and real estate, a lucrative career he would hold for the remainder of his life. He rented and sold a property called Wheeler Farm, as well as other land around the nation's capital. Ramona happily kept the house and served the community as a schoolteacher. She and Bill had friends and family over for dinner, went out to movies, and enjoyed a fruitful social life alongside their spousal life.

The two became more and more united, more and more in love. Letters between the couple expressed many tender sentiments: they enjoyed growing a garden together and watching the seasonal birds that nested around their home; Ramona once had a dream with special meaning: "I remember frequently the dream I had of walking on the water with you and the great surge of confidence that flooded my being."[37] Anniversaries came and went. In particular, their fifth anniversary was filled with yellow roses, which, "with all their rich golden beauty, are indeed symbolic of the love we bear one another and the rich beautiful years we have had together," as Ramona stated.[38]

Part of the growth they experienced as a couple was the increased expression of love, both in word and deed. Their praise for each other wreathed their marriage. For Ramona, no man could shine up to Bill:

> Really, sweet, I looked at the men in the streetcar going down town today and I thought to myself how poorly they compared with you. None of them had such lovely eyes and hair and none were as neat... You have to my mind more honor in your little finger than most men have in their whole makeup. Oh darling, in short there is no one like

you. I guess I have been half afraid to tell you that. To me it is simply wonderful that you love me and I hope with all my heart that you always will.[39]

Somehow I thought to myself—thank God for Bill. He is like a clean cool breeze compared to these desk hounds and party fiends here... I looked at that room full of men and thought to myself—"Not one of them can hold a candle to my Bill." And they could not either.[40]

Though briefer in nature than his wife's sentiments, Bill's declarations carried no less potency or affection; he often stated that she was his world:

Ramona, sweet, I love you. You know that don't you? The best part of it is I love you more every day.[41] There is nothing in this life that means so much to me.[42] I am glad you love me so, it is a help here in more ways than you know. And you should know I love you just as completely.[43] You shall always be a "lift" and an inspiration for me.[44] Perhaps, you wonder if I have time to offer love to you. Yes, I have time, and I think and speak about it often. I am a sort of advocate of our kind of love. I recommend it.[45] I love you my dear in a way that is according to the will [of] God, in the way that makes families stable and sound in the true sense.[46]

Bill's love for Ramona connected completely with his Catholic faith, creating a beautiful and stable communion between the two of them. Their spiritual union was so close that, after a while, they began to find themselves thinking as one, as Ramona recounted: "I always found great pleasure when we discovered that we were both thinking the same things at the same time."[47] Bill expressed the same, with additional wisdom about finding genuine love in a world full of sin:

> We are pretty much one spiritually and in our thinking we are able to understand each other readily, but more—we agree in our understanding. There are many things we both wish for in each other, and all these are in the perfection category. One of your last letters called for a utopian life for us. You forgot we live in a very disturbed and disorderly world. Our life must be developed within a rotten world. In dressed-up sin, and distorted virtue, as daily environment. We must find our way to true virtue and love. But no matter what is on the outside, it is possible to run in the ways of God, and enjoy the peace of a good conscience, if one learns the freedom of love. For in true love there is no evil. True love excludes evil. The two are incompatible. Where evil resides, love has departed. We desire this love, but we must honor and protect it.[48]

Though conventionally they married late—Bill was thirty-six and Ramona thirty-five—Ramona Jane Newman came into Bill's life exactly when God intended. When the doors to seminary closed, Bill undoubtedly wrestled with frustration and sorrow, but the years between the rejection from priesthood and his marriage prepared him for being a good husband, established in a career and capable of providing a comfortable home. The Carrigan's long period of waiting was rewarded in the most beautiful way as God's grace brought them together.

Blissful times such as these, however, usually give way to trials that test the mettle of those engaged; refining fires either strengthen or destroy that which is placed inside. With the Carrigans, it was no different. Hardship came for them, and thousands of others at home and abroad, in the form of World War II.

CHAPTER FIVE

WWII: Bill Begins His Service
June 1943 – December 1943

⤬

BILL LEAVES FOR WAR

I n the aftermath of World War I and the Great Depression, the United States tried to return to a normal state of affairs. Families struggled to get back on their feet after losing over 115,000 loved ones. Congress passed Neutrality Acts. Citizens voted against foreign policy decisions. The country, on the whole, took little interest in international affairs and purposefully adopted an isolationist attitude toward the rest of the world. Even when Adolf Hitler invaded Western Europe in May of 1940, the vast majority of citizens did not want America to join the efforts against the Nazis.

However, after Axis Japan bombed Pearl Harbor, Hawaii, on December 7, 1941, fewer than ten percent of citizens held onto their initial anti-war positions. President Roosevelt declared war against Axis forces just four days after Pearl Harbor. Over the course of the conflict, about sixteen million Americans served in the military in some capacity. They raced to defend their country and the freedoms of European nations.

Bill, too, was enthusiastic about aiding the war effort. Despite dutifully putting his name in the drawing pool—he took part in the third of seven total drafts in America—he was deferred. Though difficult to decipher, there appear to be two reasons Bill was disqualified from the draft: occupation and hardship to dependents not engaged in a national defense occupation (the Carrigans had no children in 1943, so presumably this referred to Ramona, who was a teacher).[1] But, forty-one years old and full of patriotism, he still wanted to do something to help, a sentiment shared by many men and women in the States at the time. So, less than two years after Pearl Harbor, Bill chose to volunteer with the American Red Cross (ARC). He had been aware of the international relief organization since the barn dances of his youth. Now he had an opportunity to put his prior leadership experience into action once again, this time on a much larger scale.

Bill began his Red Cross training in April 1943. Two months later, he was placed in a pool of applicants awaiting placement and orders. Then, on June 16, 1943, he received his assignment: assistant field director with the Service to Armed Forces (SAF) division, which included camp and hospital services. Through the SAF division, field directors and assistants resided and worked in the same regions as the military they served. If Bill had any concerns about working abroad in the same dangerous environment as the fighting men, he did not voice them until later. Only toward the end of his time with the ARC did he express that he "pulled away from American shores with feelings hardly within description. Anticipation and fears were among them. The sea, the destination, the dangers ahead were not too hard for me to imagine."[2] Regardless of his feelings, he pushed forward, wanting to do his duty.

On June 19, 1943, a few months shy of their fifth wedding anniversary, Bill left Ramona at their little Bethesda house to serve overseas. Both anticipated a separation of only six months; their parting kiss at the train station was bittersweet. Neither imagined that Bill would be away for nearly two and a half years.

❧

ARRIVAL

As a newly minted assistant field director, Bill began his journey to the Mediterranean Theater of Operations (MTO). The ship *Maraposa*[3] carried him and seven thousand others from Hampton Roads, one of two major American ports in the Chesapeake Bay, to Casablanca, one of Morocco's biggest seaports. For "eight days and nights of lonely watching" the ship "ploughed her way through the trackless sea."[4]

During that eight days' travel, the *Maraposa* sounded two warning alerts for submarine attacks. Both times, no harm came to the ship or passengers, but Bill recalled that everyone cheered for a solid thirty minutes when the first Allied anti-submarine air patrol, flying from the Azores, began to circle over their heads. These Catalina patrols—like guardian angels for the passengers and crew—flew alongside the ship, scanning the seas for threats.

"Our nerves," Bill said, "were not in the best of shape. But all in all, we had a good crossing."[5]

At long last, the ship and passengers reached the African continent. The tangle of "battleships, steamers, and freighters" crowding Casablanca Harbor made docking difficult.[6] But it gave Bill time to watch the "Arabs in flowing white trousers with red sashes and tasseled red [fezzes]" attach the *Maraposa* to the dock's hawser anchors.[7]

"A feeling of safety surged through us for a time after we disembarked," Bill recalled, "but not for long. We knew we were getting nearer to the war, and word passed to us quickly that Casablanca was still on [the Germans'] night mission map."[8] Bill and his fellow Americans arrived hot on the heels of the Invasion of Tunisia, which began in November 1942 and ended in May 1943. Allied forces seized North Africa from German field marshal Johannes Erwin Eugen Rommel and kept the Germans in a near-constant retreat until May 1943. Then, Cape Bon Peninsula in northeastern Tunisia saw hundreds of thousands of Nazis taken prisoner, their power usurped. North Africa belonged to the Allies, and they swiftly began preparing for another invasion: Sicily. Though Bill did not yet know, he and his fellow passengers were to be transported into the areas recently vacated.

Because the ARC moved with the soldiers, Bill was stationed in Tunis, Bizerte, and Mateur—all major bases of operation for the invasions into Sicily and, later, Axis Italy. Bill quickly discovered he did not appreciate Africa very much. In both an aesthetic sense and a climatic sense, it proved a source of hardship for him. In July, temperatures reached nearly 120 degrees during the day and dropped to the mid-fifties at night. The landscape was dusty and mostly barren, ugly and miserable in Bill's estimation, especially in comparison to the natural beauty he so loved back in the United States. The areas where people lived were no better. "Cities and troops and countryside are shot to pieces," he wrote to Ramona. "I live in a bomb-weakened building, machine gun bullet holes [through] the shutters, and shell holes in the roof and walls. Relics of war are everywhere, from German and French tanks to paratroopers' tommy guns."[9] Whatever beauty there might have been, it was nearly all knocked out by the hideous war. He appreciated Carthage for its historical—and Catholic—significance only.[10]

Later in the year, when nights grew colder and heavy rains turned the dirt into mud, Bill found the living situation even more uncomfortable. He suffered occasionally from bad bouts of sinus trouble and headaches in the damp conditions. A life away from what now seemed like luxuries—dry beds, warmth in winter time—wore on him as much as on the soldiers, but he rarely complained. Even on holidays like Thanksgiving, where their tables were "rough board ... covered with salvaged tin from fragmentation bomb boxes" and "*sometimes* the food [was] warm," Bill spoke gratefully about his situation.[11] Those hardships, by the end of 1943, had become routine.

HIS WORK BEGINS

Bill's work as assistant field director commenced in earnest in July of 1943, and continual labor helped keep his mind occupied. Much of his work he chronicled through letters to Ramona. If not for these epistles, his efforts—large and small—would be obscured and forgotten.

At first, a meaningful portion of Bill's work was handling communication. He made and received phone calls dealing with a variety of urgent matters for which regular mail, V-mail, or telegraph did not suffice. Many calls supplied information about soldiers and civilians who had been killed. He "delivered life and death messages" and "distributed [Red Cross] services far and wide" on a daily basis.[12] Other calls reunited families and friends who had been separated by the ravages of war or by distance. Still others served to relay information or get answers that were too urgent to be sent through the unreliable airmail and V-mails available to regular troops.

During the war, the continually shifting, uncertain conditions negatively impacted the mail system. Letters often took weeks to arrive, and sometimes did not arrive at all. Mail sent by airplane, despite moving much quicker, was expensive to transport and took up valuable space, even when the smaller, lighter Victory Mail stationery became available in June 1942. A soldier's mail might not arrive for months. And these letters were a lifeline. Those who no longer received communication from back home settled into a despair that far surpassed mere disappointment.[13] "It is sad indeed to hear a lad say, 'no one at home seems to know I'm here and would like a letter,'" Bill told Ramona; both Carrigans knew the frustration of receiving untimely, out-of-order letters.[14]

As assistant field director, Bill helped the boys who needed to relay information more reliably, thanks to his access to a telephone. In one unusual instance, he helped Allied soldiers, Tunisian locals, and Italian prisoners of war attend Sunday Mass at a Catholic church in the Tunisian city of Bizerte. Upon arriving for the early morning Mass, Bill learned that the French priest was ill, and that the Army chaplain did not celebrate Mass before nine a.m. "Such consternation reigned at the little church among the native population and a group of Italian prisoners brought in for Mass, that I almost said Mass myself to quell their anxiety," Bill wrote.[15] Instead, he "made a long-distance call" to guarantee that a priest would be available later in the day.[16]

Bill enjoyed being a "typical unglamorous Red Crosser."[17] Though making and taking calls was an important aspect of his world, there were many facets that interested him. He felt he was doing good work and his days were filled to the brim with tasks to accomplish, so much so that "enough happens in a day to fill a month of life."[18] Problems that arose—unnamed in his letters—could not dampen his spirits, especially since he thanked God daily. "It must be your Masses and prayers that make things go as they do here for me," he told Ramona.[19]

As he worked closely with the troops and officers in Tunisia, Bill became increasingly acquainted with the boys' psychology as they lived and died in history's bloodiest war. The close contact with their struggle inspired him to dedicate himself wholly to all his duties, even to the point of feeling guilty taking the ARC's salary, as he explained:

> I do not feel that I can take Red Cross money, or work under the name of Red Cross with any other motive than full Red Cross service to the fighting men first and the hospitals secondly and the rest thirdly. There are good reasons for this. I have had a chance to really see the needs in this theater. I have learned a lot about soldiers, brass hats & Red Cross people. As one example—the wounded coming back or in hospitals are not interested in murder stories, wild westerns, or thrillers. They have had all that day & night. They want nothing that will recall those horrible days and nights. They like classics, poetry—Shakespeare, philosophy, science, etc., believe it or not. Why people in the states send millions of cheap thrillers & murder tales to these boys I may never know. But somebody did not know their psychology.[20]

Bill, experienced in psychology, felt he could make a difference as an assistant field director by performing his duties seriously and with a high degree of excellence. These experiences prepared him for his biggest and most unexpected undertaking as assistant field director: doughnuts.

༄

The Clubmobile

Unsurprisingly, an enormous portion of the ARC's work overseas was caring for battle-worn and homesick troops. Among
the many services they provided, the ARC's Club Service was
frequently attended by the Allied soldiers. Of Bill's Red Cross
work in North Africa, this was the most significant operation: "In
every city and town where troops were [concentrated], our clubs
were established both for enlisted men and officers. Here, men
could find comfortable, home-like quarters, showers, barber-
shops, snack bars, game rooms, reading and writing rooms, and
plenty of activities going on, such as tours, dances, shows, etc."[21]
Clubs greatly improved morale, but when troops operated far
outside major cities, access to clubs diminished. Thankfully,
the ARC had a solution: the clubmobile. This single-decker
bus transported all kinds of home goods to the far reaches of
the troop dispersion. The clubmobiles offered a variety of comfort items: coffee, chewing gum, doughnuts, reading material,
records and record-players, cigarettes, and more. Normally, one
clubmobile would travel alongside each unit of soldiers, providing them with comfort items. To Bill, they were "a combination
of a traveling snack bar and a club on wheels."[22]

In both World Wars, the vehicles were known for being
operated by smart, encouraging, competent young women who
could both work the doughnut machines and engage the soldiers in conversation to give them a touch of home. Though it

does not appear that Bill joined the famous Donut Dollies—his staff consisted of eight G.I. men—he did personally operate a clubmobile. Conditions for driving in the war-torn desert were terrible, worse than the unpaved farm roads in Maryland he was accustomed to, but that did not stop Bill Carrigan from doing his duty.[23] He and the clubmobile hauled familiar goods like magazines, razors, and doughnuts to remote stations around Tunisia. The doughnuts, in particular, were met with great enthusiasm from the troops. "But conditions under which we work," Bill wrote in a letter to Ramona, "are not on the lines of a bakery in the U.S. I assure you, dust, water, flies, and supplies give us our headaches. But these headaches seem to pass quickly when you drive down the road and have soldiers on all sides stopping you for doughnuts—which often I do not have to give."[24] The troops reached for the supplies like they were manna in the desert, desperate for any taste of home and normalcy; the clubmobile quickly ran out of items to give. The soldiers' needs touched Bill deeply:

> If the people at home could see and feel some of these things that I do when boys who have been here for [months] without anything but army rations day in and day out ask you for 'two' doughnuts, or a 'package' of cigarettes, or a razor blade, or one or two of any of the thousands of things they were used to at home, damn—they would have a different spirit towards [these] things. I drove twenty

miles yesterday to deliver three newspapers two
month[s] old and six Readers Digests to a company
of colored troops who had nothing to read, that was
all I could get for them from our warehouse. But
they were as grateful as could be, and [they] oiled,
greased, and fixed two tires for my truck.[25]

At some point during the mid-summer of 1943, Bill stopped running doughnuts and supplies into the desert. Instead, he began
what he called "an experimental project."[26] This was "the first
detached doughnut operation in the Mediterranean Theater."[27]
Rather than move to or with one particular military unit, as clubmobiles typically did, he stayed in a primary location and served
those troops who came and went via the railways and ports.

Bill's home base was the Red Cross's Tunis Field Office.
One of the initial units that came through Tunisia when Bill was
assistant field director was the 34th Infantry Division. Part of the
34th—the 168th Infantry Regiment—had suffered extreme losses
earlier that year during the Kasserine Pass battle, where Rommel's forces killed or captured all but three hundred of the two
thousand Allied soldiers. The 34th Infantry Division got back
to its feet, however. By the time they met Bill and his budding
doughnut operation, the 34th was on its way back to Oran,
Algeria to practice for the invasion of Sicily. Staggering their
departure by separating into ten smaller groups that left one at
a time, the 34th occupied the railways near Bill's Tunis office
for ten days. Bill received the assignment to throw "doughnut

parties at the rail head each of the ten evenings."[28] On one of those nights, a British soldier—an engine crewman for the British-operated railway—pushed his way to the front of the queue and asked what was being served. Bill told him: "Doughnuts and cold chocolate."[29] The man inquired what exactly a doughnut was, much to Bill's amazement. "To think," he said with humorous exaggeration, "that I had made enough doughnuts to serve all the Allied troops in the Mediterranean, and here was a soldier who did not know what they were. Well ... I proceeded to explain. After a moment or two, light seemed to flash in his eyes and he proclaimed, 'Oh, yes, you mean those bally little things with the hole in the center?' So thereupon I figured he deserved to sample one."[30]

Toward the end of the ten days serving the 34th Infantry Division, an unnamed colonel with the 34th summoned Bill. He told the assistant field director that he wished the clubmobile could follow them for the next few days. Curious, Bill asked why. The colonel, paraphrased by Bill, replied: "'Because I'd like you to see the letters these lads write home. I venture to say 90% of them will write about the doughnut parties. These are the first touches of civilization these men have experienced in a year.'"[31]

❧

Flying Doughnuts

The Invasion of Sicily began on July 9, 1943. The Allies wanted control of Sicily, the island off the "toe" of Italy's "boot," to use as a gateway into the peninsula which had aligned itself with Hitler's efforts. Storms, generals' conflicting egos, and logistical problems arose. Nevertheless, just before dawn on July 10, 1943, the Allies began their large-scale attack on Sicily. During just the first three days of the thirty-eight-day invasion, over 3000 ships, 150,000 soldiers, and over 4000 aircraft comprised the initial onslaught against Axis powers.

Nicknamed "Operation Husky," the invasion efforts brought Bill to the docks in Bizerte to command the doughnut services for men heading into and returning from the warzone. A "gang of GIs who were knocked out in the Kassarine Pass"—a few of the 300 surviving soldiers who did not go to Oran—helped operate Bill's doughnut machine. "Night and day," Bill recalled, "we rolled the sinkers up to the long lines of lads who were marching twenty-four hours of the day onto LSTs and LCIs[32] for the rough crossing to the rougher beachheads a hundred and fifty miles away."[33] Despite frequent Axis flybys, "everybody worked hard[;] no one seemed to mind the job nor the hours."[34]

Despite enjoying this work, Bill wanted badly to be more closely involved in the Invasion of Sicily. This was the Allies' second major push into Axis territory in the MTO, and it was where most of the action was. Goods, weapons, and other cargo were flown to and from the Axis-controlled island daily; Allied boats and planes often carried wounded soldiers back to hospitals in Bizerte and Mateur and Tunis, then transported fresh, able-bodied men into the war zone the very same day. Bill wanted to be with the boys in the worst of the fighting and hardship. He even told Ramona that if she were not in the picture, he would request to be "as close to the dying and suffering boys as I could get, and I'd take my chances with them."[35]

> Even as it is, I have asked to move to Sicily at the earliest possible moment[;] four of our group are there now, and I envy them. Darling, nothing in the States, nothing in the Red Cross Training, nothing in the newspapers give the slightest picture of what is, what men feel, what conditions men live under in this horrible war.[36]

As the invasion dragged on, Bill's desire to work on the island of Sicily increased. He had already served "43,000 different men their first overseas doughnuts in those first few weeks" of operating the clubmobile and he wanted to do more.[37] Ever thinking up grand plans, he reckoned he could expand the doughnut operation and bring the clubmobile right to the front lines in Sicily. When he pitched the idea to his supervisor, however, it was initially denied. Apparently, "the generals did not want doughnut operations at the front."[38] Though he could have seen rejection from the frontlines as a setback in his hopes or a debilitating disappointment, he did not. Those suffering troops would get doughnuts, no matter how much opposition he faced. He could not shirk his responsibility, especially with multitudes relying on him. So, he sought to make his own path, using evacuation stations as his doorway:

> Well, I knew the men would like doughnuts there,
> so I set about [finding] means to get them there.
> I was soon serving the Evac. stations. Every day,
> ten or twenty C-47s would fly into Mateur from
> Sicily with men who were taken off the front line a
> few hours before. We would serve them lemonade,
> sandwiches, and doughnuts while they waited to
> be taken away for one of the dozen hospitals in
> the area. I made contact with the [commanding
> officer] of the Evac. Unit and found that every
> morning several of these big transports flew over
> to the landing strips just behind the lines to pick
> up the wounded, and they went over empty. It did
> not take me long to do a little figuring.[39]

Bill acquired permission and the very next morning was "skim-ming the Mediterranean towards Sicily" with "seven thousand doughnuts, six mail sacks of reading material, [and] a lot of other stuff."[40] With this assignment, he visited several field hospitals and two of the eight evacuation hospitals located on the island. Though several Sicilian hospitals had come under Allied control, overcrowding had forced soldiers to rest in less-than-satisfactory encampments outside the captured hospital grounds. The evac camps were little more than canvas tarps erected on top of scaf-folding-like, wooden frames with rows and rows of cots pushed near to each other, subject to deep mud and battlefield debris and targeted Axis bombing. The hospital tents were stocked with the medical gear needed for tending the injured, but they lacked home comforts for the men. So, Bill flew from North Africa to Sicily nearly every other day, bringing mail, comfort items, and, of course, thousands of doughnuts. Desperate for relief, the makeshift hospitals devoured Bill's supplies.

On one return trip from Sicily to Mateur, Bill flew with eighteen men being evacuated from the front lines. Dirty, badly wounded, and exhausted, the men were carried on stretchers into the C-47 Army evac plane. Eight hours earlier, these soldiers had been fighting on the front lines, pushing the Axis forces out of Sicily. Now, they wore heavy casts and the weight of battle. They were hoisted onto the C-47's ribbed walls, modified with racks and straps to carry three layers of stretchers, for the flight back across the Mediterranean Sea.

Bill, seeing their suffering, asked the attending nurse if these boys were allowed to have food. She said they could. Bill retrieved the items he had saved specifically for the troops flying back to Africa that evening. He made his way around the cabin, handing out reading material and doughnuts as they were desired. One man ate ten doughnuts all by himself. Another mentioned that the doughnuts were the first real food they had had in weeks. But a third refused to partake. He had been badly burned by an Axis 88 field artillery shell that had exploded nearby; his face and mouth were so damaged that he could not open his lips to take even a little bite of the doughnut. Feeling sorry for the soldier, Bill finished handing out the comfort items and sat back down.

After a few minutes, however, the burned soldier called Bill back. He motioned for a doughnut. Though uncertain how the man could possibly eat it, Bill obliged. With great perseverance, the soldier lifted the doughnut above his mouth and crumbled it into tiny pieces, letting it fall through a small opening in his lips and onto his tongue. He consumed two whole doughnuts like this.[41]

This event struck Bill deeply and ignited further determination in him: "That picture, more than anything else, caused me to get more and more doughnuts over to those men, and to eventually sell the idea of serving doughnuts in all frontline operations."[42] His frequent flights to and from Sicily became a major part of his work as assistant field director. Something so little as doughnuts, in Bill's dreamer's hands, became a source of comfort and a meaningful morale boost for so many. Toward the end of the thirty-eight-day invasion, Bill's doughnut operation was finally noticed by some of the top brass. He soon got his wish to serve doughnuts on Sicily's front lines:

> Throughout the campaign, I kept on flying [comfort supplies] over. And towards the end Mr. Stevenson, ARC Delegate for MTO,[43] came along with me on one of the trips. The next morning, he took my whole shipment of doughnuts and reading material to the Front. Two Generals were present for the distribution. The effect on the men so pleased the Brass that they ordered ARC doughnut operations

to the front[;] the next day, I was in with another shipload and Mr. Stevenson met me with an order to fly no more doughnuts over, but to fly my machine and flour over at once to start operating at the front. The Sicilian Campaign was about over, but every Invasion thereafter had doughnuts and coffee served on the beachhead within a few hours after the men landed.[44]

⁂

LEAVING AFRICA

As time wore on and the war raged across the world, Bill's highly successful clubmobile operation came to an end. The Allies pushed into Italy. The Axis forces fled the oncoming storm. Eventually, Bill was reassigned and given work in other areas of the MTO. In November 1943, he was ordered to work with the Bomber Command operating in the MTO. On December 13, 1943, he moved into Italy with the 99th Bombardment Group, one of the seven subunits of the distinguished 15th Air Force. The 99th's next post was Tortorella Airfield, a semi-permanent airstrip in the Foggia province of Italy. Constructed just a few months earlier by the U.S. Army Corps of Engineers, the airfield hunkered about ten kilometers from the Foggia city proper, and it served as a key point of departure for many high-profile missions for the 99th Bomber Group.[45] Bill, as assistant field director, was stationed at the ARC Headquarters in Foggia, Italy.

Living conditions in the Foggia region remained as bad as they had been in Africa, if not worse. In the summer, the exposed airfields were blistering, dry, and incredibly dusty; in the winter, temperatures plummeted to frigid and the environment became perpetually damp. Upon their arrival, Bill and the 99th received an icy greeting as they plunged right into the dead of winter. The men working the Tortorella airfield slept in tents and found creative ways to keep warm, such as makeshift gasoline stoves.[46] Any hot water they wanted for showers they owed to "an old locomotive boiler, stoked by an Italian."[47] Few buildings stood to provide shelter at the airfield itself, so crews were exposed to whatever punishing weather the season inflicted. Foggia's town proper was just as bleak; the buildings that remained were partially destroyed by bullet holes and mortars, and the locals were desperate enough to rob the occupying soldiers. It was miserable, but such was the nature of the job. Most of Bill's work remained there until the end of his tour of duty in November 1945. Very well, too, for God had big plans for him which involved a small, mountainside town about twenty-five miles from his base.

CHAPTER SIX

WWII: Destiny Encountered and Ministry to Soldiers

December 1943 – November 1945

∾

THE FIRST MEETING

Heavy grey clouds hung low around Foggia, Italy, signaling an approaching December snowstorm. Prepared to drive through it, Bill Carrigan and two soldiers[1] bundled into a Red Cross vehicle and set out through the wintery, wooded country toward a nearby town—San Giovanni Rotondo.

San Giovanni Rotondo, an inconspicuous town on the slopes of the Monte Calvo mountain, was without a scratch, even though Allied intelligence indicated that the Nazis hid a cache of weapons nearby. Mysteriously, no attempts at bombing the little hillside village ever succeeded. San Giovanni Rotondo seemed to be a little pocket of almost-paradisiacal normalcy in comparison to the rest of Foggia, let alone the rest of the Mediterranean Theater of Operations.

These two soldiers had caught Bill's attention with stories of a real-life, modern-day mystic. About two dozen miles from the Army's encampment in Foggia, while searching for eggs, the soldiers' buddies had stumbled into a small town—San Giovanni Rotondo. A group of local children noticed them. They introduced the American men to a stout, wizened woman named Mary Pyle.[2] They were amazed to meet her, because she was also American. She lived in a simplistic home just outside the grounds of a Catholic monastery. She offered the soldiers food and a warm hearth and several impossible stories of a mystic priest residing in the monastery.

Aside from obliging his soldiers, Bill wanted to verify those tales for himself, so he obtained Red Cross transportation. In the midst of a heavy snowstorm, he and the men set off.

Their vehicle bumped along an unpaved dirt road, flanked by scrubby bushes and a low, stone wall covered in ten inches of snow. Upon approaching the monastery, an unassuming scene unfolded before them. The courtyard, though not much more than a patch of snowy earth in front of the church building, was guarded by a single, bare-limbed tree, ringed with stones and standing watch from the left. The monastery itself was not flashy. The plain, white facade and terracotta tile roof gave the church and attached monastery an austere feel. The only adornments were a simple bell tower, a few shuttered windows, and two doors—one for the monastery and one for the little chapel. Above this latter door sat a single, ceramic image depicting the Madonna and Child.

Bill and the soldiers hurried inside. According to Bill's recollection, a Capuchin monk, identifiable by his dark habit and knotted, white cincture, welcomed them quietly.[3] The sanctuary, only large enough to hold about eighty people, lay beneath a domed ceiling and white-and-gold arches. A choir loft, decorated by a large crucifix, overlooked the quaint space. Despite the capacity, only about ten locals sat among the friars in the wooden pews. The church had a beautiful marble altar, golden tabernacle and crucifix, and triptych paintings of St. John the Baptist, Our Lady of Grace holding baby Jesus, and St. Paul. Two side altars nestled into nooks in the right-hand wall. On the left wall were another side altar and a confessional. The three Allied men received the honor of kneeling on the cold tile, close to the priest.

Shivering despite his thick, Army-issued coat, Bill turned his attention to the Mass. He had a perfect view of the celebrant: a short, serious-looking man with brown eyes, salt-and-pepper beard, and gray hair. The priest seemed to be in great pain through the consecration of the Eucharist, which "took two or three times as long as it took the average priest."[4] He ground his teeth, shifting weight from one foot to the other. As he reached for the chalice, he jerked his hand back—Bill clearly saw the stigmatic wound.[5] With tears tracking down his cheeks, the priest bit off his words, the Latin consecration *hoc est enim corpus meam*, in a clipped manner that betrayed his great agony. Before he could distribute the sacrament to the little congregation, he had to lean on the altar and gather his strength as if he had gone through an extreme physical trial.[6]

At that moment, grace touched Bill's heart. Against the bone-chilling cold, an unusual warmth washed over him. He recognized at once that this priest, "at this moment in time was in very close communion with our Lord, and ... he seemed to be so credible that I found myself hastily bringing to this altar ... my family, my friends, and those I knew were in special need."[7]

Soon, the priest seemed to regain strength, and he was able to turn and give Holy Communion to the congregation. Mass ended soon after. But to Bill, that Mass "made a lasting imprint" in his mind.[8] It was, as he later recalled, "the beginning of the greatest relationship I could ever hope for."[9]

Catching the Americans before they could leave, a Capuchin invited them into the sacristy to meet the celebrant. The local men also pushed into the room, approaching the vesting table for a blessing from this mysterious priest: "He would press his hands on their head[s] and allow them to kiss the wounds in his hands."[10] Bill and the two soldiers stood awkwardly off to the side, uncertain if they should follow the example of the Italians before them, even when the priest acknowledged their presence. But one of the locals, a count, interpreted. "Go to him," the count said, "he wants you."[11]

Though very nervous, Bill approached. He started to kneel for the blessing, but the priest grabbed his elbow to prevent him and asked *"Su Americano?"*[12] Though the Italian language Bill wrote in his recollection is almost certainly a mistranslation—he likely meant *sei Americano,* that is, "are you American?"—the priest's question was clear. Bill answered in the only Italian he knew: *"Si* Padre, *si* Padre."[13] The two men held a brief, translated conversation in which the priest asked Bill's unit and station.[14] Despite struggling with his nerves, Bill managed to answer those questions. Then the priest let him kneel, gave him the blessing, and offered his wounded hands to be reverenced. "I pressed my lips into those wounds and noted the roughness of the blood crystals which covered most of his palms and the backs of his hands," he mused.[15] Beyond this, he noted the pleasant smell of roses, or something similar to a fragrant medical disinfectant, though he did not know at the time that the scent was a holy perfume emanating from those stigmatic wounds. "I was convinced beyond any doubt," he stated, "that here was a priest exceedingly close to Christ and had been marked by Him with His own crucifixion wounds. Obviously, not for him, but for us to see. It was his sanctity which drew us, not the wounds."[16]

When Bill met Padre Pio in late 1943, the saint was unknown to the majority of the world. Bill had certainly never heard of him before, so the conclusions he drew after that first encounter were unbiased. He was one of the first uniformed Americans to meet St. Pio of Pietrelcina.

"From the day I met him..." William M. Carrigan declared, "I felt destiny between us—I was to be a part of his rise to sainthood."[17]

❧

PADRE PIO AND THE SOLDIERS

The date of that fateful Mass can only be estimated. Based on Bill's testimonies, the extensive research of renowned Padre Pio biographer C. Bernard Ruffin, the diaries of Padre Pio's spiritual director Fr. Agostino Daniele, and the historical movements of the 15th Air Force, it is safe to say that Bill first encountered Padre Pio between December 13 and December 25, 1943. In the Carrigans' letters, the first mention of the saint comes via a reply from Ramona on February 3, 1943, in which she says curiously, "I am so glad you are going to have the opportunity to see the priest you mentioned... Do tell me more about this holy man."[18] Bill's original note, written on either January 16, 17, or 24, is now lost. Nevertheless, judging by such primary sources, Bill may have met Padre Pio mere days after being transferred to Foggia.

Bill never doubted that call to destiny.[19] For the next fifty-seven years of his life, he made Padre Pio known through any medium available to him—personal conversation and letters; news articles that were some of the first, if not *the* first, to reach the United States; photographs that were printed in the news; EWTN video broadcast; speeches to schools and parishes; interviews for books and biographies; blessed medals, crucifixes, rosaries, and holy cards; and his charitable efforts, most of which he dedicated to Padre Pio. Through Bill's tireless promotion of the saint who became his friend, America came to know this living witness of Christ.

In the first month or so, however, some of the only Americans who knew of him were the soldiers in Bill's care. As soon as Bill returned to the ARC base in Foggia, he "began organizing G.I. tours to San Giovanni Monastery," to Pio of Pietrelcina.[20]

By Christmas Day, a steady stream of soldiers attended Sunday Masses in San Giovanni Rotondo.[21]

The first official tour, proposed by Padre Pio himself and approved by the archbishop Cesarano, was to be a midnight Mass on Christmas Eve—a special event for the soldiers specifically, since Southern Italians did not typically hold a midnight Christmas Mass.[22] In the meantime, Bill spoke to the chief of chaplains, a Jesuit priest named Fr. St. John, then brought him to meet Padre Pio. Evidently, Fr. St. John also recognized the saint's holiness. Soon, military chaplains in the region learned that the mystic "would welcome them at Sunday Masses."[23]

Thus began Bill's ministry. By Christmastime and onwards, dozens of men each Sunday made the twenty-five mile drive up the mountain, piling into whatever transportation Bill could arrange with the Red Cross. Curious Catholics, Protestants, and atheists alike asked to visit for Mass and confession. Bill turned away no one, and the numbers only seemed to grow; on February 26, 1944, Bill told Ramona that he "took seventy men" to Padre Pio, where most received Holy Communion and had the chance to speak with him afterwards.[24] Padre Pio gave each man a blessing, just as he had for Bill. Then he blessed and distributed the rosaries and medals which Bill brought with him. They especially liked when Padre Pio blessed their silver wings.[25] Now each man had a tangible reminder of the saint's prayers. "I know joy was brought to many," Bill wrote, "and many will be stronger from here on out."[26]

As early as April 1944, Bill wrote influential articles that soon after appeared in Catholic newspapers in the United States. Through the writings, America became slowly acquainted with Padre Pio. The articles featured examples of how the troops interacted with the Capuchins, what graces they received through Padre Pio's intercession, and how confident they were in the saint's supernatural ability to help them. The monks seemed to greatly appreciate the presence of these American and British men, and welcomed them with open arms. The Capuchins even doted on them, making sure that the soldiers sat at a "place of vantage in the church" and insisting the men sat in the "chairs around the altar and sanctuary ... because they can then see Padre Pio throughout the whole Mass and see his wounds in his hands very plainly."[27]

One of Bill's articles, written just two months after his first meeting with Padre Pio, described the pleasant atmosphere of such encounters:

> Padre Pio takes the G.I.s into the cloister, back of the altar, and gives them his blessing, a little religious gift, and a few heartening words, wishing them well, and a speedy return to home and loved ones. Everyone lingers, crowding around him, hoping for a look or a word from him. They are dazzled with his Christlike appearance and jovial manner. Some of the G.I.s who are of Italian extraction, or who have learned Italian, engage

him in conversation. Those who do not understand have half a dozen ready interpreters both resident and military to explain every word he says. His engaging smile and good humor radiate through the crowd... When he is particularly pleased with someone he will break forth with a beautiful smile, and pat the soldier on the cheek encouragingly, and give him some complimentary words.[28]

Soon after Bill's weekly pilgrimages to Padre Pio's monastery became popular, his superiors began to get wind of what was going on. Colonel John F. Laboon, Sr., whom Bill claimed was the military governor at the time, visited the field director's office.[29] Col. Laboon heard, through the soldiers, about the mystic in the mountains and wanted Bill to take him for a visit too. Willingly Bill did so. Later on, the colonel requested that Bill write an article summarizing who exactly this priest was. On Ascension Thursday—May 18, 1944—Bill typed an article addressed to his "very dear friend," Colonel Laboon. In it, he gave a brief background on Padre Pio, especially his stigmata, but focused mainly on how deep an impact the saint was making on the soldiers who attended his Masses:

His Mass is an unforgettable experience, and a sermon which stirs the depths of one's soul and awakens dormant faith in the heart. Yet he preaches not a word! *To me, and to the soldiers I took with me, Padre Pio's Mass eclipses anything we have yet experienced in this theater of War. That is not difficult to understand when one realizes that he is the very antithesis of the cause of War, and thereby the cause of our being here. In him we have found the true opposite of hate. And in the violence of this war, contact with the Love of Christ through his favored Priest is a shock to our thinking. We will remember...* When I asked him to remember the father of one of our soldiers, he said to me, 'I will pursue him with constant diligence and love.'" He never forgets a person who seeks his counsel, and he has said that he will not let a soul get away from him once that person enters his spiritual family... *All want to return again, most everyone has a buddy who wants to go, too. So the word spreads and more and more soldiers are turning to a new and better interest here. From careless, carefree soldiers, they turn to sober thought of their future, their family, and their relationship to God...* We always seek the best lawyer we can get to plead our case in civil court, but here we have a representative known to be in high favor at the Court of Christ. Who is there who would not put their case in his hands? God has endowed him with the special gift of guiding souls no matter where they are. All that is required is desire for and obedience to this guidance which one will feel and know to exist.[30]

As Bill himself said, "there were dozens, just dozens of the GIs who claimed special graces and almost instant help in their cases."[31] Many are lost to history, but not to eternity's eye.

In May of 1944, just four months after his first trip to San Giovanni Rotondo, Bill attended a morning Mass with Padre Pio. When he had a moment to write to Ramona, he could hardly express how he felt: "The description would probably be fantastic and a bit unreal in your distant place... I am seeing profound changes everywhere, especially among those I have had a hand in taking on sending to his Masses. No sermon or talking-to can do as much in the hearts of these men as attendance at one Mass."[32] Many entered the great saint's spiritual care, converted, or became stronger Catholics. Some even discovered vocations to the priesthood, and attributed such vocational direction to Padre Pio's influence in their lives.[33]

THE MINISTRY CONTINUES

As Bill carried on as field director and as he grew in friendship with Padre Pio, his work began to extend outside himself. Word of mouth helped make Padre Pio known among the Allies in Foggia, and it helped make Padre Pio known among the citizens of America. Many of the soldiers returning from the War shared their testimonies with family and friends, continuing what Bill had started. For example, Col. John Laboon, Sr. penned a long letter to Bill in the mid-1970s, telling him about his own efforts to bring awareness to the mystic. He informed Bill that he had spoken to fifty or more groups over approximately twenty years. These he did in conjunction with films shown about the saint. He was also able to show "all of those present the scab from Padre Pio's hand and the linen cloth which still retained some color of the Padre's blood."[34]

Joe Peterson and Joe Peluso, both soldiers stationed in Foggia, spent the rest of their lives lecturing about Padre Pio via slideshow; Mario Avignone of the 304th Bomb Wing of the 15th Air Force (for which Bill served as field director) had several personal encounters with Padre Pio, even after the saint's death, and spread word of Padre Pio by visiting the sick in America and using relics of Padre Pio to pray with the ill and dying; Corporal Leo Fanning, also of the 304th, received from Padre Pio a prophecy about his later ordination to the priesthood.[35]

Many American soldiers may never have received special graces or helped to make the saint known had Bill not immediately started his mission of weekly pilgrimages. As a Catholic, and a well-rounded one with experience in understanding the human condition, Bill knew that spiritual counsel helped to boost morale and make a life-changing difference more than anything else. And where better to receive such counsel than from the first priest to ever suffer so completely with Jesus Christ, the man who was a "spiritual artist"?[36]

CHAPTER SEVEN

Who Was Padre Pio?

May 1887 – September 1968

❧

PADRE PIO

In the decades since Padre Pio's passing to eternal joy, the saint's miraculous life has been written about extensively and admired by millions around the globe. The holiness and cultural contradictions of great saints like Pio of Pietrelcina always capture the attention of the world. But, perhaps due to the times—photographs, videos, and radio technologies were available in the twentieth century—his fame spread far, even before his canonization.

St. Pio of Pietrelcina was born Francesco Forgione in Pietrelcina, Italy, on May 25, 1887. His parents—Grazio Forgione and Maria Giuseppa Di Nunzio (also called Mamma Peppa)—were farmers. Though they were illiterate peasants, they possessed a strong faith and thereby had all they needed. Mamma Peppa bore seven children; two died in infancy. Of the five who lived, Francesco, named after St. Francis of Assisi, was the second oldest.

Young Francesco received a hearty Catholic upbringing, and his faith was keen, partially due to his parents' instruction and partially due to supernatural visions he experienced from a very young age. The Forgione family attended daily Mass, prayed the Rosary together, and fasted from meat three days a week, but, unlike his family, little Francesco could see Jesus, the Blessed Virgin, and his Guardian Angel, sometimes daily.[1] This was so normal for him that he assumed everyone had heavenly visions, and was surprised to learn that they did not. These experiences were formative; he decided, at a mere five years old, to pledge his whole life in service to God. He immediately began practicing difficult penances, such as sleeping on the stone floor with a rock as his pillow.[2]

At the age of fifteen, he left his father's fields and, despite many health concerns, joined the Capuchin Friars in Morcone, Italy, as a novitiate. Francesco took on the name "Pio," meaning "pious" in English, which was truly a fitting name, as his entire life was marked with special graces given only to select souls for whom God had difficult and vital missions.

After his solemn profession, but before his ordination, Fra Pio ("Friar Pious") became unexpectedly ill. He suffered "loss of appetite, insomnia, exhaustion, fainting spells, and terrible migraines. He vomited frequently and could absorb only milk and cheese. The hagiographers say that it was during this time, together with his physical illness, that inexplicable phenomena began to occur. According to their stories, one could hear strange noises coming from his room at night—sometimes screams or roars."[3] In the midst of diabolic harassment and physical weakness, Fra Pio was ordained a priest on August 10, 1910, at twenty-three years old. He celebrated his first Mass not long after. For six more years, he lived in Pietrelcina with his family, suffering intense sickness. Only when he was finally moved to San Giovanni Rotondo did the vomiting and migraines subside. Through these mysterious sufferings, God made His will known; He wanted Father Pious in San Giovanni Rotondo. For the rest of Padre Pio's austere and holy life—with the only exception being mandatory military service during World War I—he stayed in the town's small Capuchin monastery, ministering to thousands.[4]

⚮

THE WOUNDED MIRACLE WORKER

Padre Pio's striking devotion to Christ and his enormous charity for others made him well known throughout the region of Foggia, then Italy and America, and now, the whole world. Some even consider him the greatest saint of the twentieth century. Dozens of books examine his life, his activities, and his spiritual messages. Catholics and non-Catholics alike seek to understand him. Though detractors—some of whom were bishops within the Church—attempted to discredit him as a fraud, an attention-seeker, or the leader of a cult-like group of fanatics, more people than ever presented their needs and desires to this great saint. Since his canonization, devotion and petition have only grown. Hundreds of people around the globe have experienced his heavenly aid in tangible or spiritual ways: heal-ings, small miracles in work or finances, the scent of roses or violets while in prayer, even dreams of the saint. Padre Pio is active in the lives of those who seek his aid.

With the twentieth century rocked by two back-to-back World Wars, gripped in the vicious vices of greed, hatred, pride, and lust for power, and plagued on every side by violence and death, Padre Pio set a shining example of peace and mercy, virtue and perseverance, and continual movement toward eternal life despite spiritual desolation and painful hardships. Many people who came into contact with him said the same thing: he was a visible sign of Christ to the world in a way they had never before witnessed. Bill Carrigan testified that, "I found him highly dis-ciplined in the traditional practices of sanctification... His every moment of existence was to provide a channel of grace to those who sought his help."[5] Sanctity is attractive, and Padre Pio's life was no exception. He experienced a deep union with Christ, and this shone outwards in every aspect of his life.

Perhaps the most famous sign of this intimate communion manifested as the stigmata—the five wounds of Christ—which he received in a spiritual ecstasy on September 20, 1918. He had been a priest only eight years. He related the event under oath to an investigating bishop:

> I was in the choir of the church after celebrating Mass, making the thanksgiving when I was suddenly overtaken by powerful trembling and then there

came calm and I saw Our Lord in his crucified form. He was lamenting the ingratitude of men, especially those consecrated to him and favored by him. Then, his suffering was apparent as was his desire to join souls to his Passion. He invited me to let his pains enter into me and to meditate on them and at the same time concern myself with the salvation of others. Following this, I felt full of compassion for the Lord's pains and I asked him what I could do. I heard this voice: "I will unite you with my Passion." And after this the vision disappeared, I came back to myself, my reason returned, and I saw these signs here from which blood flowed. Before this I did not have these.[6]

At first, Padre Pio was interiorly troubled by the stigmata and prayed for them to be removed because they drew excessive attention to him. He could not understand why God would give him this type of humiliating, painful experience. He wrestled with God's will for a time but eventually accepted the stigmata with humility, saying "they are very embarrassing to have, but I deem it a great privilege to suffer with Christ."[7] Even more than the uncomfortable feelings, the wounds caused great physical pain for him, especially during the consecration of the bread and wine, and the agony caused his Masses to sometimes last two or three hours. Though numerous doctors examined the friar's hands, feet, and side, though skeptics dismissed the stigmata as self-inflicted with carbolic acid, science could not explain the origin of the wounds. It could not explain why the open injuries smelled like violets or roses, instead of festering blood and flesh. It could not explain why they never healed like any other bodily wound; other injuries Padre Pio sustained, such as bruising and including necessary surgery, healed as normal. The faithful, however, understood. Padre Pio was to suffer with Christ in a unique way. Other saints, male and female, have borne the stigmata, but Padre Pio is the first ordained Catholic priest to receive those five holy wounds.

Hundreds of other miracles occurred due to Padre Pio's intercession. The protection of San Giovanni Rotondo from Allied bombing was one particularly impressive miracle. Though some accounts are unconfirmed or exaggerated by rumor and fanciful imagination, other eyewitness testimonies remain of Padre Pio's bilocation. According to the research of Fr. Pascal P. Parante, S.T.D., Ph.D., J.C.B, who was one of the foremost experts on mystical theology:

> When Italian towns were being bombed by Allied planes at the beginning of World War II, the people of San Giovanni Rotondo begged Padre Pio to intercede for them with God, their town being so close to the strategic air base of Foggia. "Your town won't be touched," declared Padre Pio emphatically. These words proved true. Not a single bomb ever fell on San Giovanni Rotondo, even though many Allied planes flew over it.[8]

Some pilots of the American 15th Air Force and the RAF's 205th group experienced the "flying" friar who gestured for them to return home, or "giant" friar who took up the whole sky and protected San Giovanni Rotondo.[9] Squadron after squadron failed to drop their explosives; other accounts claim that the apparition caused mechanical malfunctions that made the bombs fall on empty fields or caused their planes to turn around entirely.[10] Even an American general (most likely USAF Commanding General Nathan F. Twining, who was in charge of the 15th AF and 205th RAF groups at the time) had seen the flying friar. When the general visited San Giovanni Rotondo after the war, the two men recognized each other![11] Though the Church has not officially confirmed these accounts, some of which seem to conflict, multiple witnesses reported a flying monk, and no attack on San Giovanni Rotondo throughout the entire course of the war ever succeeded. Padre Pio's prayers protected the town from the ravages of war.

Other miracles have been confirmed, however. Fr. Parente detailed another miraculous occurrence, this time, the cure of a girl without pupils:

> For instance, a seven-year-old girl of Ribera (Agrigento), Gemma Di Giorgi by name, was blind since birth. There were no pupils in her eyes. Her grandmother decided to visit Padre Pio and ask him to pray that the little one would be cured. She also decided to take the youngster with her, so that

the poor child might go to confession and receive her first Holy Communion from the hands of Padre Pio.

After hearing Gemma's confession, Padre Pio gently touched her sightless eyes and assured the grandmother that all would be well... True enough. The little girl received her sight soon after making her First Communion, despite the fact that her eyes were still without pupils.[12]

Dozens of other scientifically impossible cures were wrought by the confidence of Padre Pio. A woman named Paolina miraculously resuscitated on Easter Sunday after dying of illness on Holy Saturday; a twenty-seven-year-old blind woman received sight; a boy whose spine was deformed from typhus stood up straight; a woman's intestinal cancer disappeared before surgery; a man with legs immobilized by disease walked again; dozens of other similar cases—all occurred through Padre Pio's intimate communion with God.[13]

∽

FIGHTING THE HIDEOUS GIANT

As a man of great holiness, Padre Pio often suffered physical and spiritual attacks from demons, even in his boyhood. His mission, given him by God, was to labor for the salvation of souls. Of course, Satan and his army opposed this mission and tried to thwart, scare, or tempt Padre Pio in any way they could, so that he would give up the battle. In his excellent memoir *Padre Pio: Stories and Memories of My Mentor and Friend*, Fr. Gabriele Amorth recalls a story the revered saint once told him about a spiritually important incident that occurred when he was about fifteen years old, shortly before he joined the Capuchins:

> This was a vision [Francesco] had. The youngster saw a radiant, handsome man who was beckoning to him: "Come with me, because you are to fight a valiant warrior." Together they went to a huge field. On one side were handsome men dressed in white garments; on the other were hideous men dressed in black, making them look like dark shadows. Francesco suddenly found himself facing a horrible man who was so tall that his head was in the clouds.

> The radiant figure urged the youngster to fight the giant. Francesco pleaded with him to spare him from that contest, but the other said to him, "It is useless for you to resist. You have to scuffle with him. Take heart, enter the combat with trust, and fight courageously. I will be close by, helping you, and will not let him beat you."

> The clash was terrible, but thanks to the help of that radiant figure, the giant was defeated and forced to retreat, followed by that multitude of repulsive men,

who ran off hurling shrieks, curses, and deafening cries. But the other multitude broke into shouts of rejoicing and praise for the radiant figure who had helped Francesco in the unequal fight. At this point, the figure placed a crown of indescribable beauty on Francesco's head and then removed it, saying to him, "I am setting aside for you an even more beautiful crown, if you are able to fight against that giant. He will keep attacking you, but be fearless and fight him. I will always be near you so that you may always succeed in knocking him down."[14]

Little spiritual interpretation is required to understand the meaning of this vision. Indeed, Padre Pio's entire life was a constant fight against Satan and his infernal horde. Physical as well as spiritual attacks plagued him his whole life. Demons would rip off his shirt and beat him, bruising his skin. They would torment him by disguising themselves as provocative women, or attempt to strike fear in him by appearing as foul beasts or men with weapons. Numerous letters between Padre Pio and his spiritual director, Fr. Agostino, give evidence of the conflict between the holy man and diabolic powers. Satan himself even tried on different occasions to confuse Padre Pio—once, by pretending to be a penitent seeking absolution. This is Padre Pio's own account of the incident:

One day, while I was hearing confessions, a man came to the confessional where I was. He was tall, handsome, dressed with some refinement and he was kind and polite. He started to confess his sins, which were of every kind: against God, against man and against the morals. All the sins were obnoxious! I was disoriented, in fact, for all the sins that he told me, but I responded to him with God's Word, the example of the Church, and the morals of the Saints. But the enigmatic penitent answered me word for word, justifying his sins, always with extreme ability and politeness. He excused all the sinful actions, making them sound quite normal and natural, even comprehensible on the human level. He continued this way with the sins that were gruesome against God, Our Lady, the Saints, always using disrespectful round-about argumentation. He kept this up even with the foulest of sins that could be conjured in the mind of a most sinful man. The answers that he gave me with such skilled subtlety and malice surprised me. I wondered: who is he? What world does he come from? And I tried to look at him in order to read something on his face. At the same time I concentrated on every word he spoke, trying to discover any clue to his identity. But suddenly, through a vivid, radiant and internal light I clearly recognized who he was. With

a sound and imperial tone I told him: "Say long live
Jesus, long live Mary!" As soon as I pronounced
these sweet and powerful names, Satan instantly
disappeared in a trickle of fire, leaving behind him
an unbearable stench.[15]

For all his believable excuses and sly argumentation, the Devil
could not proclaim the names of Jesus and Mary, Padre Pio's
two greatest loves. Despite the incredible, frightening attacks
against him by demons and the Prince of Lies himself, God
never permitted them to best Padre Pio. With the frequent
assistance of his guardian angel and other saints, by close obser-
vation of his interior life while having such supernatural experiences, and by the grace of Christ in his soul, the Italian monk
battled evil on every level. As the radiant figure in his vision
promised, Padre Pio was never defeated; no matter how difficult
the fight, the wicked giant fled every time.

∽

A MERCIFUL CONFESSOR

Padre Pio's confessional was, as many penitents could corrob-
orate, a place of healing. The saint certainly practiced patience
in that ministry: there were times in his life when he heard
hundreds of confessions every day. He suffered no ridiculous-
ness in his confessional and was known to remove people who
refused to repent or who did not take the sacrament seriously.
However, the Holy Spirit gave him many words of wisdom

for honest penitents, and he was also known to be gentle and fatherly. He did not sugarcoat the Truth for anyone, but frequently gave mercy where severity was unhelpful. He took his duty as a confessor with utmost seriousness and demanded the same of his penitents.

Many conversions took place after penitents saw Padre Pio for the sacrament of Reconciliation; some are famous, some less so, but all are incredibly important. Jesus spoke of heaven rejoicing over the return of one wayward son; often, Padre Pio had his work cut out for him as he sought to bring those lost sheep back into the flock. Perhaps the most famous conversion-via-confession Padre Pio encouraged in Italy was of a highly active Communist by the name of Italia Betti, who was very effective in bringing new members to the Party. Italian journalist and author Stefano Campanella, quoting information from several Italian newspapers, explains it thus:

> "[Her family] discovered that [Italia] had cancer. Her younger sister, Emerita, the only one who had 'inherited' the faith of their mother, after much insisting, convinced her to go to San Giovanni Rotondo. 'In front of the Capuchin friar, to whom are attributed so many prodigies, Professor Betti felt strangely bewildered; she confided to her sister who was close by that she felt as if she were being pushed toward the altar where Padre Pio was celebrating Mass. Even after the function was

over Professor Betti did not want to abandon her sacred place. Only after the insistence of a friar did she decide to leave, but only after having made an appointment for confession the next day... The next day, driven by impulse and emotion, Miss Betti, without waiting her turn, rushed to the confessional and publicly recanted her materialistic ideas and her past."[16]

Padre Pio's dedication to the sacrament of reconciliation consumed much of his ministry, yet his love for souls did not stop at their spiritual well-being. He devoted himself especially to the sick, for whom he developed a supernatural charity. In 1914, before his ordination, he was drafted into the Italian Medical Corps during World War I. He served for two years. During that time, he was discharged due to health concerns, then recalled to the Medical Corps over and over, until he was finally considered unfit for military service and sent back to his monastery. Many years later, he initiated the construction of a hospital called *Casa Sollievo della Sofferenza*—the House for the Relief of Suffering—in San Giovanni Rotondo. His spiritual sons began the undertaking as soon as they heard of Padre Pio's desire. When two of these men showed him the building plans, he gave them a blessing and said, "My great work on earth begins this evening. I bless you and all who will contribute to my work, which promises to be ever bigger and greater."[17]

His hospital was near and dear to his heart, as it was a place where both physical and spiritual healings could take place. In fact, Padre Pio believed it was a place where his "psychosomatic principle" was practiced. Bill Carrigan wrote that principle down for healthcare professionals to remember: "Love is the first ingredient in relieving suffering. Let the patients see and understand that they are really loved. They will soon try to return that love. God's love enters and suffering is abated. God's love is activated and this creates a spiritualized environment ... a result of God's love in action. Both patient and nurse experience spiritual grace ... God's work becomes our own."[18] Officially established in 1956, the House for the Relief of Suffering still operates today.

Furthermore, Padre Pio paid attention to the needs of both unemployed adults and uneducated children in San Giovanni Rotondo. He constantly sought to alleviate the pains of the poor and destitute, and one of the practical ways he did this was by instigating the creation of a Center for Professional Development. During and after World War II, many citizens needed jobs. Padre Pio noticed the crowds that gathered at the monastery doors to receive a few hundred *lire* here and there. When he discovered that these people sought work, but that there were no jobs for them, he spurred his fellow friar, Padre Carmelo da Sessano del Molise, to find a way to help them, to teach them to work.[19] After some time and several petitions, the friars were allowed to "create, in the area of the district of Sant'Onofrio, the Center for Professional Formation."[20] In a short twenty-five years, just under 3500 students graduated with qualifications in seventeen different fields.[21]

But this was not the only learning center Padre Pio and the Capuchins were responsible for creating. Under his guidance, spiritual sons and daughters, as well as local teachers, built three different Catholic kindergartens in three different districts of San Giovanni Rotondo, replacing the one unsatisfactory Catholic kindergarten and beating out the Protestant schools which sought to undermine the Truths of the Faith.[22] Padre Pio had a strong belief in Catholic education, and he did not want to see children deprived of such a treasure.

∾

THE ULTIMATE PRIEST

St. Pio of Pietrelcina lived a life of extraordinary grace and devotion to Christ. He worked so many miracles for the glory of God that detailing even a quarter of them could fill a book cover to cover; through the graces given by the Holy Spirit, he healed the blind, cured illnesses and injuries, provided people with material needs, prayed constantly for conversions, and even spiritually adopted souls. His prolific advice is timeless and inspires hundreds upon hundreds of people to take their spiritual lives seriously. He was a true witness of Christ. Perhaps no one articulated Padre Pio's life better than Pope St. John Paul II, who canonized the stigmatist in 2002. "The life and mission of Padre Pio," the pope said at Padre Pio's canonization Mass, "prove that difficulties and sorrows, if accepted out of love, are transformed into a privileged way of holiness, which opens onto the horizons of a greater good, known only to the Lord."[23] St. Pio of Pietrelcina is, as Bill Carrigan came to understand, one of the holiest saints of the twentieth century.

CHAPTER EIGHT

WWII: Bill as Field Director

February 1943 – November 1945

❧

PROMOTION

I n February of 1944, not long after his initial encounter with Padre Pio, William M. Carrigan received a promotion with the American Red Cross. He became a field director, the head of Foggia's ARC Field Office. Almost immediately, his work increased—and so did his ministry revolving around Padre Pio.

It was not a job for the fainthearted, the lazy, or the easily overwhelmed. He wrote home about how his days were "filled with every conceivable type of request. Locate Hungarian, Romanian, Russian, Greek, Jew, etc. etc. in all parts of Europe. Find a grave of a friend or brother, decorate a grave for someone requesting it back home, [get] transportation for a man to Belgium for purposes of finding his family, etc. etc."[1] And that was just one portion of the job! He also made arrangements with the Vatican to "handle communications" for noncombatants "seeking prisoners of war [and] families in Europe, as well as soldiers who have families in German occupied [and] lost territories."[2]

His important communication efforts did not decrease as he stepped into his new role[3]; however, the greatest service he carried out, judging by the detailed information he often conveyed in his letters to Ramona, were the discipline and personal counseling he provided for the men in his care. In a way, Bill waged his own war against the sufferings and evils around him—particularly the moral evils. That war began with his doughnut operations in Tunisia and Sicily, but it took on a different character as he settled into his role as field director and became better acquainted with Padre Pio.

～

TOURS AND TALKS

As part of the Service to Armed Forces division, Bill was often responsible for providing entertainment to his soldiers. In two key ways, he made sure the boys had something other than death and war to contemplate: tours to significant historical sites, and community talks that helped the men make sense of themselves and their situation. He had begun this service in North Africa—visiting Carthage, for example—but it expanded rapidly when he became a field director. As a great lover of history and art, Bill considered the tours a chance for him to exercise his own knowledge, too, as well as increase his public speaking skills, since nearly all his speeches were extemporaneous![4] Apparently, he worried about keeping "an audience interested" and the tours with historical lectures helped him gain confidence.[5]

He gave only the best to his boys, as noted in a letter to Ramona on June 1, 1944: "I just returned from a long sight-seeing trip with a group of my men. I cannot name the place, but if you know me[,] I go to the best places. We had a very satisfactory tour."[6] Though letter censorship prevented him from specifying the locations of his tours, he strove to provide intellectual enrichment in as high a quality as he could. Rome, unsurprisingly, was his favorite stop. As early as September 1943, only a few short months after his arrival in Africa, he hoped to be sent into Rome.[7] Perhaps he wanted to be close to the fighting, like during the Invasion of Sicily. Perhaps he wanted to be close to the ancient historical sites, the relics of martyrs and great saints, and the numerous, beautiful Catholic churches. Though the Army Post Office (APO) codes on Bill's letters and the content of his missives indicate that he did not receive a long-term aid assignment to Rome, he nevertheless was lucky enough to visit the Vatican more than once; there, he enjoyed the Papal Garden and from it plucked multiple flowers, including a rhododendron and a rose—gifts he sent home to Ramona.[8]

Along with the tours, Bill sometimes hosted American celebrities who performed for the soldiers. In March of 1944, for example, he "entertained Hollywood's John Garfield and Jean Darling, along with some lesser lights...before and after they put on a show for the Group."[9] Showing off his sense of humor, Bill then joked, "You see I mingle with these celebrities so much now that I've lost interest in such things as autographs!"[10]

As well as coordinating American stars, the Red Cross also "provided speakers for many of the programs in our area."[11] If a guest speaker was not available and no one else was scheduled for a group discussion, responsibility fell on Bill himself. He found this work engaging and intellectually stimulating, not only for himself but also for the troops. His discussions covered everything from geography, to art, to the Christian history of particular sites or regions, to morality and Catholic theology.[12] The former seminarian half-joked, "I feel I can handle the average man when it comes to theology. I might not change his views, but I can give him something to think about."[13]

Most talks, however, centered on one highly favored topic: the future. Everyone wanted to talk over what post-war life might be like, how they would conduct themselves on political, moral, and spiritual levels after the war concluded. In one instance, Bill gave such a talk to about sixty men, all of whom seemed willing to listen to their field director extemporize for an hour and a half, then participate in questions and answers. A distinctly fatherly attitude pervaded his discussion. He proudly told Ramona about it:

> One group of fellows told me afterwards that I left them plenty of food for thought [and] that they were already putting their minds to work on some of the things I said. One fellow said it was like a match starting a fire, it was spreading fast. Well, I do not think they will lose much sleep. But if I can

take their minds off sex and the pin-up nakedness
in their quarters for tonight and put them talking
[and] thinking about their own future, perhaps I've
done a good job. I tried to put them straight on a
few things at home. A few pointed remarks about
the portion of life that is being shaped for us, and
some of the angles about our problems, pressure
groups, politics, etc. etc., even a point or two on
sex in answer to questions. We had an interesting
evening.[14]

Once the 15th Air Force became acquainted with Padre Pio, the
saint also captivated their minds and hearts. The talks, evening
conferences, and "frequent G.I. group discussions" Bill led after
Christmas of 1943 often centered on the great saint and the
graces flowing from him into those who visited him.[15] In his
May 18, 1944, letter to Colonel John Laboon, Sr., Bill explained:

When the soldiers board their trucks and begin the
winding trip down the mountain, [there] is much
silence and deep thought. When conversation starts,
it is always about Padre Pio and what effect he
had on them. Reactions vary greatly, but everyone
reports an undefinable change in their being. One
said that he found Padre Pio looking at him as he
entered the Sacristy and in that moment, he felt
that Padre Pio could see right into his mind, and

the sins of his whole life seemed to flash into his consciousness. Another man told me that he felt that his soul was given a profound shaking and his mind put to work at right thinking. Back in camp the soldiers think and talk about this wonderful Priest and what he must be.[16]

⌇

MORAL GUIDANCE

Though part of his Red Cross job, personal counseling did not always come easily to Bill. True, he possessed a university-level education in psychology, a strong sense of Christian morality, and experience with giving guidance, but he also admitted that he did not always know what to say.[17] Despite his concerns, however, he always tried to right wrongs where he could, with varying degrees of success. And he owed much to his saintly friend: "I don't know what I would do if I did not have Padre Pio to settle some problems," he declared.[18]

Padre Pio was such a spiritual gift to the men in Bill's care that often the field director referred stubborn disciplinary cases to the saint. And who better to send them to than the "designer of souls," the "spiritual artist," who was so intimately united with the Lord?[19] At one point, Carrigan recalled a soldier who became a discipline problem.[20] At Bill's urging, the man agreed to see Padre Pio. After fifteen minutes with the saint, "the soldier's attitude changed radically."[21] Later that day, the man noticed impoverished children playing in Foggia's streets and

learned that the displaced kids "spent their time robbing soldiers or inviting them, for a fee, to their sisters' beds;" not long
after, Foggia received a large donation of sports equipment,
including baseballs and basketballs.[22] Once a discipline concern,
the soldier became the enterprising organizer of a children's
recreational program.

But problematic soldiers were not the only ones Bill urged
to see the saint. Anyone he thought might benefit from Padre
Pio's holiness he directed up the Monte Calvo. A traveling new-
lywed couple whom Bill hosted, for example, received such an
invitation. "I've convinced them a trip to Padre Pio tomorrow
will add greatly to their honeymoon," he told Ramona. "They
are going. I am evidently a convincing fellow."[23]

Sometimes, the soldiers and their civilian lovers went to Bill for
one-on-one advice. One such example he wrote about in late
1944. Throughout the course of the day, two different soldiers
came to him to ask about marriage to local Italian girls. Of the
two marriages, Bill saw only one as being advisable: "It's interesting, but this morning I assisted in getting one soldier married,
and this afternoon spent some time trying to dissuade another
from a similar course. Not exactly that, but rather to impress
him with the tremendous obstacles to marriage over here in
war time."[24] It appears that Bill was unsuccessful in swaying the
man from his desires. Instead, he "got part of an answer [from]
him—a promise to go with me to Padre Pio and talk with him

about it."[25] And of the married man, he wrote: "I devoted my time to providing transportation and personal attention to one of our soldiers who married a local girl. He was sold on the idea. Being of Italian extraction, he is right at home. He has a nice girl and they are both Catholics, married at Mass, so perhaps it will work out."[26] Noticeably, he did not forbid or bar the first man from getting married; he did not attempt to force the man to this or that course of action. Instead, he simply tried to make the man aware of the dangers, and convinced him to visit the best spiritual guide available.

As if new marriages were not complicated enough, infidelity in pre-existing marriages was also a problem during the war, prominent on both sides of the Atlantic. Nuptials celebrated before and during the war fell apart as men were held overseas longer than expected. Wives at home decided they had waited long enough; they were not going to "go through another winter without a man."[27] Even families with children began to split as the "magnanimous girls [gave] their men their 'freedom.' ... Divorce seems to be the easy way out. I do not know what comfort to offer these men," Bill wrote.[28]

Prostitution also ensnared some of the soldiers, married or not. This greatly angered Bill; he treated the topic with the utmost contempt and hatred. Toward the end of his assignment in Italy—July 4, 1945, to be exact—Bill wrote a scathing letter home in which he detailed the less than patriotic day and the manner in which soldiers were choosing to honor their country. He lived right across from a clinic with a sign reading *V.S. Army*

Pro Station; here, soldiers could obtain medical intervention to avoid sexually transmitted diseases. According to Bill, who had a full view of the place, visitors were infrequent.[29] Though the American army attempted to tactfully encourage soldiers "on grounds of patriotism, unit pride, faithfulness to loved ones at home, and personal self-interest" to avoid wrongful sexual contact, over six hundred soldiers fell ill with various venereal diseases daily in 1944.[30] And, since VE Day, May 8, 1945, Bill claimed that venereal disease had been "on a rampage," passed around by the "ladies in the business."[31] Why should the Fourth of July be any different? There were no real celebrations—no fireworks or sparklers—but he could be sure that the soldiers were having their fun in another way. "It stinks to high heaven— the whole dirty business," he wrote, disgusted. "They told the boys in the beginning they could have their cake and eat it, because health measures were fool proof... The days of Sodom and Gomorrah are returning."[32] It must have been particularly frustrating for Bill, since he consistently encouraged the troops to practice virtuous sexual conduct.[33]

To these matters of infidelity, divorce, and cheap promises, Bill could not truly relate, which made it difficult for him to offer comfort. He did not have to worry about losing Ramona; she told him that she was a "one-man woman."[34] Though it appeared "cruel at times to be away," he could not help but thank God for his situation of separation.[35] He and Ramona both knew faithfulness to one's spouse could be accomplished. "There are a lot like us, just the same," he wrote to Ramona. "They are the ones doing a good job silently—silently suffering out their separation."[36] Quite the contrary to many of the issues he saw around him, Bill reported that her dedicated love, frequent Masses, and prayers fueled his ability to counsel the soldiers: "A lad told me this evening I was the first one who ever gave him a hand and encouraged him to hang onto his ideas and live right. So you are giving strength to others through me."[37]

⌬

CARE OUTSIDE THE ARMY

At times, Bill's counseling and care extended beyond the American soldiers of the 15th Air Force. His free time was limited; it was not often that he finished enough pressing work for the military to allow him to assist outside causes. His "first duty" was to the troops, and he had precious little time for what he called "extracurricular activity."[38] He sometimes had to limit himself from speaking with the misfortunate local citizens while he was in Africa so as not to become distracted: "The native people I have had little to do with, for different reasons. I'm soft-hearted[;] I'd have to do something for them if I became friendly, and I'm pledged to work for the soldier."[39]

He likely felt the same way about the people of Foggia. His interactions with the locals in Italy were not frequent, but he did write home about a few notable occurrences that edged out of military work. One such instance: in May of 1945, nearing the end of Bill's European tour, three Italian women came into his office, each one pregnant. They inquired if Bill could get in touch with the soldiers who had promised to marry them. Bill, a bit miffed, asked "if they ever thought that marriage was supposed to come before pregnancy rather than after?"[40] The girls just smiled, acting as if they knew nothing of the sort. Bill then had three pregnancies to "look after now and it is something, I assure you."[41]

Another instance: across multiple letters, Bill asked Ramona to mail over household items such as sewing needles and handkerchief fabric for a group of local nuns. He drove the consecrated women to a city whose name is unknown due to military censorship, and he thoroughly enjoyed serving them. "There is so much pure Christian virtue in these nuns in [Italy]. I am amazed they can do so much with so little... I find myself enjoying life more when I am doing little things for these holy children of Christ than when I do anything else."[42] In addition to the friendly aid to the nuns, he also provided humanitarian aid to the destitute local community. In June 1945, only a few months before the end of the war, Bill was put in charge of distributing items that the troops left behind as they began returning home. Clothing, food, and many other things he allocated to schools and orphanages, taking care of the most vulnerable in any war-torn society: the children.[43]

⤙⤚

A WITNESS TO GREAT SUFFERING

In the two years that he was with the ARC, but especially as a field director, Bill witnessed significant suffering. Though he had a "tough military exterior," at his core, he was gentle-hearted, with a special compassion for people who were hurting, regardless of their nationality or social class.[44] However, having compassion, by very definition, meant that Bill suffered alongside those around him. From his vantage points in both Tunisia and Foggia, he watched historic events take place, but he also saw the aftermath of those events. He "took the last will and testament of the chief [bombardier] on that very secret, very historic first mission to cross over to Russia."[45] He saw B-24 bombers leave Libya for Operation Tidal Wave, which sought to destroy a critical Axis fuel deposit at the Ploesti oil fields in Romania; saw B-25s depart for the Brenner Pass, the Axis' resupply lines in the Alps between Italy and Austria; saw the "quiet and beautiful morning sky" that was an hour later "rent ... by the terrible bombing of Monte Cassino Abbey," which he heard; saw planes take off to bomb Vienna, Berlin, and more.[46] When visiting the ruins of Monte Cassino Abbey, founded by St. Benedict in the fifth century, the surviving monks told him that "five hundred civilians still remained buried beneath the rubble."[47] Not always from a distance did Bill experience the viciousness of war. Sometimes, his stations in North Africa came under attack by Axis forces; he described the experience in 1945, only a few months after he returned to the United States:

> The violence of battle in this war cannot be described. The atmosphere itself at times would become so hostile that the very air around one

seemed to tear at one's clothing and skin. The splitting, shrieking, vibrating air in a bombardment was often more frightful than the sight of the explosions. The violent shifting of air masses would push and pull the brain in its cavity so viciously that a man would become angry, mad, and frightened without knowing exactly what was causing it, and not a few died from concussion.[48]

This was death on a large scale, but Bill also watched deaths on a smaller, more personal scale. Though he did not often tell Ramona about the tragedies he witnessed, probably preferring to give her an upbeat report so as not to unduly worry her, certain instances slipped into his writings. In a few snapshots to her and others, he painted a painfully clear picture of seemingly pointless suffering.

Men who went to him for assistance one day died the next. In April 1944, Bill wrote home to Ramona that he had witnessed a Catholic soldier die by flak burst. This man had just recently asked Bill to "find out how his wife was getting along" as she was pregnant and due to give birth soon.[49] Difficult situations of this nature occurred more than once. Each time, Bill could not help but think of the family back home who would have to bear the terrible loss. "This war strikes fast and wickedly at any moment and it isn't choosy," he wrote.[50] On another occasion, Bill cared for traumatized soldiers returning from a mission where nearly half their unit was gunned down by Nazis on the way to Rome.[51] And, at times, he witnessed civilians hurting just as much as, or even more than, the Allies. He wrote home one day about his "many serious jobs" including transporting a local woman whose back had been broken. His vehicle was a "broken-down Italian ambulance" and the atmosphere one of "inhuman disregard for the gravity of the situation... Her back was broken three weeks ago and no one would lift a hand to help her."[52] After personally orchestrating her admission to a comfortable hospital, Bill told Ramona his theory, which he first put into action in 1933, building the St. Vincent's swimming pool: "If you have a good work to do, the people who have the means will help, if it is put to them in the right way."[53] This philosophy pervaded his work with the Red Cross.

Around 313,000 Allied soldiers died in the Italian Campaign, which lasted from 1943 to 1945. To grasp the scope of this loss, the New York Yankees stadium holds about 60,000 people; approximately five and a half Yankees stadiums' worth of Allied men died over the course of two short years. Those who escaped death often returned with unimaginable injuries of body and mind. It was these men with whom Bill consorted on a daily basis while in Italy. It was these men who went to him for moral, material, or mental help. Looking at these statistics, it is not hard to imagine that many of the jobs Bill worked involved neglect for human life, fear, worry, and trauma. He was no stranger to these problems, nor was he often shocked by the harsh circumstances.[54] Much of it, maybe even most of it, was pure suffering—little to nothing could be done to prevent or improve the circumstances. Bill understood this. He was, in many ways, "up close and personal" to the damage of war, and he could not always provide relief.[55]

The heaviness Bill carried was perhaps made a little lighter by the knowledge that it was not wasted suffering. Very rarely did Bill complain about his circumstances while in the warzone. He carried his cross with a dignity inherent to someone who trusted in God and in himself, who sought after things that were eternal rather than temporal, who worked good on earth while keeping his eyes on heaven.[56] He saw that "suffering could be redemptive," an experience which "hardened him and toughened him and prepared him ... to be the man of character that he became."[57]

∽

THE MASS

While the conditions around him were dire, Bill considered one thing his anchor and solace: the Holy Eucharist. It was a source of great comfort and strength for him. The graces he received at the altar fueled his ability to do his job as both assistant field director and field director. While in North Africa, he wrote home about the little church the soldiers used for their services:

> It is a very interesting Church; as I said before it is shell-pocked and chipped almost beyond repair, but it is being repaired. I was all alone there before a beautiful altar, and my visit with our Dear Lord

was most satisfactory. I felt a great happiness there, as I have felt on a great number of occasions in my life. I could not help but pour out my love for Christ in the Blessed Sacrament for the very numerous blessings I have received from Him.[58]

Less than a year later, he stated, briefly but powerfully, that he "enjoy[ed] Mass very much," because it helped him reconstruct his life and his connection to Ramona.[59] It brought relief and interior peace, no matter the conditions under which the holy sacrifice took place, which were rarely what he was used to seeing in the United States. For one, regulations were not as strict. "We can go to Communion at this evening Mass even though we just ate dinner," he told Ramona. "It is a little odd at first, but so many changes make it easy to take a few more."[60] For another, Mass was not always in an ancient church or a beautiful cathedral! Once, Bill wrote about holding the service in a bar room: "We just [threw] out the drunks and took over for a half hour, while the boys cooled off outside. That is the tempo we work under. Next week we may have Mass in a stable, a cave, on a truck, or in a Church, one never knows. But we have Mass," he added. "That is essential."[61]

Bill touched on something that the great saints of history have spoken about at length. Attending Mass and receiving Jesus in the Blessed Sacrament was his way of finding peace amidst intense personal and societal suffering. Padre Pio's services, more than any others, impacted Bill on a deep spiritual level. After one morning Mass in May 1944, Bill hurriedly penned a letter, striving to capture his feelings about his experience. "The experience has *added up to everything that went before and piled a little more on top*," he stated.[62] He then detailed the unusual fortitude he noticed in himself as a result of Padre Pio's holy Masses:

> No words are necessary when Padre says Mass. I could go into some wonderful descriptions but I almost fear writing what I really feel and think about him. I've questioned myself about the permanency of this new strength, and, somehow I think it will be *very* permanent. So again I find in trying to help others to better living, I come through with the knowledge that I have gained far more than I put into it. That seems to be the common experience when one tries to give others a hand.[63]

Even the Masses he did not attend, such as the ones Ramona offered almost daily for him at their parish in Maryland, settled his heart. He relied on grace to make sense of things in a period of senselessness—and the violence, fear, pain, and anger that could and did drive men mad. The reconstruction he mentioned attests to his openness to God's grace. Though he may have been often full of sorrow or pain—given his sensitivity to others' suffering—grace prevented him from despairing.

Bill once expressed to Ramona his hopes that his work, especially his talks with the soldiers, would mean something later on. "Maybe something will evolve out of this war and my experience which will take us whirling through new, uncharted regions of experience and adventure," he said.[64] The answer to that speculation, that hopeful perspective, came through Padre Pio, the Holy Man of Gargano, who completed and surpassed the good Bill had started.

CHAPTER NINE

WWII: Bill's Personal Experiences with Padre Pio

1944 – 1945

∽

MAYBE MIRACLES

In numerous letters and later presentations, Bill indicated that, during his overseas work in World War II, he frequently interacted with Padre Pio. He was honored to be an altar server at Padre Pio's Masses on numerous occasions. The two of them spent time in conversation, even though Bill knew little Italian and Padre Pio knew little English; divine aid may have translated for them. After all, Padre Pio possessed the gift of xenoglossia—speaking and understanding languages he had not learned—and Bill recalled: "Padre Pio didn't have any language facility except what he called his very poor Neapolitan Italian... We had many conversations when ... nobody was around, and I don't know just how we communicated, but we did."[1] Bill even ate with him at his one daily meal—"It is a joy to sit beside him for dinner," he wrote—and slept in the monastery cell beside the saint's: rare privileges indeed.[2] He wrote often of his growing friendship with the Italian mystic. "Darling," he told Ramona in one letter, "you have no idea how it feels to have a saint embrace you and throw a deep radiant smile at you. Well, I think I get more than the usual amount of it. For he really gives out when I visit him."[3]

In a note about himself, probably designed as a short biography for a newspaper or memoir, Bill wrote that he "went behind the many facades (false and true) which sprung up ... to find the real Padre Pio. I have been most fortunate to have had direct contact with Padre Pio during and after the war, whenever I was privileged to go to the monastery... To kneel in night prayers with the community beside him and his arm buckled in mine—unforgettable moments."[4] Through the many hours of time spent with the saint, Bill became, as the Capuchins later told him, Padre Pio's best American friend.[5]

This intimate connection put Bill in a unique position as one of the few Americans—indeed, one of the few laypeople in general—who "really knew Padre Pio through personal contact."[6] It seemed he would have the chance to witness many miracles and supernatural phenomena, but he related, "In all my experience with Padre Pio, I never, *never* observed anything miraculous."[7] Personally, Bill did not witness any instances of bilocation, any fights with demons, any incredible healings; he was quite disappointed by the frivolous misconception that Padre Pio was some kind of "fairy godfather" who "knew everything and could do everything."[8] The saint was not the Lord God any more than Bill himself was, and Bill disliked the notion that all the good works were due to Padre Pio's power rather than to God's grace. To this point, Bill even recorded Padre Pio's desires to direct thanksgiving toward the True Giver, which were later published in *The Catholic Standard*: "To those who wished to thank him for graces received: 'If you have received a grace, do not thank me, but go and thank our Lord. He is the one who gave it.'"[9]

Perhaps in defiance of the fantastical notions that rose up as Padre Pio became more and more popular, Bill possessed a healthy skepticism for the miraculous. He was a level-headed man, not one to fall prey to propaganda, hazy claims, or empty promises; he was not a fanatic in his devotion to Padre Pio. Bill simply knew what he had witnessed. Because of this, he was hesitant to believe every single miracle or grace that petitioners claimed to experience.

Despite his skepticism, Bill did recount a pair of personal experiences with Padre Pio's supernatural gifts, though he was not sure they could be attributed as miracles. He related these via an interview with C. Bernard Ruffin, whose excellent research and writing shine through in his book, *Padre Pio: The True Story*.

The first occurred when, while writing at his desk in Foggia, Bill noticed a very particular smell. He "'had no trouble in identifying the aroma as that of Padre Pio... It wasn't something you could confuse with any other odor.'"[10] Indeed, that scent, often compared to roses or lavender, was a sign of the saint's presence, even when he was not physically present and even after he passed away. It is one of the well-known phenomena associated with Padre Pio's holy wounds. Bill would come into contact with that distinct aroma again while facilitating someone else's minor miracle.

The second curious experience was "the closest thing to a supernatural manifestation" Bill ever personally witnessed.[11] Sometime between early 1944 and late 1945, the Red Cross told Bill that he was being reassigned. A new field director, fresh from the United States, would take over in Foggia, and Bill would transfer to Leghorn, a port city in Tuscany, Italy, nearly 450 miles away from Foggia. Whether the change upset Bill can only be speculated, but not long after he received the news, he met Padre Pio in the friary garden and "told his priest-friend that he expected to be transferred soon to Leghorn."[12] After a long pause, Padre Pio "gazed across the valley illuminated by the setting sun. Then he made a cryptic statement: 'He will go, and you will stay.' Although Carrigan has been deeply hesitant to attribute this statement to supernatural wisdom, it happened as Padre Pio said."[13]

Though Bill had reservations about his own outwardly mystical experiences, his letters tell a slightly different story. He absolutely believed in the passage of grace from God, through Pio, to himself. That was never a doubt. Numerous times, he expressed complete certainty that Padre Pio was a living saint whose intercession with the Lord was powerful: "Special graces are flowing our way... But always I try to gather grace for you too. I want you to have more, and still more, spiritual comfort. We have a saint, very definitely, on our side."[14] Through this grace, Padre Pio began to deeply impact

Bill's perspective. The middle-aged field director tried to see things from the saint's spiritual point of view. While he was overseas, even after a year of knowing Padre Pio, he sensed Padre Pio's hand in his life, giving him strength to carry out his work and to withstand his long separation from his beloved wife. "Needless to say," he wrote to Ramona, "Padre is a very close friend of ours. He will not forget us in his Masses and prayers as long as he lives... To me, no one on this side of the Atlantic means a thing in comparison to him. He is a great man in the truest sense."[15]

Of all the encounters he had with Padre Pio, one of the most important occurred during his final meal with the saint in November of 1945. The monastery was chilly, as it often was during the later months, so Bill wore his Army overcoat.

As they finished dinner, Bill decided that he wished to keep some memento of Padre Pio for when he returned to the United States. Boldly, he asked if he could keep the saint's spoon, picking it up from the table. Padre Pio gently took the utensil from Bill's hand and instead placed his empty wineglass into Bill's deep overcoat pocket. Then he sliced a piece off one of the Italian rolls served with the meal, blessed it, and handed it to Bill with the statement, "With these, you will not want."[16]

Surprised, Bill accepted the gifts. After their meal ended and the guests exited the refectory, Bill asked a Hungarian priest, another visitor to San Giovanni Rotondo who had witnessed the exchange, what he thought Padre Pio meant. "Well," the priest said, "Padre Pio has worked out a lot of symbolism to convey ideas... You shouldn't have any trouble with that one."[17]

And Bill did not. He understood at once that Padre Pio referred to the Holy Eucharist, the bread and wine that became the Body and Blood of Christ. "I think that his statement was very true in my case," Bill mused. "I just can't account for a lot of things that have happened in the last forty-something years. And I feel a responsibility to pass the word along that Padre Pio was no ordinary priest. He is the ultimate priest, and one who can help you as well as he's helped hundreds of thousands of others." He paused, then added, "And me."[18]

FAVORS BILL DID FOR PADRE PIO

Bill's heart for generosity and service extended assuredly to the monks in San Giovanni Rotondo, made more fervent by his friendship with the saint. For example, one Christmas, he orchestrated the cutting of pine trees for the soldiers, then donated a few to the monastery for the priests there.[19] However, he had two recorded incidents of special favors that he performed specifically for Padre Pio.

On June 4, 1944, Bill and others were able to visit Rome, recently recovered by the Allies, on one of apparently several tours to the Eternal City. He told his holy priest-friend about his travel plans, saying "Padre, look ... I'd like to see the Pope when I go up there. Padre, come on, let's go. Come with us. See the Pope."[20] In response to the invitation to travel, Padre

Pio declined with the surprising statement that "they" would kill him![21] Bill later explained the mystic's unusual statement: if the people of Italy knew he was traveling to Rome, "every town and hamlet" would have turned out and "surrounded him."[22] But, to Bill's desire to see the Pope, Padre Pio replied, "Yes, you will and give him a message... Tell him I pray for him and love him."[23]

With that message in mind, Bill left Foggia for Rome. When they arrived, the whole city was filled with Allied military. Not only were they the triumphant liberators, but they were also guests—Pope Pius XII was holding an open house for the Allied servicemen. Bill did not know this until they had almost reached the Vatican. Accompanied by a lieutenant, he entered a large room inside the Vatican. "The place was absolutely packed and we just got inside the door and that was all," he explained, "so the possibility of getting anywhere near the Pope was ridiculous."[24] It seemed he would have no chance to deliver Padre Pio's message. At the back of the crowd, Bill would never have had a chance if not for the "highly dressed guard" who came through, asking if there were any French individuals there; "a few held up their hands."[25] The guard then pointed to a door right behind Bill, indicating that the Pope would speak to those individuals privately. Bill turned to the lieutenant, asking "You understand French?"[26]

Upon hearing the lieutenant's affirmative answer, Bill cried, "Let's go!"[27]

He and the lieutenant joined the twenty or so people who left the extremely crowded exterior room. Pope Pius XII greeted the Frenchmen, then hurried with them from that room's stage to another room's stage where he was going to meet some Americans. Bill continued:

> I walked right alongside him, held out my rosary, and had him bless it as we walked along. He walked very fast. I was able to come right in with him on the stage, and I was standing right up on the stage as he talked to the crowd. Then he made a quick, quick sweep around the circle on the stage, would hold out his ring to anybody that wanted to kiss it, and then say a word or two. And when he came to me, I took his ring, kissed it—I said, "Your Holiness, Padre Pio sends his love." He stopped and ... he leaned over and he said, "Padre Pio! How is he? We haven't heard anything from him."[28]

Once again, Padre Pio's prediction came true, and Bill was able to deliver the message as requested. This favor was relatively minor, though, for the other recorded instance had Bill in much higher stakes: for this life-or-death matter, Bill was asked to ignore the rules of the military and ARC.

Bill's "special mission" was to help a woman named Mrs. Abresch.[29] The war was almost over at this point, as Bill recalled. The British army had "pushed the Germans north, past Ancona,"

Italy, which was over two hundred miles away from Foggia.[30] Bill did not ever expect to make that trek, but his holy friend specifically commanded him to take Mrs. Abresch to Ancona. She was dying—seemingly from hemorrhaging that required surgery—so, Padre Pio called Bill to help. He informed the Red Cross field director that he ought to take an ambulance to a hospital in Ancona, where a special penitent of his, a doctor, would take care of her. Bill thought it was a crazy request. He and Padre Pio knew the rule: Red Cross evacuation vehicles were not to be used for civilians. "We can't do it," Bill said.[31]

Padre Pio replied firmly, "Get an ambulance and take her up there."[32]

That night, Bill slept poorly. He knew there was a hospital in Foggia from which he could obtain an ambulance, and he did not know any of the officials at that hospital ... maybe he had a chance. A slim chance, but it was something. "When I got up and had my breakfast," he said, he finally decided, "I've got to do *something* about this. So I went over to the hospital and introduced myself to the [Commanding Officer], a colonel there, a doctor."[33]

Bill explained his tale, telling the colonel about Padre Pio— had he heard about the mystic? Yes, the colonel, though not Catholic, had heard the stories. So Bill told the officer in all frankness, "He is very insistent that this woman will die if we don't get her up to that hospital [in Ancona]."[34] The colonel reiterated the rule: no evacuation vehicles for civilian purposes.

Feeling he had failed, Bill started to leave. But before he could, the colonel suddenly spoke up.

He said, "There's another rule that we have in the hospital, that we're supposed to help Red Cross... I'll put in an order to the motor pool for an ambulance and a driver."[35]

Knowing it was outside the demands of his regular ARC work, knowing he was using his day off to make a long, difficult trip, knowing the colonel was going out on a limb to loan the ambulance, Bill set off. His gratitude he expressed to Ramona, stating that it was a "very good gesture on his part ... for there are no rules in the book [by] which he would be obligated to follow in my demands. He could refuse me easily. I am sure Padre is engineering the whole thing."[36]

At six-thirty in the morning the next day, the ambulance transported Mrs. Abresch out of Foggia; Bill and a nurse accompanied her.[37] For even a healthy person, the roads were punishing—a product of previous heavy bombing—and they were forced to drive over two streams when the road was too damaged.[38] Though the drive was long and painful for poor Mrs. Abresch, her condition mercifully did not worsen. They reached the Ancona hospital eleven hours later. The sick woman was taken away for "the best care available at this time," Bill reported. "She will be there several weeks building up and taking blood transfusions before operation... Padre Pio and this doctor both feel she will be o.k. after the operation."[39]

In his later recollections of the special favor for Padre Pio, Bill mulled over the way everything worked out so perfectly.

"I think Padre Pio had a special hand in the whole thing," he declared. "I never secured an ambulance before... The doctor, on arrival there, told me he knew I was going to bring her, as Padre told him so some two weeks before."[40]

> And the next morning we came on back [to Foggia] and I returned the ambulance. Nobody ever knew what happened. As far as I was concerned, I thought I might be called up for court martial or something. But it was fine, and that is very good! I was hoping that that was over, but about a month later, Padre Pio sent for me again.
>
> He said, "She's well now, go up and get her!"
>
> I said, "No, Padre, please! I was lucky the first time."
>
> Well, we got the ambulance, went up, and again, nobody knew anything about it.[41] Things happen strangely every once in a while.[42]

SPIRITUAL FATHER AND SON

Bill and Padre Pio shared a close friendship where both enjoyed the other's company, as evidenced by many visits during and even after Bill's service with the ARC. The mystic seemed to show special attention to his Red Cross friend; even in a crowded room, he would ask for Bill specifically, or ask him to visit after Mass, with a "simple friendliness" that brought Bill nearly to tears each time.[43] "I've asked him to do so many things," Bill wrote, "and I believe he does them as if they were his first concern. And I know thousands seek him out."[44] Even five years after Bill left Foggia, Padre Pio asked whether Bill would be visiting that year. The Capuchin's superior, who often wrote on Padre Pio's behalf, noted: "So you see, that in spite of the hundreds who are coming here this year, Fr. Pio has not forgotten Mr. [Carrigan]."[45]

In that friendship, Bill was sensitive to Padre Pio's humanity as well as his intense spirituality—he sent Padre Pio pineapple juice when he was ill and long underwear for the winter to help him stay warm. That Bill was devoted to and loved Padre Pio was no question, but they were not merely a mentor and a student. A letter written on July 14, 1947, by the Capuchin's superior at San Giovanni Rotondo, gives evidence that their relationship extended deeper: "He always remembers you with that love which a father feels for his son and he will ask the Lord to shower blessings and grace upon you and Ramona."[46]

Padre Pio also personally demonstrated his paternal care. One day, Bill served at the altar during one of the stigmatist's Masses. Afterward the liturgy concluded, Bill was about to leave, but Padre Pio stopped him and, "taking a beautiful, deep red rose from the altar ... he gave it, saying: 'This rose represents the great love I have for you.'"[47] It was a simple gesture, but one Bill held dear. It impressed upon him the depth of their spiritual relationship.

On the receiving end of such care and attention, Bill grew increasingly aware of his unworthiness, yet encountered such tenderness and mercy in Padre Pio that his response was prayer rather than despair. "I am not a holy man and I have many sinful weaknesses," he confessed to Ramona, "but he seems to not be harsh with me because of my sins... Sweetheart, let us draw close to Our Lord and always have Padre Pio as our interpreter and guide in that august court of Heaven. I am sure we cannot do better. Charity and obedience should be our will as shown us by our conscience and all will be well for us."[48]

He wanted to always remain under Padre Pio's guidance, for he was *in persona Christi* more visibly, more tangibly, than any other priest Bill had encountered. From this holy friendship sprung a well of strength, as Bill mentioned on multiple occasions. Peace, too, was a likely result of his friendship with the saint, since Padre Pio occasionally reminded Bill not to worry so much.[49]

BILL'S SPECIAL REQUEST

As Padre Pio's best American friend, Bill Carrigan enjoyed a close relationship with the great Italian saint. It was a privilege that afforded opportunities to know Padre Pio personally, which meant Bill had many pieces of advice, many stories, and many truths to share with the world. From that friendship, Bill drew many graces for himself and for Ramona, joining the flow of grace from God; and he had a particular favor he wanted to ask of the Lord through His servant Pio.

Bill had been away from his beloved Ramona for nearly two years, with the exception of a brief leave in late 1944. The separation was, at most times, incredibly painful. When it was milder, it was a dull ache. They had no children, which was a source of sorrow for both of them. So, while still serving overseas, Bill took a particularly sensitive request to both Ramona and his spiritual mentor.

Chapter Ten

July 1943 - November 1945

∽

A Painful Separation

" **I** never realized until I came here how one woman has captured my whole life and my whole future," Bill Carrigan wrote to his wife. "I hope this damn war will soon be over and you and I can again be together."[1]

On September 3, 1943, the very same day that the Allies began their invasion of Italy, Ramona Jane Carrigan sat down at her typewriter to compose an anniversary letter to her husband. It was the first time in five years that the Carrigan couple were not side by side on that special day, and a now-familiar sensation of grief settled into Ramona's heart. Along with her sorrow was a deep gratitude for the anniversary gift which Bill had arranged to be delivered to their home. "My dearest love," Ramona began, "As I write this letter, your lovely yellow roses are right by my side and their fragrance fills the room. Darling, there is nothing that you could have thought of that would have pleased me as much as yellow roses."[2] After several pages of news from home and answers to his questions in previous letters, interspersed with declarations of love, she concluded: "Bill, I love you more than all than all the world... Good night, my dear, and I wish with all my heart that I could lie as I did in your arms five years ago. I send you my heart in a yellow rose petal."[3]

When Bill parted from Ramona on that bittersweet morning in July 1943, he had no idea that he would be away from her for over two years, with only one brief leave period to visit her in late 1944. Had the couple known the future, they may have chosen a different path, but unexpected goods came out of those painful times. During those years' separation, the couple exchanged hundreds of letters. Both Bill and Ramona expressed that, despite the distance, they felt they grew closer and more vulnerable with each other. Barriers that sometimes exist in face-to-face conversation broke down and they communicated more openly than before, especially about their admiration for each other. Distance makes the heart grow fonder, indeed. Through every letter, short or long, from Bill's hand or Ramona's, the sweet aroma of love prevailed. The Big Dipper constellation and the moon, visible in both Maryland and the Mediterranean, became the couple's messengers, referenced often in their missives. Whether writing at the makeshift desk in his tent, at a proper table, or on his knee, Bill started many letters with "Ramona darling" or "my sweet." Hardly one letter from either ended without a sentence or two about the depth of their love and how much they disliked being apart.

Yes, their union was admirable—a source of happiness and a model of both longevity and devotion, even while apart—but that did not excuse them from difficulty, and their marriage, like any, was not perfect. As the war dragged on, issues small and large came to light. They faced the challenge of navigating personality flaws, the untimely death of a close friend, and painful childlessness, all while over 4,500 miles apart.

∞

A LOVE CRUCIFIED

Of course, the separation itself caused both spouses heartache. Like removing the hand from the wrist, the parting of the husband from the wife was painful; both suffered periods of intense loneliness and concern for the wellbeing of the other. Bill tried to encourage Ramona not to worry—"There are dangers in this business, and I am not shirking my share of them," he said, "but I feel I'll come through all right... So do not be anxious about me."[4] She worried anyway. She had struggled interiorly with his decision to go. Though she supported her husband's desire to make even a small difference and did her best to set herself and her desires aside, his departure deeply saddened her. Soon after Bill left Bethesda, Ramona typed him a letter detailing her true feelings:

> Sometimes I hate myself for not begging you to stay here instead of trying to be understanding and broad about it when my heart was breaking at the thought of your going. You were so excited at the idea you didn't even notice it. I keep telling myself that I will get used to it and I won't miss you so badly but that doesn't work. It gets worse instead of better.[5]

Over the course of the war, Ramona did her best to maintain her mental health by keeping busy around the house and continuing to participate in social and professional life.[6] Other times, she "sat alone here on the little porch ... and wept for loneliness and desire" for her beloved's return; she sometimes tired of "trying to look and act as if I really do not mind your being so far away when every minute of the day I miss you."[7] She missed his affection, his help with housework, his company at parties and at Mass, his closeness, his little routines. The union of spouses was more than just belonging to each other materially; the two became one spiritually as well, so much so that Ramona felt incomplete in Bill's absence, like she existed only partly without him.[8] "There are not many couples, darling," she wrote, "who can bear such a separation without damage."[9]

Bill, for his part, missed his wife in waves as well. Often, his life was so full that, from waking to sleeping, his daily duties took his mind off the separation. Other times, his loneliness seemed to be all he could write about: "I feel sick and lonely too—don't ever think I don't—sometimes it is worse than other times, but it does not improve."[10] In fact, over a year after his initial deployment, Bill described the physical distance between them in a time of great evil with a striking analogy: "Our married life and our love is being crucified by this separation, caused by a crucifying war which has the world upset and violently destroying itself without reason or knowledge of the result."[11]

Whether due to insecurity or the marital issues he saw in the soldiers around him, Bill sometimes expressed concern that he was not the kind of husband he ought to be.[12] He worried that Ramona, who so exuberantly poured forth her admiration of him, had begun to idealize him, cramming him into a mold he did not fit and thereby setting them both up for disappointment—a trap that many separated spouses fell into as the war progressed. He was acutely aware that he was not perfect: "I am not a holy man and have many sinful weaknesses."[13] He wondered if she had sufficient reason to love him. Furthermore, he felt bad for being away and delaying their life together.

Though she frequently desired Bill to return home, Ramona responded to his worries with nothing short of complete confidence. "You amuse me by wondering if I have good reasons for loving you," Ramona replied in a typewritten letter. "I am not all worried about having visualized an ideal and just fitting you into it. It is just the other way around."[14] When surprised by his personal discouragement, she chided him gently: "What in Heaven's name do you mean? I have never complained about the husband I have. Far from it, for I always thought I had the best in the world. If I said something to make you think otherwise, you are surely taking it in a different way than was intended. I love you, Sweet, with all my heart."[15]

Their love they communicated through letters and words, of course, but also through prayer. Ramona attended daily Mass, with only a few misses, the entire time Bill worked overseas, remembering him always in her intentions. She missed having him at her side, placing his pinkie finger over hers as they stood and knelt, but those prayers benefitted them both. The graces they received connected them across thousands of miles and eased the pain of separation even a little. Whenever Bill had Mass, he made it a point to raise Ramona to the Lord's sight, asking for her good as well. One morning in September 1943, he attended Mass and breakfast, then sat down to write. He told Ramona that he had taken Holy Communion and prayed for peace:

> I have united my Mass and Communion with yours today, and with all the Masses throughout the world, through all time, and all these in union with Christ's sacrifice on the Cross for cessation of this senseless war, and the return of joy and peace to the hearts of man. I went to the altar after Mass and asked our dear Lord to ease your lonesomeness and give you comfort to take my place until my return... On many occasions here I feel direct comfort that I feel is of Divine origin. I know your prayers are of special help. Darling, you know I felt it would be very hard to be away from you, but I find some compensation every day to make it easy to bear our separation... Sweetheart, we have blessings of a spiritual kind which we are slow to recognize, but are there nevertheless. Let us thank God a thousand times for these. Life is such a shallow thing without a truly daily spiritual life—an understanding of the spiritual helps bridge the awful gaps of our existence.[16]

The spiritual character of their marriage gave them strength, though it did not always alleviate the feelings of pain and loneliness. Nevertheless, Bill reminded Ramona often of his love; he praised her for managing their home affairs so thoughtfully[17] and frequently urged her to pray for assistance.[18] "You put your hand in mine," he wrote lovingly, "and we both will put ours in the hands of God—then I'm sure everything will be well for us."[19]

THE DEATH OF CATHERINE SAUNDERS

Besides the obvious trial of being apart, Bill and Ramona also struggled with the length, content, and timeliness of their letters, especially in the beginning months of separation. Some of the mail trouble was in their control. For example, shortly after Bill left Bethesda, he wrote to Ramona several times about the content of her letters. He felt put out because her missives were on the shorter side and double-spaced; he wanted more of her thoughts, more knowledge about what was happening at home—enough to fill multiple pages.[20] Longer letters, he must have thought, would help bridge the oceanic gap between them. Ramona, on the other hand, indicated that his critical treatment was painful, because "even a little slap gains great strength by the time it has traveled across the ocean."[21]

But some of the mail issues were out of their control. The postal services during the war found it hard to transport large letters and packages overseas; Bill suffered similar communication troubles as the soldiers he assisted. Anything over two ounces could not be sent quickly. Even the smaller, lighter V-mail some-times took weeks to arrive. This meant that the Carrigans' letters frequently came in out of order and information between sender and receiver was lost. This type of delay caused great interper-sonal strife between the couple when a freak tragedy befell a beloved family friend. The Carrigans were very close with the Saunders family. Both parties held the other in exceptionally high esteem ("Remember," Bill once told Ramona, "Saunders were *my family* for many years before you and I were married and I feel a great indebtedness to them."[22]), and it appears that they had in common the Catholic faith. They frequently shared meals and other social activities before World War II began.

In late September of 1943, while at his Tunisian station, Bill received an out-of-sequence V-mail from Ramona. It came nearly three weeks after it had been written. Containing infor-mation about the Saunders family, it insinuated that something terrible had happened:

> When I look at Catherine Saunders' children and think that she will never have the joy of seeing her children grow up, it just makes me sick to think of it. Love is a strange and wonderful thing, dear. There is so much joy and sorrow too bound up in it. Joe Saunders will never again be a really happy man. Life can never be the same for him and I feel so sad for him. Patricia always had such happy sparkling eyes and to see them yesterday so clouded with

sorrow was a sad sight indeed. Mrs. O'Leary called me today, or rather this morning, and I'm going down again this afternoon to be of some help, I hope. The phone is ringing constantly and it is very hard for the family to try and answer it and give such a sad message again and again. I do not know all of the arrangements yet and I will do our part you may be sure. I feel sure you would want Masses said. Maybe you might even like to have a Mass said in one of the churches there. Of course my love, I am only mentioning that and I wonder why, for you are so much more thoughtful than I am that you need no suggestions, I am sure.[23]

Though filled with detail, it left out the most important piece of information: what happened to Catherine? Why were Bill's wife and friends grieving? On September 20, 1943—likely the day Ramona's V-mail arrived—he wrote a cold and critical response. In past letters, he had asked Ramona to "double up" on the details of top-priority information by writing the most important facts in multiple letters—hopefully, that would ensure that he had all the pertinent facts ready at his disposal, no matter what order the letters came in. Because she had not, to his perception, followed this request, his reply was angry, fueled by worry for his friends and irritation at having to repeat himself. "This is exactly what I have referred to on several occasions," he wrote. "I cannot answer this letter to [Joe] Saunders' family, because I do not know whether or not Mrs. Saunders is dead, paralyzed, blinded or what. I suspect the first. But how? I am in the blackest ignorance... I expect details in some later letter which may reach me one or two months from now."[24] Despite apologizing for the sharpness of his letter, which he rushed to send the very same day he got Ramona's, he reinforced his request for repeated information, then finished: "Tell Saunders I'll have Masses said as soon as possible in the most famous Church in all Africa, the Cathedral of Carthage, and in the boyhood home of St Augustine, overlooking the site of the martyrdom of Sts. Perpetua and Felicitas... Please forgive the severity of this letter... Love, Bill."[25]

He also returned her initial V-mail so that she could see the matter from his perspective. Just two days later, however, Bill received two V-mails from Ramona that she had written on September 7, 1943, only one day after the accident. Deeply grieved to have to relay dreadful news, she gave all the necessary details in sequence: that Catherine Saunders, the family's matriarch, had left for New York, intending to visit an ill friend. She boarded the Congressional Limited, a train traveling between Washington, D.C., and New York. It "wrecked outside of [Philadelphia] in the worst wreck the line has ever known."[26]

Catherine's husband, Joe, and his son Joe, Jr., went to the site of the accident in an attempt to locate his wife. No word came from Joe for several hours, so Ramona stayed with the Saunders' grieving younger children. Around 6:30 that night, Ramona and those at home received word that Catherine

Saunders had indeed passed away in the railroad accident. Ramona wrote: "That poor boy had to look through all the bodies at the morgue and was about to give up when they said one more body had just been brought in. Joe Sr. recognized in the man's hand Catherine's ring and the wristwatch he had given her, so he knew his terrible fears were confirmed."[27] To the family's meager relief, Catherine's body had not been mutilated, though it was severely bruised. She died of internal injuries. Ramona ended her letter by apologizing: "I hate to burden you with it but I know you would wish to share in the grief of these dear friends and I do want you to know that I will do everything that I can do to help them."[28]

These V-mails, filled with details and relevant information that gave the fullest possible picture of the horrible accident, prompted Bill to write a letter of apology. He regretted sending that critical letter; in hindsight, "I should have waited until morning. I hope you get this first. Your two Vs ... have been excellent reporting. There was hardly another question unanswered in them... Forgive my criticism and let's try to coordinate all this information between us."[29]

The couple smoothed over this argument and forgave fully. After all, only one other letter contained Ramona's thoughts about criticism, either before or after Catherine Saunders' death. In that note, she said she had destroyed a sarcastic response she had written.[30] Clearly, she was attempting to repair a situation rather than let pettiness or hurt feelings perpetuate the difficulty between them. Bill also stated, months later—indicating that he thought frequently of his temper—that he felt badly for being so severe in some letters.[31]

Thankfully, most of the letters passed across the Atlantic did not contain such terrible news or interpersonal strife. The frustrations of delayed mail remained, but Ramona's letters grew longer and more detailed. They poured their feelings out to each other in an increasingly intimate manner. Like messengers from Cupid, the cherished epistles spoke often of deep affection. Bill especially liked to praise his wife's virtues and devotion: "If every married soldier overseas had a wife like I have in philosophy & love ... us R.C. men would almost be out of a welfare job unless the army permitted us to act as cupids and carriers of love messages."[32] Their mutual adoration of each other fueled their relationship even while apart for so long and made it easier to smooth over misunderstandings or arguments such as the issue with information across letters.

❦

A REQUEST FOR PADRE PIO

Perhaps the biggest trial the Carrigans faced as a couple was that they never had children. It is not clear why. Perhaps one or both of them suffered from infertility; perhaps their ages—both nearing their forties when they married—played a factor. Perhaps it was due to spending their first five years of marriage in "a deep [rut], and a very selfish one, too," as they focused on things other than starting a family.[33] Regardless of the reason, it was a source of deep regret.[34] Bill wished he could start over, wished he had met

Ramona twenty years earlier, wished that he had not left her side: "I wonder why we are making the sacrifice! At a time when we should have a family wisely started—with children laughing and delighting us with their ever new and individualistic patter—we are separated for duty towards others—you toward other children, I toward their brothers and fathers!"[35]

Nearly as soon as he left for Europe, an unusual idea proposed itself. Bill had always been a dreamer, finding ways to solve problems and provide relief to those around him; as his hopes for having his own family dwindled, he suggested his idea to Ramona. He felt strong hope that she might agree. In all his life, God led him, even in failures. "To take care of one of those failures," he wrote to his wife, "I prayed this morning for another wonderful thing to happen to me. This time it involves you too... Darling, I have asked Our Lord to help me find two little orphan children of good birth and of holy parents, preferably French, a boy and a girl, that we may offer them something of that life, education, religion, & happiness they would have had, had not this cruel war killed their parents and ruined their home."[36] Keenly aware of the joy they lacked, yet not wanting to force his hopes if she did not agree, he beseeched Ramona to send an honest response.

That was precisely what she gave. Bill's letter came, no doubt, as a huge shock, especially since it appears the couple never considered adoption at any point before this letter. On August 2, 1943, about two weeks after Bill sent his proposal, she sat down to reply. At such a distance, Ramona found it hard to discuss. Though she understood his generous motive, the suggestion hurt her, made her feel inadequate as a wife and as a woman, "for it means to me that you have given up any hope of having a family of our own... I talked the matter over with the doctor the last time I was there and he said there was no reason to feel I would not have a family."[37] Moreover, she worried that she would not sufficiently love the adoptees, despite her fondness for children. She put the letter away for the night, too overwhelmed with emotion to continue.

Later the next day, likely after much prayer and reflection on her inward feelings, she continued her thoughts in another letter, articulating herself more carefully and thoroughly:

> Beloved, the question of children touches a spot more tender than you know. You see it is a bitter disappointment to me too. I realize that it is for you too and that makes my sorrow the deeper. The first year we were married, I did not mind for I thought we could easily wait a while; so when we had no children then, I did not give very serious thought to it, feeling that of course we would later. The discussion is a deep one and very difficult at such a distance. I do hope and pray you will understand how I feel. I am a poor hand at explaining my feelings and that is a handicap. However my dear, if you find two such children as you have in mind, I will pray that they will take the place of our own if

it is God's wish that we have none of our own. Bill,
please know that I love you very deeply and your
happiness is of the greatest importance to me and
I will do all that I can to add to that happiness.[38]

After sending her letter, Ramona could do nothing but wait for
Bill to receive the painful but honest missive. Nearly a month
later, thanks to postal delays, his reply arrived. He thanked her
profoundly for her frankness and praised the letters as being
some of the best she had ever sent. "Darling, I'm very sorry
about the letter regarding the children," he said. "[I] think we
might forget the whole episode. But I'm glad in one way you
wrote that letter. It tells me a lot I didn't know or wasn't sure
of about you."[39] He was disappointed, to be sure, but consoled
himself by saying, "perhaps I shall never find any [children]
that would meet my standards."[40] Besides, he had not given up
hope that he and Ramona could conceive their own children.

He ended his letter with another apology. "I know I pained
you much in that letter, but I did not think you would draw that
interpretation... Stay ever in my love, darling. I'd suffer untold
anguish if you didn't."[41] Ramona apparently left the discussion
at that, for she did not mention the matter again. For a time, they
did not discuss it any further, though Bill kept a secret hope in
his heart for a couple more years. In 1945, nearing the end of
his time in Europe, Bill turned to his spiritual father for advice
about adoption. Apparently, he asked several times:

I just returned from an hour with Padre Pio, the first in nearly three weeks. I had a long visit with him. I prayed with him in the choir, and talked with him later... I had absolution from him, and again promises of constant assistance on our behalf. He is a wonderful man and is very good to us and our friends. I asked about children again, and again he said for us not to adopt any—they would obstruct our vocation unless they were our own. So if we have a family they need must be our own.[42]

Bill trusted Padre Pio's perhaps prophetic judgment on the matter and finally let go of the idea of adopting orphans.

After the war, Bill and Ramona never did have children of their own. This reality, however, did not stop them from supporting children. They loved their nieces and nephews. While Bill was abroad, he always sent home Christmas gifts for "the children"—referring either to extended family or the children Ramona taught at Oyster Elementary School. Ramona's students loved hearing from Bill. He sent them German and Italian propaganda pamphlets as visual aids for what was happening abroad, as well as "invasion money" for their collections. He sent them pictures from some of the historical places he visited, like Vesuvius. He wrote letters to them around Christmastime and Eastertime, and they wrote him letters back. He even obtained prayers from Padre Pio for the children, especially those who were not Catholic.[43] One of Bill and Ramona's neighbors, Steve Critzer, knew the couple when he himself was just a boy. Whenever he could, young Steve would run over to visit, usually leaving with sweets and sodas and the lasting memory of their affection.[44] "You could feel and see the love that they had for one another when you [were] around them," Steve recalled.[45]

⁓

LOVE BEGETS LOVE

During the war, and perhaps due to it, Bill leaned all the more heavily on God's direction of his life. He tried many times to predict when the war would end and he would be able to go home. Though he had been allowed to take a short leave—the *USAT Henry Gibbins* brought him from Naples to New York on August 3, 1944—he had to return to Europe all too soon. The leave may have felt like a tease, a taste of what he could not yet enjoy fully. But, in March of 1945, not long before he completed his tour of duty, he expressed that he had surrendered it all to God:

> Darling, I do not know when I can plan on returning to you. I hope soon. But from here I do not know. I will leave it pretty well in the hands of the Lord. I'd rather let Him decide what is the best time for me. I wish Him always to direct me [in] both ... work and travel. I'm not a very good Christian and I do not merit such guidance but I

hope to have it out of the great charity of Christ. So you see how I feel; if the Lord thinks it better for me to go home soon, well and good—if to stay a little longer—well and good.[46]

As much as their marriage was tested during their two years apart, communicating almost exclusively through letters, it also grew stronger. War raged. Marriages broke apart. Mail arrived late or out of order. The Carrigan couple felt their lack of children and their separation keenly. Still, they stayed firm. To combat loneliness, they found ways to demonstrate their affection even across an ocean. The mature and sensitive love, the humble apologies and forgiveness, the spiritual connection, and the hundreds of letters exchanged between Bill and Ramona certainly made their situation more manageable, even if the ache never went away fully. By way of a philosophy of their marriage, Bill encouraged Ramona to continue in the way of love—for each other as spouses, and for those around them—while the world was in convulsions of agony: "Hate begets hate. Love begets love. Let us try to stay by the latter, even though we may have to live with the former for a while."[47]

CHAPTER ELEVEN

Bill's Ministry Reaches America
August 1944 – November 2000

∽

AMERICA MEETS PADRE PIO

During Bill's brief leave in the late summer of 1944, he expanded his Padre Pio ministry. After obtaining permission from the Capuchin's superior, Bill gave presentations about Padre Pio at churches around Washington, D.C., garnering interest from the citizens of that area. Bill's leave most likely lasted only a month, as that was the typical arrangement for those working with the armed forces, but in that timeframe, he made quite an impact. His talks, along with his articles which had circulated in Catholic presses, piqued the curiosity of American laypeople and clergy alike. No longer was it just the military men overseas and the local Italians who were privy to Padre Pio. When he returned to his station in Foggia, hardly a month passed before he wrote to Ramona about how "Padre Pio is getting letters directly, and through the Vatican and through me, from people in the U.S."[1] The steady stream of mail all mentioned the articles Bill had released earlier that year, and all begged Padre Pio's intercession in their various affairs. "I am very happy to realize my article has reached the hearts of our people," Bill reported.[2]

On November 1, 1944, a week before concluding his ARC mission in Italy, Padre Pio's Superior gave Bill permission to continue his ministry, in addition to offering "a promise of cooperation and permission for a translation of his life."[3]

In his own words, Bill "became Padre's man Friday in developing the 'American Connection'," referencing Daniel Defoe's classic novel, *Robinson Crusoe*.[4] Here, in the nation's capital, Bill's ministry flourished. He found a curious and eager audience—people of all ages and walks of life seeking the Truth of God. Interest in the mystic grew exponentially. With intense devotion and unflagging energy, Bill spent the remaining fifty-five years of his life sharing the Good News of Christ to others by introducing them to the holiest priest he knew.

∽

Returning Home

At the port of Naples, on the cool, clear morning of November 8, 1945, Bill prepared to board a ship and, after more than two years abroad, return to the United States. The vessel, the *USAT Sea Snipe*, waited in the harbor. It had served as a transport ship in the Southwest Pacific Theater, particularly between California and Australia. With the war officially over, the *Sea Snipe* made several trips from various European ports to Hampton Roads, carrying U.S. troops back to their homeland, and it was about to cross the Atlantic again.

Bill seemed to know that his time in Europe was drawing
to a close as soon as July 1945, when he started sending items
home.[5] By November, his work with the American Red Cross
had concluded; some of his final jobs included the distribution
of leftover American goods to destitute Italian locals. With his
duties complete, he felt ready to go home. As he waited his turn
to board, he penned a brief note to Ramona:

Darling,

I can put in a line to you before I board this
morning. It is a beautiful morning. I went to the
Jesuit Church here for Mass and Communion
yesterday and today, it was very nice. I always like
to have Mass and Communion before a trip.

Sweetheart, I am glad to be on my way—there
are no regrets about going now. I've completed
my tour of duty and brought it to a good head.
Everything is satisfactory at Hq. and they feel I've
done a good job too. Well, I know my own feelings
are that I put in satisfactory work here.

I'm leaving on the *Sea Snipe* and will arrive at
Norfolk somewhere around the twenty-first. I'll be
in Washington within twenty-four hours. Please do
not go to Norfolk as processing and other difficulties
would not permit you to meet me anyway. The

military does not want the families coming to the ports. You prepare for me at 4814. I'll see you there. I'd rather it be at home anyway.

Darling, I hope you will get this before I get home and I hope it will give you the "lift" you have been waiting for.

All my love till then, dear.

Bill.[6]

Nearly two weeks later, Bill reentered the United States. Though the reunion of the Carrigan couple is not recorded, one can only imagine the joyful meeting on the front step of their Bethesda home and the peace it brought both spouses to be once again whole.

As Bill readjusted to regular life, his enthusiasm for Padre Pio burned brightly. He considered the Capuchin monk to be a "credible sign to our time" of Christ's suffering and love, a true witness, "a channel of grace."[7] Through the years, Padre Pio became an integral part of Bill's daily existence, not only because he asked for prayers both during the saint's earthly life and during his eternal life, but also because he spent hours talking to anyone who would listen about Foggia's holy man. As W. Shepherdson Abell, Bill's friend and lawyer later in life, said, Bill was tireless. "He talked to everyone he met about Padre Pio," Abell recalled. "He wrote letters and newspaper columns, organized Masses in Padre Pio's memory, sponsored books and videos. I was once told that he had distributed over 1 million Padre Pio prayer cards."[8]

From his home in Maryland, Bill traveled far and wide to give talks on Padre Pio, noting some of the most important things about the saint. He began in his local area around Washington, D.C., and Virginia, going to "every church ... at the request, the invitation of a sodality or Holy Name Society or some other religious group."[9] He insisted that he would travel anywhere to relate his stories of the mystic, and this he did. He spoke at educational institutions like the Catholic University of America, Mount de Sales Academy, Christendom College, and Belmont Abbey, at secondary schools, and at churches who specifically asked for him. He gave presentations to students, to war veterans, to prayer groups that he himself founded, to curious adults, to those interested in Padre Pio's relics, to anyone who wanted to know more. Bill's nephew Chuck Furr estimated that Bill gave over five hundred talks on Padre Pio after returning to the United States. Every time he offered a lecture, he would bring blessed medals. According to him, "there'd be a hundred people or more there, and then ... after I gave each one [a medal], I'd have a whole lineup coming back to get one for mom and one for grandma and one [for] papa."[10] These were "especially well received, because they were in the hands of Padre Pio."[11] Sometimes, after a talk, the group would approach him and people, especially the elderly women, would ask to kiss his hands, because he had touched the hands and stigmata of Padre Pio. Bill always denied these requests, stating with a laugh: "Forget it!"[12] He did not try to claim credit for his part in helping others. "I have always tried to introduce Padre Pio as someone [they] can go directly to, not to me," he said.[13]

In addition to medals and sometimes rosaries, he always had prayer cards featuring rare photos of Padre Pio taken by Frank Abresch, a photographer friend of Bill's, and sometimes Bill himself. He gave these out in copious amounts to anyone and everyone who was interested.

Relics also came into his possession, given to him before his Red Cross service ended in late 1945. The first: the paired wineglass and bread slice, second-class relics. The second: a scale of blood that had fallen off Padre Pio's wounded hand, a first-class relic. The blood crystal, as Bill called it, was a precious memento given as a gift. As Bill was leaving the San Giovanni monastery for the last time, one of Padre Pio's fellow priests ran after him and pressed a small envelope into his hand. "Keep this," the monk told him. "One day Padre Pio will be canonized."[14] Inside, Bill found the scab. Under normal circumstances, blood rots, giving off a foul odor.[15] Padre Pio's blood, however, retained its original form for over seventy years, never rotting or reeking. All these methods Bill utilized to spread awareness of the stigmatist priest.

THE FLOW OF GRACE

As part of the lectures, paraphernalia, and information which he disseminated between 1945 and the late 1990s, Bill distributed the holy priest's wisdom. All Padre Pio's messages united into one all-important theme that the saint wished everyone to know, and which he told Bill specifically to pass on: "Tell them 'God loves them.'"[16] Those messages deeply impacted those who witnessed them. Like the soldiers whose faith grew deeper or who were inspired to make changes in their lives, the American people who encountered Bill's efforts experienced similar effects, even though they may never have actually met the saint in person. "I've had people come up and say, 'Well, you made Padre Pio alive for me. I feel I was there, I feel I know him,' just from the pictures," Bill said.[17] It became a constant theme in his life to be a conduit of grace.[18]

During his talks, even children felt Padre Pio's impact through Bill. As many of his lectures occurred at schools, he developed a strategy for bringing his holy Italian friend to local fifth, sixth, seventh, and eighth graders: "Take over their religious class, and show them the slides, and tell them about Padre Pio. But I had to concentrate on a part of Padre Pio's life, so I concentrated on the Mass, because I had beautiful pictures of Padre Pio at the Mass."[19] He used those images and Padre Pio's example to explain what the Mass was, what it meant, and how one should approach the holy sacrifice. Then, having already obtained permission from the teacher, he asked the students, "If Padre Pio means anything to you, will you sit down ... sometime in the next few days and write me a single page letter to tell me how you feel about Padre Pio?"[20]

Bill received a multitude of responses. For example, one girl wrote him a letter, saying, "Mass bored me. I never enjoyed going to Mass. And now seeing the pictures of Padre Pio at Mass, and hearing the stories of Padre Pio, of how he loved the Mass, I don't think I'll ever be bored again at Mass."[21] Another little missive, emblazoned with words *Thank you, Mr. Carrigan* beside a cross colored with brown marker, intimated that the seventh grade girl had gone home and told her family "about Padre Pio and how he got the stigmata and they liked it so much they asked me to tell it over and over."[22] He retained many of the notes which students penned for him and read them over and over in difficult times.

"That one conviction in a single half hour," Bill said contemplatively, "that might move a person for a lifetime."[23]

Beyond the extensive lectures, healing and hope occurred through the other avenues Bill pursued too. For example, Padre Pio's intercession—his spiritual, paternal care—touched Bill's extended family during a period of difficulty and loss which began with the death of Bill's sister, Loretta Marie, in August of 1949. Chuck Furr—Loretta Marie's son, Bill Carrigan's nephew, and the impetus behind this biography—recalled the story. He was only eleven years old at the time of his mother's passing.

Loretta Marie Furr (*n.* Carrigan), married with eleven children, lived on sprawling, rented farmland in Waseca, Minnesota. Her husband, Charles Everett Furr, Sr., worked at the Chicago Northwest Railroad, and farmed as well. In all, the family made a decent life for themselves in their small community.

The large Catholic family had no electricity in their home, so they relied on kerosene for lamps and their kitchen stove for warmth, heat, and cooking. As was routine, a delivery man came one morning to fill the Furr family's thirty-gallon kerosene barrel. Unbeknownst to him, and to the Furr family, he had forgotten to empty the hose which fed into the barrel. It had been previously used to deliver gasoline to the farmer next door. So, by complete accident, eight gallons of gasoline mixed in with the twenty-two gallons of kerosene.

On the evening of August 23, young Chuck, the eighth child, trekked to the barrel and pumped two gallons of the gasoline-kerosene mixture into their five-gallon kerosene can. He set it on the front porch as normal and went on his way.

That night, Loretta Marie went to bed musing about the sleepover that one of her daughters was hosting. A thought struck her—she had forgotten to frost a cake for the next day, so she got up again. The house was dark and quiet. "Usually," Chuck recalled, "[Loretta] would pour four or five ounces [from the kerosene can] in a bean can or something, and take it to the stove and start it."[24] But that evening, rather than taking the time to pour kerosene into a lamp and light the lamp, she brought the whole bean can to the stove. She did not know there was a spark already in the stove. "Kerosene does not explode," Chuck said, "but this mixture blew up."[25]

Loretta Marie sustained second and third degree burns across two-thirds of her body. One of her sons, Tom, woke and rushed to help—he wrapped his mother in a raincoat to put out the fire—but she died of her burns about forty-eight hours later on August 25, 1949.[26]

Upon hearing the terrible news, Bill Carrigan traveled to Minnesota from Washington, D.C., for the funeral. Loretta Marie was his younger sister, the child immediately following him in birth order. She was an excellent homemaker and "had an exceptional ability to improvise and meet the needs, whatever they were," of her family.[27] Bill compared her to a maypole. Each of her children was tethered to that maypole, and each would be tugged back into line if he or she got "tangled up with the others."[28] During the critical time of grief right after Loretta Marie's death, Bill took over that role. He ensured that the children continued their lives—their homework, their farm work, and so on—and encouraged them to pray the rosary. Even after returning home, he did his best to be a solid foundation for his nieces and nephews, especially Chuck, who felt a "very significant void" and subsequently "kicked up the dust a few times," according to Bill.[29]

On top of caring for his distraught extended family, he immediately sought the efficacious intercession of Padre Pio. The saint had once stated that, once a person was recommended to him, he would not forget to pray for him or her. Banking on this promise and perhaps seeking consolation, Bill wrote to the

Italian mystic about the terrible accident. Not long after, a return letter, written once again by the Capuchin's superior on Padre Pio's behalf, arrived. It included this passage: "Your account of the tragic death of your sister Marie visibly moved Father Pio, and he promised to pray for her, for her husband and the children. He added, 'Let us hope she will soon be in paradise.'"[30]

Through Bill's letter, Padre Pio became the spiritual patron of the Furr family. Initially, the grieving family had no knowledge of the saint's intercession. Chuck himself, who met his Uncle Bill for the first time at his mother's funeral, did not learn of it until many, many years later. Yet, when he found that response letter from Italy in a stack of Bill's papers, Chuck stated that it touched him immensely to learn of the saint's prayers for not only his poor mother, but also for himself, before he even knew Padre Pio existed.

Albert Synder, a family friend of the Carrigans and an employee of a Supreme Court judge in Washington, D.C., received a special grace through a holy card of Padre Pio. Albert was not Catholic, but his wife was, and the Snyders were Bill and Ramona's good friends. They often celebrated holidays like Thanksgiving together. One day, when the two couples were spending time together, Bill used the opportunity to tell his friend about Padre Pio. Though Albert appeared not to be paying attention—his focus remained on the newspaper he was reading—when Bill offered him a holy card of Padre Pio, he accepted it.

Years later, Albert and his family left Washington, D.C., and moved to Philadelphia. Due to personal circumstances, Albert's mental health declined. He packed a suitcase and walked down toward the nearby river, planning to commit suicide. The hot weather and traveling with luggage made walking along the river difficult, so Albert found a bench and rested for a little while. "For some reason or another," Bill said, "he opened his wallet. And the picture of Padre Pio slipped out on the bench."[31] Albert picked up the holy card and regarded it for a while, contemplating the saint. Only God knows the thoughts that ran through his head, but after a time, Albert Snyder tucked the card away, stood up, and spent the afternoon in prayer at a nearby chapel. Following his change of heart, he started attending Mass with his Catholic wife.[32]

Though Albert's mental health improved thanks to Padre Pio's intercession, he never formally joined the Catholic Church. This caused Bill some consternation, and he even told Albert that, though he was "going through all the motions," he was still missing the mark.[33] Albert insisted he knew what he was doing. Bill did not feel confident about that answer; he considered Albert "kinda tough" when it came to religion! So, he did what he knew best: he told Padre Pio about Snyder's story while visiting San Giovanni Rotondo in the 1953. The saint calmly stated, "Well, you keep pushing and I'll keep pulling."[34] That was enough for Bill. "I'm sure the Lord is taking care of that situation," he said.[35]

Of the relics in Bill's possession, at least one miracle has been strongly suspected, this one at an all-girl's Catholic high school in Catonsville, Maryland, named Mount de Sales Academy. At some point prior to the incident, Bill had donated the blood crystal, the slice of bread, and the wineglass relics to the school. Though there is no official documentation from the Church, since the principal at Mount de Sales Academy, a Dominican nun named Sr. Philip Joseph, O.P., was unable to follow up, she strongly believes Padre Pio's relic contributed to the healing of a young lady from a neighboring high school.

The girl suffered a tumor on her pituitary gland. To remove it, doctors needed to perform a dangerous surgery. Having heard about the blood crystal of Padre Pio housed at Mount de Sales Academy, the girl's parents drove her to Catonsville, praying desperately for the tumor to either disappear or shrink significantly. Sr. Philip Joseph "placed the relic on the back of her neck [and] head and we prayed to Padre Pio. When she went for her next doctor's appointment to schedule surgery for the tumor, the tumor was gone."[36]

One day, a woman who had heard one of Bill's talks on Padre Pio asked him to visit her friend, Mrs. Cullen. This woman, a fifty-two-year-old widow with no children, suffered from "one of the worst cases" of mouth cancer that Bill had ever seen.[37] Over the course of several years, the cancer became so severe that doctors had to surgically remove part of her jaw on the left side, as well as part of her tongue, which made talking difficult.[38] Mrs. Cullen had no family and few consistent friends. There was even concern among the staff that she might commit suicide.[39] Though she wanted badly to visit Lourdes, France, in hopes of a miraculous cure, her condition prevented her from traveling, adding to her utter dissatisfaction with life.

As requested, Bill met with Mrs. Cullen at her hospital bedside. He told her about Padre Pio. Because she could not go to Lourdes, Bill made a suggestion: why not send Padre Pio a letter explaining this situation?[40]

Mrs. Cullen agreed. "Some weeks later," Bill said, "she called me on the telephone."[41] The ailing woman, though struggling to speak, confidently stated, "I'm going to have a miracle."[42] She then related that Padre Pio had written her back, and that the morning after she received the reply, she recognized a "strange aroma" similar to the one Bill had described as emanating from Padre Pio's stigmata.[43]

Ever the rational skeptic, Bill decided to test the verity of this phenomenon. He held a brief interrogation—what did it smell like? Flowers. Maybe there was a vase of flowers in the hospital hallway? No, she had looked. Perhaps there were flowers outside the hospital window or in the yard? No flowers around at all. Did anyone give her any perfumes recently? But no—no perfumes either. Mrs. Cullen remained adamant that the pleasant floral scent signified Padre Pio's spiritual presence.[44]

Sometime later, the doctors told her that she needed another surgery. During the operation, she kept with her a picture of

Padre Pio and a crucifix which Padre Pio had blessed specifically for special occasions like Mrs. Cullen's.[45] Bill had given her both items. The surgery was successful, and Bill noticed a profound change in the widow's attitude. Despite now suffering from complete muteness, she let Bill know that everything was alright with her. She reached her final days in peace.

After her passing, Bill attended her funeral, acting as a pallbearer. He left with some others in the undertaker's limousine and found himself sitting across from Mrs. Cullen's friend, the one who requested that he visit her. She was one of the only people to visit her while she was ill. As they drove, the woman hesitantly asked if she could keep the crucifix that he had given Mrs. Cullen.[46] Aware of how kind this woman had been to the late Mrs. Cullen, Bill agreed—luckily for her, because she already had the crucifix in her possession. After a moment, the woman spoke again, saying, "You know, I'm not a Catholic, but since I got to know this lady, especially since Padre Pio came into her life, I saw a change... I felt that Padre Pio had a lot to do with her situation." She paused, then continued, "My eleven-year-old son, my husband, and I are now taking instruction."[47]

"So you see," Bill concluded, "how the flow of grace doesn't stop; it just keeps on going."[48]

CHAPTER TWELVE

An Important Assortment of Charities
1950s – November 2000

∾

RICHES TO GIVE

Before and during World War II, Bill Carrigan held a career in real estate. The work suited him, since he had developed skills that made him capable of envisioning improvements or plans and executing them effectively. Among other property-related matters that included acquiring and selling, Bill maintained at least two homes that he rented out, one of which he called Wheeler Farm, or Wheeler Road. While he was away, Ramona took over the management of the Wheeler Farm property; she battled lazy workmen, cheapskates, constant upkeep and repairs, and men who thought they could dupe her because she was a woman. Rarely was Bill displeased with her efforts; he often praised her for thinking along the same lines as he thought and acting as he would have acted, were he home.

Upon his return to the United States, he expanded his career and "became a successful developer of commercial and industrial properties in the D.C. area."[1] Bill possessed the vision to see the post-war expansion of Washington, D.C., and Virginia.

He would "buy land ahead of that movement, develop it—put in culverts, roadways—and sell it to another developer" who would then erect strip malls, stores, houses, and so forth.[2] He became a land consultant for Archbishop (later Cardinal) Patrick O'Boyle of Washington, D.C. He even bought and owned a radio tower. For a time, on top of this property business, he and Ramona also owned an antique shop on Route 211 in Washington, Virginia, called the Washington House of Antiques (sold in 1972). These sources of income, wisely handled, made William M. Carrigan a millionaire.

Yet, where many individuals in high-earning positions might hoard the money or use it to satiate their lust, pride, or greed, Bill did the opposite. In fact, he was known, especially in his old age, to live continually below his means. Chuck Furr related that, as a product of the Great Depression and two World Wars, Bill was the type of man to dry paper towels for later reuse.[3] Fr. Michael Sliney, L.C., a priest-friend of Bill's in the 1980s, said that his attire was austere: flannel shirts, plain slacks, beat-up old shoes, and glasses that might have been taped at one point.[4] He provided a comfortable living for himself and Ramona, bought a small, historic manor in Virginia, filled his homes with antiques and books and Catholic art, *and* turned his income outward, extending financial assistance to both organizations and individuals. He viewed money as a tool intended for Good; it should not remain in the pockets of the earner, but should be used to enable a positive difference in the world. Upon learning that Bill Gates was a billionaire, Bill Carrigan cried, "I haven't done enough. If I had a billion dollars, there's so much more I could do!"[5] Though Bill preferred Catholic causes, he also funded several non-religious humanitarian causes. Most donations were made under his *and* Ramona's names. Padre Pio always inspired their love for prudently distributing their wealth to those who needed it.

༻

SECULAR AND RELIGIOUS CAUSES BILL SUPPORTED

In the later years of his life, from the war years until his passing in 2000, Bill extended his philanthropy to a number of organizations and individuals, some documented and some not. W. Shepherdson Abell, the lawyer who managed Bill's estate, stated that he was "astonished to discover that [Bill] had dozens—maybe hundreds—of private charities," that is, gifts to individuals.[6] These gifts consisted of "whatever it took to help the person keep going."[7] Most of those instances consisted of paying people more than they technically earned, loaning money without stressing about documentation, or gifting a sum, large or small, without expecting it to be repaid; Bill was the type to see someone's need, offer to pay, then "figure out the paperwork later."[8]

Tom Cunningham, a recipient of one such gift, explained how Bill's generosity impacted his life. Tom had been working with the Family of the Americas Foundation as a software developer in the early days of the Internet, and when he finished the project which the Foundation had hired him to do, he wanted to start his own company. Before he could, Bill asked him to create a website about Padre Pio. Tom willingly did this—it took him maybe ten hours total—and Bill paid him five thousand dollars for his efforts![9] After opening the check in his car, Tom went right back into Bill's house, feeling he had not earned such a sum. But Bill insisted Tom keep the money, saying, "Tom, no, no, no, *I* want you to have this money, and *Padre Pio* wants you to have this money."[10] That was Bill's mentality about his charity. It was not just his own desire to give, but it was Padre Pio's desire as well. His treasure, just as much as his time and talent, he considered at Padre Pio's service—and therefore at the Church's service, at God's service.

With that five thousand dollars, Tom Cunningham started his company. It grew into a successful business in the late 1990s, and he expressed deep gratitude for the gift which so far exceeded the normal payment for a relatively small job: "In the annals of Mr. Carrigan history, nobody really cares if he gave Tom Cunningham five thousand dollars, but ... it made a significant impact in my life... And I think there are a lot of people like that. Some simple, well-timed gift made a big difference that nobody ever cataloged anywhere, you know? I think that's a lot of his story."[11]

During his lifetime, Bill developed what he called a "healthy suspicion in dealing with people."[12] That "red light," consisted of a keenly honed ability to discern, to "hold up until I can check out the difficulty."[13] Much like his skepticism of miracles, this skill enabled him to choose the causes which would enact the most good for society and for God. Through generous gifts, he facilitated the production of good work in international healthcare, education, religious services, pro-life care, parish construction, and more. The support he offered impacts the Washington-Virginia area to this day.

⤞⤝

THE INTERNATIONAL EYE FOUNDATION

In the 1960s, Bill became acquainted with the International Eye Foundation (IEF). Bill was good friends with Dr. John Harry King, Jr., M.D. Dr. King, a Roman Catholic, had served in World War II, in both the Pacific theater and in Italy. When his war career concluded, he worked as the chief ophthalmologist at the Walter Reed Army Hospital in Washington, D.C., and founded the IEF in 1961.

Bill and Dr. King may have met at the same church in Maryland; since both men were prominent figures in their Washington-Virginia community and shared similarities in their overseas service, it is no wonder they became friends.[14] Dr. King introduced Bill to the IEF, and the intrepid Mr. Carrigan became a founding member. For several years, he held a position on the board of directors.[15]

Though connected with the organization, Bill did more than just serve as a board member—he financially supported the IEF and its eye care programs in third-world countries through a restricted endowment of $400,000. Having a "real affinity for Latin America," Bill specified that the endowment, plus its growth, was to be used only for Latin American healthcare programs.[16] Called the William M. and Ramona N. Carrigan Endowment, it primarily funded, in perpetuity, the Magi Eye Clinic in San Pedro Sula, Honduras, which had been established by Dr. King in 1983 and which was attached to the government hospital in that same region.[17] Named by Bill himself, the clinic was able to set up, train employees, hire an ophthalmologist, and care for "little things like conjunctivitis or having glasses, but also cataract surgery and glaucoma surgery" in an area with little access to such services.[18] Inside the facility hung a small portrait photograph of Ramona.

The money from the Carrigan Endowment also enabled the IEF to send a doctor to St. Kitts in 1986, and to give a grant to the "Catholic University of Chile in Santiago to support and equip a new pediatric eye clinic" in 1992.[19]

Bill's aid did not extend only to the Latin America programs, however. In the 1970s, the IEF had a program in Kenya, setting up an eye clinic in Central Province, where there had not been one before. Dr. Randolf Whitfield was in charge of that program, where he "helped train ophthalmologists and set up a national service, and do outreach surveys to try and assess the prevalence of blindness" in that area of Kenya.[20] The program was eventually very successful, but in the beginning, it struggled. The IEF had to pay Dr. Whitfield's salary, provide a vehicle for him, gather local support in Kenya, purchase medical equipment, and so on. Before obtaining a grant from USAID in 1976, "it was up to Mr. Carrigan and some of the board members to support the program."[21] He did so for four years—1972 to 1976.

Possibly connected with the IEF's relief programs was another of Bill's generous endeavors. Through a young seminarian (now priest) named Michael Sliney, Bill cut a deal with a budding preschool in the Maryland area. Part of that deal was that the Shamrock School would take charge of mailing eyeglasses and educational books to various countries in the African continent, most likely in exchange for his financial support.[22] Fr. Sliney attested, "Every month, tons of glasses and tons of books would be arriving to our center—we were in charge of boxing them and packaging them and bringing them to the post office and sending them."[23]

Bill's work with the International Eye Foundation, whether through significant financial contribution, organization and donation of needed items, or simply by connecting the right people to each other, reached across the world. As usual, he offered vital but quiet background support; he allowed others to take the spotlight.

❧

Donating Land to Various Causes

As a land developer, Bill was able to buy, sell, and rent parcels of land to both individual and religious causes. Before serving in World War II, Bill granted the Fathers of Mercy two plots of land for the Novitiate in University Heights, a neighborhood adjacent to the Catholic University of America campus.[24] He also donated land to Camp Castleton in Virginia, which now hosts Catholic youth camps for more than two hundred boys and girls yearly.[25] These gifts were no small matter, yet they were only the beginning of his property donations.

Another significant benefaction enabled the construction of a small, predominantly African-American parish called Holy Family Church. As often was the case, the situation was intimately connected to Padre Pio and the flow of grace.

While serving in Foggia, Bill asked his saintly friend what he could do for the Catholic Church in America. How could he help? Padre Pio responded to the question with a question: was there something he could give?

Carrigan mentioned that he owned some beautiful property in rural Maryland, just outside of Washington, on a hilltop overlooking the city. He had thought before of how wonderful it would be if this property could be a place where people could come together to adore Christ in the Blessed Sacrament—like that Biblical image of the shining city on a hill. Padre Pio told Carrigan that this was indeed what he should do. He then gave [Bill] a Miraculous Medal of Mary, and told him to bury it on the property, and to ask the Blessed Mother for her prayers that God would bring this dream about—and he told Carrigan that he would pray for this intention too.[26]

After returning to the United States, Bill buried the Miraculous Medal as instructed and prayed. Three years later, following Bill's inquiries, Archbishop Patrick O'Boyle surveyed the land. Moved by Bill's story, the Archbishop accepted the gifted land; on November 14, 1952, "the parish was canonically established."[27] Construction began on November 24, 1956, and the first Mass was celebrated a year and three days later. The church, rectory, school, and convent—far more than Bill's original intention—opened November 27, 1957, "thanks to the generosity of William Carrigan and the prayers of St. Pio, our patrons!"[28] Holy Family Church operates to this day.

❧

MAGI LITURGICAL ARTS CENTER AND SCHOLARSHIPS

In the 1980s, Bill and Ramona decided to give back to the college from which they both graduated. Bill possessed a deep love and appreciation for Catholic art, especially works that encouraged contemplation of Christianity. In fact, an article from *The Register* stated that Bill was an art collector who was "no neophyte when it comes to arts patronage. His home is filled with paintings and sculptures—many of which he commissioned."[29] Ever one to see a need and work to meet it, he found himself dissatisfied with the religious art that was being produced in the years just after the Sexual Revolution and the Second Vatican Council. The arts were, and still are, "the most effective and lasting method of communication between peoples," he wrote.

"The history of the arts also reveals that creative minds found the greatest challenge in the areas of religious themes ... generation after generation is inspired by sacred art, and it becomes for them a lasting silent sermon."[30]

With these considerations in mind, he decided to promote education in the liturgical arts. The William M. and Ramona N. Carrigan Magi Endowment Fund for the Catholic University of America consisted of one million dollars for the creation of a liturgical arts center and scholarships in order to promote a return to Truth, Goodness, and Beauty in Catholic art. "Hence," Bill wrote, "the creators of this Endowment Fund believe that the promotion of religious art, by spiritually oriented artists, will help people in their search for spiritual fulfillment."[31]

Three programs fell under the Magi Endowment Fund. First, a half-tuition scholarship (still available today) for students whose "postgraduation goal is to serve the Catholic Church as a teacher, composer, choral director, sculptor, craftsman in bronze or iron or some other mediums."[32] Second, support for high-quality "publications in the field of liturgical arts."[33] And third, the establishment of a liturgical arts instruction center called the Magi Liturgical Arts Center where students of various mediums, including TV and theater script, clay, and fabric, could apprentice under "spiritually oriented" masters of the discipline the individual student wanted.[34]

His devotion to Catholic education also shone through other donations to different institutes of learning. For example, various Native American schools in the United States received a total of $1,700 in 1993. Between 1994 and 1996, Bill gave nearly ten thousand dollars to Oakcrest School, an all-girls institution serving students in grades six through twelve. Based in northern Virginia, they lean into the spirituality of Opus Dei and strive to form the whole person through the Catholic Church. In 1997, Bill sent one thousand dollars to his friend Archbishop Charles J. Chaput, O.F.M., Cap., specifically for the care and keeping of St. Thomas More High School in Rapid City, South Dakota.

CENTER FOR THE APPLIED RESEARCH OF THE APOSTOLATE

Among the many Catholic organizations he backed, Bill supported the Center for the Applied Research of the Apostolate (CARA), which was originally located in Washington, D.C. Connected to Georgetown University, CARA was officially founded in 1964 and has served since then as an organization dedicated to researching social science within the Catholic Church. Their mission is threefold: "To increase the Church's self-understanding; to serve the applied research needs of Church decision-makers; and to advance scholarly research on religion, particularly Catholicism."[35] Through their research and consulting, they serve "dioceses, parishes, religious communities and institutes, and other Catholic organizations."[36] They are committed to letting their findings speak for themselves. Their research has helped track the changing moral climate in the Western World, has documented major religious issues in the Church at large, and has covered many specific or local concerns.

Bill served for a brief stint as the chairman of CARA's national committee, which showed both his support for the organization and his devotion to the Blessed Mother. On at least one occasion, Bill requested a specific study be conducted. In 1977, for example, he was the impetus behind a two-year research program about Marian devotions. The study had three main objectives: "To offer scientific support for the devotion to the Mother of God under the title of Our Lady of Guadalupe, patroness of the Americas; to give support of the Mexican people and to all other Catholics of Latin American cultures in the United States; and to foster an increase in devotion to the Mother of God among all Catholics."[37]

Bill fervently believed that the "devotional life of the Church is in possession of the poor, and that it could be helpful to research and restudy the basis for certain devotions and their impact on people," hence his desire for this study to be accomplished.[38] He financially sponsored the project; it resulted in educational pamphlets about Our Lady of Guadalupe and was considered a success.[39]

༒

THE INTERNATIONAL BOOK SERVICE

For over 35 years, Bill was the founder, president, and director of a unique operation conducted at the Catholic University of America. Called the International Book Foundation, the organization and its volunteers focused solely on providing books, particularly theological ones, to those in impoverished countries. Publishers would donate books, and the International Book Service would send them around the globe.[40] All the letters that arrived at Bill's home in Kensington, Maryland, contained heartfelt pleas: books for seminarians, for new monasteries, for libraries seeking spiritual and educational materials, for priests trying to better shepherd their people, for recent converts looking for Christian literature to bolster their faith journeys. Requests came from the Philippines, Nigeria, India, Malawi, Zimbabwe, Malaysia, Indonesia, and Kenya. A million books traveled overseas and into the hands of missions around the world, thanks to Bill's generosity. Most of the information about this charitable endeavor is lost now, but twenty-two surviving letters of petition give credence to how far-reaching Bill's charity was.

Pro-life Work

Bill did much for the community around him in Washington, D.C., Maryland, and Virginia; one of those things was upholding the right to life. As lawyer W. Shepherdson Abell said of him, "He was intensely dedicated to the pro-life cause."[41]

Bill Carrigan, straightforward in his logic, stated, "you can't make a good conclusion out of the bad syllogism... The difficulty with abortion is the confusion about the difference of 'right to bear children' and 'the right of a child [that] was conceived to be born... That is the difficulty that most people are having today: that a child, once conceived, has a right to be born.'[42] If a woman did not want to risk conceiving a child, particularly outside marriage, she should exercise her right to her body by practicing chastity and abstinence. If she did conceive, then that baby had an undeniable right to be born, to live. Armed with this moral logic, Bill fearlessly called abortion centers to argue for the rights of the unborn. He thought often about the issue.

He also donated to, wrote for, and gave patronage to many publications that actively spoke out against the murder of infants in the womb, such as *The Triumph*, run by Christendom College between 1966-1976. To the Family of the Americas Foundation, an organization seeking to educate couples on Natural Family Planning among other worthy causes, Bill donated a total of $270,500 between 1991 and 1997. He also donated a total of $32,200 between 1990 and 1997 to the Northwest Center, a pro-life pregnancy and post-birth assistance center in Washington, D.C., that still operates today. In 1997, his reach extended into other parts of the United States and encompassed pro-life matters beyond anti-abortion activism. In 1997, he gave one thousand dollars to the Priests for Life, a Florida-based, anti-abortion group still working out of Titusville. In 1998, the Women's Injury Network received a significant fund—$100,000. Also in 1998, Bill gave an unspecified donation to Morality in Media, a national organization that combats pornography and sex trafficking while promoting human dignity.

DAUGHTERS OF ST. PAUL RELIGIOUS
COMMUNITY

Religious communities, too, saw Bill's charitable hand in their affairs. Around 1991, Bill made a large donation, approximately $10,000, to the Daughters of St. Paul in Alexandria, Virginia. When the sisters called to thank him, he invited them over for lunch, and from then on, he was friends with the "media nuns." He also helped them "on a local level in obtaining funds for ... evangelization efforts" in the community.[43]

During one visit to his home, Sr. Joan Paula Arruda, F.S.P., a newfound friend of Bill's, noticed large boxes in the front hall. When he opened them, he revealed stacks of videos, probably VHS tapes, for children. "I had noticed the label," Sr. Joan recollected, "It was from a company called CCC of America, which produced at that time in the nineties ... children's videos, saints' videos in particular, and I just connected that he must have been a funder of this particular project."[44] That was Bill Carrigan—ever the supporter of educating children in the Faith.

His impact on the "media nuns" did not end with the $10,000 donation, nor the evangelization efforts for children. He also funded a purchase necessary for the nuns' own evangelization process: he bought them a machine which put staples in the spines of magazines that the sisters produced. Moreover, his undisclosed donations to both their motherhouse and the local house in Virginia encouraged the sisters to honor him at one of their fundraiser dinners. At that benefit dinner, he offered to match whatever amount was donated that night. He did so much good for the nuns and was so generous in his charity that he was named the St. Paul Person of the Year in 1992 "by virtue of his lifelong devotion to the Catholic Church as well as his generous support for the Daughters of St. Paul."[45]

❦

PADRE PIO'S HOUSE FOR THE RELIEF OF SUFFERING

Aside from the items he frequently sent to Padre Pio, such as pineapple juice and long winter undergarments, Bill gave money to help build Padre Pio's one earthly dream: the *Casa Sollievo della Sofferenza*, his House for Relief of Suffering. Padre Pio brought many people to Christ, the Divine Physician, and he wished for them to have physical relief as well as spiritual. Bill, like many of Padre Pio's spiritual sons who invested time, talent, and treasure into what is now the largest hospital in San Giovanni Rotondo, sent at least one check overseas. In March 1953, the Capuchin's Superior at San Giovanni Rotondo wrote to Bill, thanking him for his unspecified but obviously welcome donations: "Fr. Pio was pleased to receive your note and thanks you heartily for your gifts to the hospital. He thinks of you and remembers you, esp. at [Holy] Mass."[46]

❦

THE PADRE PIO PROVIDENZIA TRUST

The Padre Pio Providenzia Trust was part of Bill's last will and testament, "a charitable trust ... to distribute the proceeds of his estate according to his wishes."[47] Upon the event of his passing, Bill wanted his estate to be given away to schools and programs of Catholic education, to eye care, and so on. Paperwork and testimonies from Chuck Furr and Mark Eggert, two of Bill's nephews, give three examples of how the Padre Pio Providenzia fund was used in the spirit of Bill's charity.

On July 10, 2001, about eight months after Bill's death, his estate loaned two paintings to the Holy Family Academy in Virginia; on December 31, 2008, the Padre Pio Providenzia trust was "pleased to convey the oil paintings to the Holy Family Academy as a gift."[48]

Two more organizations received art via the Padre Pio Providenzia Trust: the National Centre for Padre Pio in Barto, Pennsylvania, which received an oil painting of Padre Pio; and the Blue Army of Our Lady of Fatima, which received a watercolor painting of Padre Pio. Previously, both paintings had been on loan to the respective organizations, but the Providenzia Trust conveyed the art as permanent gifts. The Blue Army sent a letter of thanks, in which they detailed that the painting was placed "near our confessionals, a reminder of Blessed Padre Pio's great dedication to the Sacrament of Divine Mercy."[49]

Through the Providenzia Trust, even Catholics in Hawaii felt Bill's helping hand. Through Bill's nephew, Chuck, the Serra Club of Honolulu received a $10,000 gift.[50] The Serra Club of Honolulu is a sector of the USA Council of Serra International, which draws its inspiration and name from St. Junipero Serra. It is "a worldwide Catholic organization of lay men and women dedicated to promoting vocations to the priesthood, diaconate, and vowed religious life."[51] Given that Bill possessed tremendous respect and love for priests and religious, it is perfectly fitting that part of the trust fund in his will would go toward an organization promoting vocations.

∽

OTHER CAUSES BILL SUPPORTED

There are likely dozens of other organizations Bill supported that are now lost to time and faded memory. However, his comprehensive and decidedly Catholic support for dozens of different causes shows just how generous he was with his money. He gave cheerfully and without reluctance or compulsion. God's grace flowed out in abundance for and through Bill's good works. The following chronological list demonstrates further causes Bill Carrigan supported, both Catholic and secular:

The Heritage Foundation ($900) in 1996

Crisis Magazine ($25,000) between 1996-1997

Providence Hospital ($50,000) over a decade time period and in 1998 (at which Bill also started a Padre Pio Prayer Group)

Anchor Mental Health in 1998

Medical Mission Sisters in 1998

Legion of Christ in 1998

The Dominican Sisters in 1998

The Catholic Relief Services (a friend of Bill's from CARA, Gerry Early, suggested that Bill was a principal benefactor for this humanitarian agency)[52] Malta House ($50,000) over a decade time period.

William M. Carrigan was, in the ideal sense, a conservative capitalist: a man who achieved wealth through legitimate means and who continually looked out for those needing help. John Ciskanik, the current Executive Director of Planned Giving at Christendom College, once thought Bill was a "very competitive fellow" whom one would "want to watch out for," because Bill was known to drive a hard bargain and to stubbornly advocate for what he knew was right.[53] However, John found that Bill was not the kind of man to crush others under his feet in a mad struggle for money. He instead saw a man whose heart was on fire with charity and fueled by Padre Pio's example.

No matter what cause Bill chose to support, it always received his full intention. He believed that resources were to be shared, that money was a tool for the execution of good deeds rather than something to be hoarded. And, though his charity reached far across the world, he was especially generous with those close to home.

CHAPTER THIRTEEN

How Bill Impacted Rappahannock County,
Virginia
1960s – 2003

∽

REVITALIZATION BEGINS

Washington, Virginia, is a part of Rappahannock County. It is a peaceful town full of winding roads, stately forests, and birdsong. Many of the people who live there are down-to-earth, blue-collar types. The community sits nestled among nature, far from the busy city hubbub of Washington, D.C. The Carrigan couple took great pleasure in nature; many of the war letters between them mentioned the beauty—or woeful lack thereof, on Bill's side of the world—around them. Perhaps it comes as no surprise that the quiet countryside attracted Bill's attention in the early 1960s.

After moving from Bethesda to Kensington, Maryland, Bill and Ramona bought a second home: a manor in Washington, Virginia which was called Avon Hall. Built between 1796 and 1803, it "thrived for many years as Thorn's Tavern before being relocated to its current setting near the entrance of Town."[1] Here, it came into the possession of the Baggarly family.

Franklin Clyde Baggarly was an agent with the U.S. Bureau of Investigations (the FBI's predecessor) before and during World War II. He eventually settled in Washington, Virginia, where he lived until his death in 1961.[2] Avon Hall was Clyde's personal home in both childhood and adulthood. It is believed that Bill bought the home directly from Baggarly. As such, Bill only considered himself a custodian of Avon Hall, seemingly out of respect for its historic lineage.

This white, "evolved Colonial Revival-style manor home" still stands today.[3] It has recently undergone restorations to bring it back to its former glory: two stories tall, graced with an elegant portico supported by four regal, Roman-Tuscan columns. This historic building seemed to speak of grand old countryside times. A soft, green lawn dotted with trees sloped down from the house to a one-acre pond which Bill kept well stocked with fish. Birds chirped cheerfully around the roof and the wind rustled the leaves of the magnificent trees beside and behind Avon Hall.

After Bill and Ramona moved in, they decorated their manor home with a great deal of commissioned art and rare furniture. Though they could easily have closed themselves off from society, preferring the company of the wealthy alone, they did not. Bill's generosity and fervent faith trickled out into Rappahannock County, permanently altering the community in a positive way. He had two main circles of influence here: the local town of Washington, where he owned his second home, and the larger commonwealth of Rappahannock.

As was his penchant, he also provided many opportunities for the county to expand. The first thing Bill did upon arriving around 1960 was buy a run-down property in the town center and restore it, turning it into a small store, then into "The Inn at Little Washington, Rappahannock's premier restaurant."[4] From that point on, "the revitalization of Washington officially began."[5] Bill helped establish the local library, for which he received in September 1984 the DAR's medal of honor—the highest award offered by the organization.[6] He "helped to create the Rappahannock County Historical Society" and even provided water for local residents during a drought in 1983.[7]

He also invested money into the real estate around the area. Steve Critzer, a long-time resident of Rappahannock County, the former Vice Mayor of Washington, Virginia, and a personal friend of Bill's, indicated that Bill "invested in some properties by purchasing them—a major subdivision that was built in the mid-sixties."[8] When the original developer ran out of money, Bill jumped in with his own funding to help. Steve continued:

> With Mr. Carrigan's financing, [the developer] was able to complete the subdivision and get the road taken into the state system and start marketing the lots. I believe Mr. Carrigan received quite a few lots for his participation rather than money... I can imagine in other areas he made it possible for someone to own a home or own a piece of

property by providing financing to the folks that maybe couldn't go to a bank and get financing for one reason or another.[9]

And, perhaps most importantly, thanks to Bill's charity and passion for the faith, the Catholic Church was established in Rappahannock County for the first time. All his good works earned him the county's Man of the Year award in 1981. Though only a "part-time resident of the county," he paid close attention to the needs of his community: "Full-time interest, full-time energy, full-time dedication and full-time generosity... He was the wheel that started the renovation in the town of Washington rolling."[10]

⌁

Fourth Of July At Avon Hall

In Rappahannock, Bill's philanthropy and patriotism connected. As Bill's inclination was ever to share his resources, Avon Hall's beautiful, sprawling property became the site of a beloved annual Independence Day picnic.

Bill was a true patriot. As a son of the twentieth century, he lived through some of America's most defining historical events as either an observer or a participant—two World Wars, the Great Depression, the Cold War, the first space flight, and more. As the grandson of Irish immigrant farmers, he understood the value of meaningful work and proper distribution of wealth and the American Dream. All his experience, alongside his Red

Cross work, inspired in him a strong sense of honor for and pride in his country. Ramona, too, shared patriotic sentiment. As a member of both the Daughters of the American Revolution and the Daughters of the American Colonists, she could trace her lineage directly back to both the first English settlers in America and the brave fighters for independence.

It seemed only natural, then, that the Carrigans would be responsible for the annual Fourth of July party at Avon Hall. Originally a fundraiser for the local library, it soon became incredibly popular; guests even came from other states.[11] For over twenty years, he and Ramona threw "a birthday party: not only for their neighbors in Washington and fellow citizens of Rappahannock County, but for the entire country."[12] Hundreds of people sat on Bill's sloping lawn, going in and out of Avon Hall to get potluck meals and drinks. Those who received personal invitations from the Carrigans were privileged to sit on Bill's front porch to enjoy the show. The local band and high school attended.[13] And it did not stop there—the whole town joined in the celebration:

> There was something to be enjoyed by everybody: children's games, pony rides, hot air balloon rides, auctions, book sales, white elephants, antique automobiles, free movies, art shows, costumed pageants, bluegrass music and dancing. And talk about food: bake sales, ice cream stands, and sidewalk cafes kept busy dishing up barbecue

and lamb sandwiches, hot dogs and hamburgers, cake and pies, washed down with iced tea and lemonade.[14]

On one or two occasions, Bill even used his connections with the Army to bring in helicopters for people, especially children, to learn about and admire.

Just before the end of the night, special guests—such as Senator Eugene McCarthy, one time—and other heads of the community read the Declaration of Independence, reminding the audience of the nation's origins and guiding philosophies. Sometimes the readers dressed in historical regalia to look like founding fathers! Then, at 9:15 pm, everyone gathered on the lawn for the finale: a grand fireworks display that sent shimmering light over Avon Hall and the surrounding woods.

Many attendees had fond memories of being at these Fourth of July parties. For some guests, the celebrations gave a good estimation of Bill's personality, of his mission "to share everything he had with everyone around him."[15] After accepting a personal invitation to Avon Hall, Mark and Clare Cohagan of Mount de Sales Academy in Catonsville, Maryland—and their young children—visited for the event. While there, the Cohagans noticed that Bill chose to remain out of the spotlight. The only time he appeared in front of the crowd was to recite the Pledge of Allegiance and the Gettysburg Address.[16]

"He was the host," Mark said, "but he was not the reason. He was the one that actually was able to make it happen, and so he did. But he didn't want ... to be out in front and all."[17] Clare added on, saying Bill "was bringing everyone together but keeping us focused on why we were there."[18]

After approximately thirty years of part-time living at Avon Hall, Bill sold the property. On July 4, 1991, Bill gave a farewell speech, in which he reminded the gathered crowds that "[Ramona and I] have never really owned Avon Hall. We are only custodians for a little while. People may hold title to Avon Hall but they, like me and Ramona, will only [have] been custodians."[19] Eventually, the legislators of the Rappahannock Association for Arts in the Community took over the Fourth of July celebrations, and Avon Hall was turned over to the local town government; from then on, the town took charge of the famous Independence Day parties.[20] Such celebrations were, to the Cohagans and likely many other guests, "absolutely the [most] quintessential Americana Fourth of July that I've ever experienced." Clare then added: "And I'm sure I'll never experience anything like it again."[21]

∽

Bringing The Catholic Church To Little Washington

Of all Bill's charitable endeavors, one of his most striking is that he enabled the Catholic Church to come to Rappahannock County. The Catholics living in the Virginia county sorely needed a functioning local parish, but they had nothing. They were forced to attend parishes in other counties, as Steve

Critzer explained. "The Catholic Church was in Front Royal, Culpeper, Warrenton," Steve said, "and there was none here in Rappahannock."[22]

It appears that Bill and Ramona initially offered Avon Hall as a site for Catholics in Rappahannock County to gather for Mass.[23] At the very least, they had a priest come frequently for private Masses. The priest who celebrated the services for Bill and Ramona, Fr. Maurice du Castillon, was well familiar with the sleepy town, "alternating services between Oscar Lindgren's Jessamine Hill and William Carrigan's Avon Hall."[24]

Bill became increasingly aware of the need in Rappahannock County for a Catholic church. To meet this need, Bill donated two small buildings: a former schoolhouse and its cafeteria.[25] He named the makeshift church "St. Peter's Wayside Chapel."[26] It was not big, and often people had to run snakes, mice, and rabbits out before Mass, but it accommodated them well enough.[27] In the late summer of 1979, the first Mass was celebrated. Within the space of just over one month, the community grew so rapidly that a second Mass was added to the Sunday schedule![28] In the spring of 1981, the congregation grew large enough to merit a name change— "Wayside Chapel" was officially changed to "St. Peter's Catholic Mission."[29]

Bill agreed to lease the land for five years, and he also handled most of—if not all of—the utility bills and mortgage. As time passed, Bill and the council of locals, including Fr. du Castillon, all agreed that they wanted to have a permanent church building—an actual church—and attached property. After all,

Bill was aware that this building was "very inadequate, even as a temporary chapel."[30] In the first ever business meeting of St. Peter's Catholic Mission, one council member, perhaps concerned that so much work would amount to very little, asked: "Is there [a] break-even point in numbers generally agreed upon to estimate the chances of success?"[31]

Ever aware of the truths of the faith, Bill answered swiftly: "St. Peter's in Rome started with just one."[32] The minutes went on to record more of Bill's thoughts: "Having a permanent church building will attract Catholic families, and it was pointed [out] that if there is access to the highway, signs indicating the presence of a Catholic Church and the times of Masses will attract people traveling through."[33] On this matter, Bill and the council appeared to agree. There should be a better, permanent parish. Figuring out how to accomplish that goal, however, put Bill and the committee at odds.

As more and more families joined the parish—by 1988, the tiny Catholic community had flourished to contain seventy families—the committee debated their next move. Some members wanted to expand and renovate the land they already obtained from Bill, and some wanted to find new land on which they could build a parish from scratch. Perhaps unsurprisingly, Bill preferred the former option.

When the committee received an offer of free land, with stipulations, Bill advised against accepting it, feeling the gift was a poor business move. As a property assessor for Cardinal O'Boyle for many years, he knew what to consider when buying land for a new church. In his estimation, the free gift was too good to be true. The ground itself was inadequate for sewage and plumbing, and the fire department next door held weekend shooting contests—not exactly a favorable environment for peacefully celebrating the Mass. Despite holding different points of view, Bill and the council reached a compromise: though they would not renovate the existing property, they would accept Bill's expertise and reject the free land. It took St. Peter's Catholic Mission several years to find sufficient space. A new church was built and that little parish, which still exists today, owes its birth to Bill. "And now," Steve Critzer concluded, "there is a Catholic Church here in Rappahannock County."[34]

⚬⚬⚬

Further Benefits To Rappahannock County

Bill made two other notable contributions to the area around Avon Hall. First was a time capsule. This pyramid, about as tall as an average person, was placed on the grounds of the public library, of which Bill was director of the Board of Trustees. He allowed local schoolchildren to fill the capsule with letters and drawings, mementos and newspaper clippings, anything that would give an indication of the era. Then, "a sealed copper box containing artifacts and messages was placed in a concrete, water-tight vault in the stone-faced capsule. The vault was sealed in a special ceremony on July 4, 1983, to be opened on July 4, 2083."[35] He intended it to be a reminder of a perhaps humbler past for children of the future. It was a curious and creative way to encourage an education in history.

On top of facilitating the time capsule, Bill also donated some school property to the Child Care and Learning Center (CCLC), which still serves Rappahannock County's families today. In the 1980s, the CCLC offered "a recreational program for 40-50 children every day after school, and full-time during the summer."[36] Taking care of the youth—such was Bill's *modus operandi*. Due to their hefty support of the community in so many ways, the *Rappahannock News* named Bill and Ramona the 1981 Persons of the Year.[37] It was a thoughtful way to honor the Carrigans' generosity.

∾

In July 2003, three years after his death, Bill still kept on giving, this time through the auctioning of his belongings and estate at Avon Hall. This provided the community with "financial success and a wonderful time for more than 500 buyers who came to bid on the contents of the Avon Hall estate."[38] Some bidders telephoned in from as far away as Utah, giving evidence to the value and desirability of Bill's possessions. By the auction's end, all "the contents of the historic home sold for a total of $163,000" and "the town would retain $140,000 to $145,000" of that sum, no doubt to be put to good use in the community.[39]

Without a doubt, the Carrigans—true patriots and true Catholics, true givers and true lovers of the Gospel—permanently impacted Rappahannock County. He and Ramona are still periodically remembered in the *Rappahannock News*, which often looks back in time at the important people and events in the area. And, incidentally, Rappahannock was not the only area of Virginia that changed forever due to Bill's influence. Front Royal, home of Christendom College, also met with William M. Carrigan.

CHAPTER FOURTEEN

Saving Christendom College and Resurrecting
Mount de Sales Academy
1970s – 1980s

~

A Vocation To Education

ill's generosity was far-reaching, but also prudent and, in a way, cautious. He lent money often, but he was careful to support worthy causes; he wanted to know that the recipients were dependable, honest, and truly well-meaning, especially when the beneficiaries handled the education of the next generation—a matter of major importance to Bill. In his wartime group lectures with his soldiers, they pondered many questions. Why the war? What good or evil would it produce? How would it affect the future of each person and each nation? How must one live after returning home? How can another war be prevented? Bill and the boys decided, seemingly unanimously, on a single answer to the latter question: education in virtue. From the dozens of group discussions, Bill distilled their thoughts down to two principles: the necessity of working to live, and the dire need for "everyone in the world to recognize the rights of others to secure economic, religious, and political freedom" based on the Ten Commandments.[1] "Until people can learn of these principles," Bill stated, "they cannot use them, nor put them into practice. So, before true peace can come into the nations of the world, a vast educational campaign must be launched."[2] He held onto this belief for decades after the war.

Undoubtedly, this grand vision set the parameters for many of his later philanthropic endeavors, driving him to support many schools and teaching organizations. Indeed, as Shep Abell attested, Bill's "greatest joy—aside from the cause of his beloved Padre Pio—was Catholic schools."[3] Of Bill's many beneficiaries, two large and well-known Catholic institutions received special attention: Christendom College in Front Royal, Virginia, and Mount de Sales Academy in Catonsville, Maryland. Both sought to bring the truths of the Catholic faith to children in an orthodox manner. Without Bill Carrigan, it is highly likely that neither school would exist as it does today.

❧

SAVING CHRISTENDOM COLLEGE

Bill had ties with Christendom College since the 1970s. He had been a donor for the *Triumph* magazine, an orthodox Catholic publication associated with Christendom College, which combated many moral and liturgical issues cropping up in American society after Vatican II. During the Sexual Revolution, the magazine spoke out fiercely against contraceptives and abortion. As a staunchly and actively pro-life man, Bill was happy to donate to the magazine.

In the late 1970s and early 1980s, however, Christendom College was struggling. The tiny college in Front Royal consisted of fewer than forty students (far below what they needed for financial stability), who learned in rented classrooms and who lived in rented apartments instead of dorms.[4]

Dr. Warren Carroll, the man who first proposed the idea of an orthodox Catholic college in Front Royal in 1976, wanted to purchase a tract of land on which to build a permanent campus. Dr. Carroll and his companions dreamed of expanding, of putting down roots, so to speak. They found a parcel of land they liked, but the asking price was "$450,000, which was absolutely impossible for a school hanging on by its financial fingernails."[5] And, as Dr. Timothy O'Donnell, the current president of Christendom, said, "The college had virtually no endowment, virtually no money, and was very, very small."[6]

Dr. Caroll and his companions worked hard; through a series of fortunate connections, they managed to get the price halved—$275,000 and no lower. It was good, but not good enough; that was still unattainably high for the young school. Moreover, the land's seller, George Meany, stipulated that the college had to supply the payment by a certain date or else the deal would not stand.[7] So one of Christendom's board members, Sean O'Reilly, asked banks in the area for a loan. He was turned away. They did not want to risk a quarter-million dollars on the little Catholic college. Sean asked individual donors. They declined to help. No one was left. No one but one man—William M. Carrigan.

Following the testimony of Sean O'Reilly's wife, Anne, as recorded in Laura S. Gossin's excellent biography, *One Man Perched on a Rock: A Biography of Dr. Warren H. Carroll*, everyone tried to dissuade Sean from approaching Bill. True, Bill had funding to spare, but he did not "give his money to an organization that wasn't worthwhile."[8] With Christendom's existence so tenuous, it seemed unlikely that Bill would step in to help.

Sean tried anyway. After numerous phone calls regarding "Catholic education and how wonderful it was," about which Bill always agreed, Sean decided he could not avoid the point any longer.[9] At the end of one such conversation, O'Reilly boldly declared: "Either you believe in Catholic education and you're going to help us, or you don't mean what you say."[10] Finally, Bill Carrigan agreed: he would handle the brunt of the land's price—the mortgage, which cost $200,000—and Dr. Carroll could figure out how to attain the remaining $75,000. Then, "In Dr. Carroll's presence, Mr. Carrigan took out his checkbook and wrote out a check for the entire amount of the mortgage ... thus making the land and the buildings Christendom's property."[11]

On March 9, 1979, having obtained all necessary funds, Christendom College and Bill Carrigan purchased the land. The new campus officially opened later that year and began to grow.

By the time Dr. Timothy O'Donnell stepped up in 1992 as the third President of the school, Christendom College had "a very large debt, over half a million dollars, and the college was not ... able to pay that off at all."[12] One of his biggest challenges as a new president was to significantly reduce that debt, which had not decreased much due to the high interest that Bill charged. The pressure to bring the school into better financial straits inspired Dr. O'Donnell's frequent trips to Bill's house in Kensington, Maryland, to strike up a relationship. Bill was nearly ninety-five years old, and dementia was beginning to set in—yet Bill never forgot Padre Pio, who had died in 1968. Dr. O'Donnell knew of Bill's friendship with the saint, since he was Bill's favorite conversation topic. "I really needed to bring in some powerful heavenly aid," Dr. O'Donnell recalled. "I took [a statue of Padre Pio] out of the library and brought it to Bill ... and I said, 'Well, you know what? I'm going to leave it with you so long as you give it back to us when you go to see Padre Pio in person.'"[13] Bill placed the statue of his old friend next to his preferred sitting chair and would, during conversation, constantly touch and place his hand over the head of the statue—a "beautiful sort of sacramental image."[14]

Dr. O'Donnell prayed often, asking Padre Pio to inspire Bill to forgive the debt that burdened the school. He "knew that things were always going to work out," but one final push was necessary.[15] William M. Carrigan was an honest man who took care to speak the truth, even if it was hard, and things with Christendom College had reached a point where the frank truth was required. Dr. O'Donnell visited him and told him: "You know, Mr. Carrigan, you're not going to be able to take it with you."[16]

Evidently, Dr. O'Donnell's words reached deep into Bill's heart; he "proceeded first to cut the interest rate on his loan, and then designated that whatever amount the college still owed at the time of his death would be forgiven."[17] And that is exactly what happened.

Bill's humility in yielding to the truth showed John Ciskanik, the current Executive Director of Planned Giving at Christendom College, an estimation of Bill's character. Ciskanik illustrated a story of Bill's childhood and how it had originally colored his view of Bill and the loan situation: a competition for a gold or silver coin placed atop a greased pole.[18] While the other young boys rushed and failed to climb the slick pole, Bill waited for his opportunity. Soon, the grease was gone. "And as they were getting closer and closer," Ciskanik related, "he stepped up—climbed up—over the shoulders of everyone and got the coin."[19] After hearing that story, Ciskanik assumed that Bill was the kind of man who would be willing to step on people, willing to let them do the hard labor, in order to succeed personally.

Once John Ciskanik heard about Bill's forgiveness of the loan and interest, though, his opinion changed. To clarify his belief, he made the distinction between a job and a vocation. "A job is where you exchange time for money," Ciskanik claimed.[20] It is a means to an end, and some people are willing to do whatever it takes to reach the top, including abusing or dehumanizing others. "That," he continued, "was not Bill Carrigan."[21] Rather than use the interest payments Christendom College owed him to line his own pockets at the expense of others, Bill "was actually using those payments to make [a] life for the students at Mount de Sales. *Our money went to Mount de Sales*,"

Ciskanik emphasized. "What I saw and what I realized was actually true—Bill lived a vocation: it's Catholic education."[22]

Continuing to operate in the flow of grace, yielding to God's truth in his own heart, Bill enabled Christendom College to become the acclaimed, orthodox university it is today. In honor of his generosity and humility, a monument stands outside "the new St. John the Evangelist Library on Christendom's campus ... which reads: 'Without him ... Christendom College would not exist today.'"[23]

Resurrecting Mount de Sales Academy

In the 1980s, Bill became closely associated with another institute of Catholic education. Around the same time that he was working with Christendom College, staff of Mount de Sales Academy reached out and asked if Bill would give a talk about Marian shrines located around the world. Having traveled to various European Marian sites—and San Giovanni Rotondo—with Ramona in 1953, he possessed first-hand experience on the topic. Bill willingly obliged the all-girls' high school. Perhaps something about the school caught his attention, but Clare Cohagan, the Director of Development at Mount de Sales Academy, said with a chuckle, "I don't think we impressed him very much."[24]

There certainly was not much impressive about the school at the time. It appeared that the Academy had seen its heyday. Once, it had been like the Biblical city on a hill; Mount de Sales Academy perched on the highest point in Baltimore, towering over the city proper. The original structure was built in Catonsville, Maryland, by the Sisters of the Visitation of Holy Mary. These cloistered religious established the school in 1852. Though these nuns remained closed off from the world (the Academy still retains some of the original grilles and turn-stiles from the cloisters), they opened the minds of the girls they served. For over a century, it offered education, but in 1979, Mount de Sales Academy received a heavy blow when the Visitation nuns were reassigned elsewhere. Determined to keep the school afloat, alumni and the parents of both alumni and enrolled students rose to the challenge. They bought the school to ensure that it would continue to serve and assembled themselves as a Board of Trustees. Soon after, they became a private, Catholic, all-girls' high school.

It did not take long for the immense task of running a high school for approximately one hundred and fifty girls to take its toll. Funding became more and more difficult to find, especially as the school building and former cloister deteriorated. By the time the 1980s rolled around, the four-story, double-winged complex had long since lost its luster. Window shutters hung crookedly, where they hung at all; exterior paint along the building's trim flaked off; interior paint and plaster crumbled off dilapidated walls, even in the chapel; the roof leaked; one back stairwell flooded every time heavy rains hit Catonsville. In the winter, the schoolboard was forced to preserve funding by turning off the heat in the west wing. The long, curving driveway had so many potholes that cars and buses struggled to make it through the gates and up to the school.[25]

As if that were not bad enough, the staff became aware that one of the small, adjoining buildings was being misused. The Old Infirmary was so named because it had once been a medical center for the students. But in the 1980s, police informed the administration that, judging by the markings on the walls and the paraphernalia inside, the old clinic had become a ritual site for satanists.[26]

In May 1986, Sr. Philip Joseph Davis, O.P., a sister with the Dominican Sisters of St. Cecilia in Nashville, Tennessee, found herself in charge of Mount de Sales Academy. The Dominicans had arrived in 1985 and quickly picked up where the Visitation nuns had left off, but things were slow to improve. Some classes, such as the English literature course, were taught well below high-school levels.[27] Others were infrequent—the religion classes met only twice per week. They had no cafeteria, no accreditations or strong pre-college curriculum, and no special focuses except an academic track and a business track. Getting seniors into local colleges was nearly impossible. Principal Sr. Philip Joseph recalled that she "had to call and go visit admissions offices of local two-year colleges, not to mention the University of Maryland, who did not want to even *look* at a student from Mount de Sales." In short—the school was a mess. "Truly," Sr. Philip Joseph said, "I can say that it was only by the grace of God that the school was still operating. There was no sensible reason it was still open."[28]

But despite all the exterior decline and the struggle to keep going, Sr. Philip Joseph noted that "the school had a special spirit."[29] They were dedicated to quality Catholic education and possessed a fervent determination to continue in the right path despite difficulty. Bill likely sensed the zeal for education and service, two missions close to his own heart.

Through a series of fortunate events, Bill Carrigan became involved as a financial benefactor. God works in mysterious ways and often places people together to work for the greater good. In such a way, the Lord orchestrated the pathways for the benefit of Mount de Sales Academy.

The first connection between Bill and Sr. Philip Joseph came through a man who served as both the president of the Academy's Board of Trustees and the president of Christendom College's board: Chris Cuddeback. Chris told Sr. Philip, "There is a gentleman named Bill Carrigan who lives in Kensington, Maryland, and who would write you a check for one million dollars and never miss it... You should go down to his home and meet him."[30]

She did just that. Their conversation lasted for three hours, and Bill mainly talked about his Red Cross work and Padre Pio, as was his penchant, but just before her visit ended, Sr. Philip Joseph informed him of Mount de Sales Academy's financial needs. She said that Bill "listened attentively" and "said he would pray [that] Jesus would send someone to help."[31] There was, at the time, a litany of people seeking aid from Bill and,

ever the astute businessman, he had to be convinced that invest-
ment in the failing school would be worth his time and effort.

It was not exactly a firm "no," nor was it a definite "yes." For
the summer months, Bill did not connect further with Mount de
Sales. Sr. Philip Joseph returned to the St. Cecilia motherhouse
in Nashville and received a new assignment to serve in the
motherhouse's sacristy.

During this summer break came the second connection in
the flow of grace. The motherhouse's chaplain, after hearing
Sr. Philip Joseph talk about Mount de Sales Academy and their
endeavor to obtain assistance from Bill, brought her a book on
Padre Pio. Reading the book inspired her to reach out again.[32]
She penned a letter to Bill. In it, she suggested that, if he would
buy the contents of the library from the recently-closed Immaculata High School in Washington, D.C.—the desks, the chairs, all
the shelving, and about thirty-five thousand books—they would
name their new library after Padre Pio.[33] Fifteen thousand dollars was the projected cost. She ended the plea with a single
sentence: "How do you know that you are not the person Jesus
is sending to me to help Mount de Sales Academy revive?"[34]
She posted the letter in June and waited.

In late August, right around the beginning of the school year
and the sisters' return to Mount de Sales, a response sat on Sr.
Philip Joseph's desk. The very brief note read: "Please call William Carrigan at this number when you return from Nashville."[35]

Thus, Bill came to deeply love Mount de Sales Academy.
He saw the vigor and piety. He liked the historic nature of

the building and the school's mission to educate future generations in virtue as well as the typical school subjects. But
what really sealed Bill's desire to work with the Academy were
the Dominican sisters' charisms for study, prayer, community,
and preaching. Like a gardener "would care for the sprouting
garden," as Mount De Sales Academy's Director of Operations
Mark Cohagan illustrated, Bill stayed with the school "because
he needed to care for it... And he always talked about it in
terms of the orchard... We have to care for these things. That's
the only way they grow."[36] Clare added that Bill began to feel
more connected to the school because he was able to share
the message of Padre Pio with students and faculty who were
genuinely interested.[37]

In fact, Padre Pio played a large part in how Bill chose to
assist the struggling little high school. Clare Cohagan recalled a
pivotal moment in Mount de Sales' history and in Bill's efforts
to fund the school's renovations. In one of his many discussions
with Clare, Bill related an "extremely vivid" dream: "Padre Pio
was holding an umbrella over top of the school. *Clear* message
to Mr. Carrigan that, before he did anything else, we needed
a new roof, which was absolutely true. We were in dire need
of a new roof."[38]

Bill at once set about finding out how he could complete
Padre Pio's task; how could he ignore such a clear request from
his spiritual father? With the heavenly umbrella in mind, Bill
personally picked a company that would install a red, standing
seam metal roof, which looked very similar to the original roof

built in 1852.[39] The new tin roof was twice as long as a football field. All the leaks that had caused flooding and interior water damage no longer existed.

Over the course of eight years, Bill donated over $370,000 to Mount de Sales Academy. Upon the request of an additional $750,000 to fund a fine arts building, he opted to donate land instead; though, for their own reasons, the school was unable to keep the land and it sold for exactly the amount of money they needed, bringing Bill's total financial support of Mount de Sales Academy to well over one million dollars.[40] His funds touched nearly every part of the school. There was a long list of needs, of little things that built up to bigger things due to neglect and other changes; here, Bill applied the principle he learned as a boy restoring manual typewriters in 1915: "It's the little things that need to get fixed to make the whole thing work again... Just take care of all the little things and the big part will take care of itself."[41] His heartfelt desire was "for Mount de Sales to become the shining example of what a Catholic school can be and should be."[42] And by the grace of God, he was going to do his part to make it so. To demonstrate the scope of Bill's remarkable generosity, Sr. Philip Joseph submitted a list of the restorations made possible by his gifts. Among a great many endeavors he accomplished at the high school, these are some of the more significant ones.

As Sr. Philip Joseph originally requested, Bill did purchase the contents of the Immaculata High School. In addition, he renovated the entire first floor of Mount de Sales' west wing so that a library—named for Padre Pio, of course—could be constructed. This included adding new flooring because the original could not sustain the weight of all the books and shelving. Ten years later, he paid for the complete repainting and re-carpeting of the library, as well as the computerizing of the library catalog.[43]

Bill also supplied a bell system to announce the end of classes and an intercom system for campus-wide announcements, both of which are in working order today. Irked by the amount of potholes in the long, sloping driveway leading up to the school, he had the entire blacktop repaved. Where paint peeled and flaked on the exterior of the building, he had it scraped and repainted. He also refurbished the second and third floors of the school's west wing, turning nuns' cells into additional classrooms. The exterior entrance of the building, including the columns and portico, and, above it all, the cupola from which the entire campus and the city of Baltimore can be seen, were remodeled as well. Plus, Bill's aid allowed the school to demolish the walkway between the main building and the Old Infirmary, physically severing the satanists' ritual site from the school.[44]

With his aid, Mount de Sales installed a complete computer lab in the west wing's second floor library. This library was dedicated to Theresa Carrigan, Bill's older sister who died in a freak railway accident. He helped refurbish the science labs and classrooms with upgraded tables and functioning equipment.[45] Liturgical arts also felt his assistance; Bill supplied materials for the third-floor art room and paid for the salary of a teacher who was an expert in liturgical art, making sure that the students received a high level of instruction with quality tools.[46]

In addition to the extremely generous financial support, funded, in part, by the payments Bill received from Christendom College, Bill cared also for the physical and spiritual wellbeing of the students and staff. For example, Bill told the administration to inform the teachers that, if they wrote a list of items they needed for the next school year, he would supply at least one of the things for each teacher.[47] He also worked with Mark and Clare Cohagan to bring oranges and apples to students during the Thanksgiving holidays—a special treat at a time when the price of citrus and other fruits was high.[48] He cared for the students like a grandfather, and it seems that the students similarly loved him.

To cap off the impressive financial donations that enabled the school to undergo such extensive and necessary renovations, Bill completed his charity by introducing Padre Pio to Mount de Sales Academy. Of course, his dream of Padre Pio holding the umbrella over the school made an immense impact. He gave occasional lectures to both students and adults on Padre Pio. He donated the first-class relic—the blood crystal given to him in 1945—and the second-class relics—the hardened but intact bread and little wineglass Padre Pio offered. And, he gifted a special piece of art: a mosaic.

During Bill and Ramona's whirlwind Marian shrines tour and visit to Padre Pio in 1953, Bill filled several rolls of film. Many of the photographs featured Padre Pio. Hardly any people were permitted to photograph the saint, but Bill was one of the trusted few.[49] "He evidently lost one roll of film specifically of Padre Pio," Sr. Philip Joseph recounted.[50] Nearly thirty years later, Bill rediscovered the film and, with a great deal of emotion, realized that "in *one little corner* of a frame, a picture of Padre Pio distributing Holy Communion appeared."[51]

Sometime between 1984 and 1986, unbeknownst to anyone at Mount de Sales, Bill commissioned an artist friend in Colorado to create a mosaic based on that one photo of Padre Pio offering the Eucharist to a woman. Just a year later, in April of 1987, Bill called Sr. Philip Joseph. He asked, very excited, if the Academy wanted the mosaic, "which had just arrived [at] his home."[52] Sr. Philip Joseph did not hesitate to say yes, but she was concerned about how realistic the mosaic would look. After all, "it is one thing to render a mosaic of someone we don't know or have never seen. It is another thing to render a mosaic of a known person who has been shown in many photos throughout his lifetime."[53]

Later that very same day, Sr. Philip Joseph looked out her office window and noticed Bill, at eighty-four years old, hauling a huge crate by himself up the steep front stairs of the Academy. "What dedication," she exclaimed. "With the help of our ... maintenance personnel, we took it to the library. It was not small. I estimate about two feet by four feet. When [Bill] removed the wood crating, those of us looking on gasped because it was so lifelike. It was placed over the mantle in the main room of the library and it fit perfectly. We had no previous idea of its size."[54]

After the mosaic was hung, Sr. Philip Joseph felt that a small miracle occurred beyond the obvious matter of the mosaic's perfect fit above the fireplace. Though the Old Infirmary had received an exorcism after the police discovered the satanic activities, a malicious feeling still remained. Following the mosaic's placement, however, she and her fellow sisters noticed that the lingering "presence of evil" was lifted.[55]

Truly, Bill lived a vocation to Catholic education. He and Ramona, though childless, adopted Catholic schools and their students. Mount de Sales Academy's girls he especially loved; Bill gave a graduation address for the class of 1990, in which he told the girls, "If I were your father, I would be very proud of you. Yes, and I am very proud of you even though I am not your father."[56] His connection with the all-girls high school truly extended beyond that of a donor. He became a surrogate father.

CHAPTER FIFTEEN

The Final Years

1990 – November 30, 2000

❧

PAPAL RECOGNITION

As the 1970s passed and the 1980s drew to a close, Bill felt the gratitude, lauds, and bittersweet endings that followed his lifetime of charity and striving for virtue. One such honor he was awarded in 1973: after decades of tirelessly promoting Padre Pio through every available channel, the Catholic Church recognized him for his efforts. He received from Pope Paul VI the *Pro Ecclesia et Pontifice* Papal Award. The highest honor bestowed upon laypersons or clergy, this award is given to those who demonstrated outstanding service to the Church. In Bill's case, his instrumental work in "making Padre Pio known throughout the western world," and "his generous support of the works of the Church," won him this Cross of Honor, as James Cardinal Hickey of the archdiocese of Washington stated.[1] The shining mark of gratitude for his ceaseless efforts certainly did not give Bill the idea that he could rest on his laurels, though! For the next twenty-seven years, he continued to tell everyone about the Italian stigmatist, the "ultimate priest."[2]

For the last decade or so before his passing, however, Bill faced sufferings that arguably outmatched many of those that had come before. Though dementia trailed its fingers in the waters of his life, though he experienced a singularly great loss and an attack on his person, though his independence and management of both personal and business affairs dwindled, he never lost his spirit. "I never heard him complain, never heard him be negative," Fr. Michael Sliney, L.C., mentioned. "He bore his cross with great dignity."[3]

❦

Losing Ramona

Of all the griefs Bill suffered throughout his life—his siblings' deaths, his parents' deaths, injury to friends and family, losses of fellow Americans in war—Ramona's passing impacted him the most. Their approximately two-year separation during the war had been painful enough; the eleven years after her death were immeasurably lonelier.

Ramona had suffered a health scare once before, around April of 1945 when Bill was still overseas. She wrote to Bill, informing him that her doctor indicated she had a weakened heart. Anxious, her husband promised to speak with Padre Pio right away, and subsequently recorded the saint's response.[4] "I talked with Padre Pio," Bill wrote, "and he said I need not worry, you will be [alright]. Your welfare is in his hands. He was very quick in giving an affirmative answer. I hope he is right."[5] The situation quieted, and Ramona lived well for the next forty-four

years, accompanying Bill on a tour of Marian shrines, upkeeping their homes, and participating in her husband's charities.
As she reached her early nineties, several bouts of unknown
illness necessitated care at the Potomac Valley Nursing Center
in Kensington, Maryland. She remained there for three months;
during that time, the schoolgirls of Mount de Sales Academy
sent her cards and flowers and offered Masses and prayers—a
testament to how beloved she was to the school and the young
women there. Then, on May 9, 1989, due to complications
stemming from diabetes, heart ailments, and a stroke, Ramona
passed away.[6]

Though Bill resolved to "use Ramona's [funeral] Mass ... to
help others understand the spiritual life," evidencing his inner
desire to make good use of his own pain, the "sun rose and set"
on Ramona.[7] Her death left a gaping hole in Bill's heart and in
the community.

A faithful and devoted Catholic, Ramona attended Mass
daily, or near daily, for many years. She was a philanthropist
in her own right—not only as Bill was, distributing their goods
alongside him, but also in her maternal care for others. None
were spared from her kindness. She was intelligent and humorous and a deep feeler, a forward-moving woman who managed
real estate, held chairwoman positions with the Daughters of the
American Revolution and Daughters of the American Colonists,
sang, cooked, advocated for teachers, and maintained activity
at her local parish. She rarely used coarse or strong language;
in fact, Chuck Furr attested that he only once heard Ramona

swear.[8] She dressed impeccably, carried herself with dignity. Her conscientious personal conduct and sense of humor radiated outward, as did her self-giving sensitivity. And her marriage to Bill, fifty-one years long, was admirable for the Christ-centered love which passed between them.

The Carrigan couple's marriage served as an excellent example for those with whom they came into contact. For the girls of Mount de Sales Academy, it was a particularly powerful witness to the sacrament of marriage and its indissolubility; on Bill and Ramona's fiftieth wedding anniversary (September 3, 1988), Mount de Sales Academy honored the Carrigan couple with a special Mass and celebratory cake. At that joyful event, Bill spoke about his experience with love—particularly his and Ramona's love which matured throughout their marriage. In an age of possessing things and throwing them out when they are no longer interesting, satisfying, or useful, true love is not disposable, Bill claimed.[9] Rather, genuine love draws the other to itself in eternal honor and dignity.

After Ramona's passing, Mount de Sales Academy held a very different type of Mass and ceremony, no doubt bittersweet to Bill. On September 29, 1989, the school officially dedicated their new science wing to the late Ramona Carrigan. Today, a burnished gold plaque hangs on the wall underneath a beautiful black and white photo of Ramona. It reads:

> My dear students, you honor me here. I thank you
> for all your prayers and Masses—they helped me
> bear the pain. "Build strong character... You are

the custodians of virtue." True love and happiness will adorn your life. I love you for eternity. Ramona Carrigan.

It is likely that Bill wrote the text for the plaque based on Ramona's private words, and he included the message that Padre Pio had for American women—that they are the guardians of virtue in society.[10]

Fr. Lorenzo Albacete, a Puerto Rican priest, theologian, and teacher, gave closing remarks to all the young women and staff present at the Ramona Carrigan Science Center ceremony. In them, he noted that, even though he had not often spoken with Ramona, the flow of grace through her, through Bill, and through Padre Pio into Mount de Sales Academy was impossible to miss. He also detailed an account of the woman who had so captured Bill's heart:

> In her presence, frankly, I did not find it necessary to speak. I found that there was such a soothing and powerful warmth emanating from her—even in the time of her greatest suffering, indeed, especially then—that I did not want to speak. I just wanted to *rest in her company*. I know this incredibly attractive aura that surrounded her was due to her transparency to God's love. It literally came out of her. It was not difficult to understand why she had such a tremendous impact on the life of her students during the ... years of completely selfless

service as a teacher. She was guided by ... devotion to Padre Pio, who knew that truth and spirituality were not credible without love for the sick and the weak... But because it was God's love that moved her, her teaching work had that healing power and that convincing solidarity which the Lord tells us [are] indispensable for the proclamation of truth.[11]

Ramona's funeral Mass was held at Holy Redeemer parish in Kensington, Maryland. Attended by many who loved her, the service was, as Bill put it, "a truly spiritual event."[12] He felt particularly touched by the beauty of the singing provided by the girls of Mount de Sales Academy. Even the priests, twelve in total, commented about it. "You will never know what all this did for Ramona and me," Bill told the students in a later speech. "She had asked me before she died to be sure and thank those beautiful girls, teachers, and sisters at Mount de Sales for their prayers and gifts... She loved you."[13]

Ramona Jane Carrigan is buried in Rock Creek Cemetery in Washington, D.C., and her family and friends hope her soul is in the eternal rest of heaven.

✺

THE AFTERMATH

A deep grief—"a solitude and a heaviness"—settled over Bill's life.[14] Though he carried on with business and his charitable efforts, he returned time and again to the many letters he and Ramona exchanged during World War II. There, he found traces of his wife which he no longer had access to; touched by the depth of her love, he wrote his thoughts on the envelopes of a few of his favorite letters: "Ramona always sent much love. Had we only reviewed these letters together again before she left me ... how much love we would have recovered."[15] Sr. Joan Paula Arruda, F.S.P. noticed how intimately Bill remained connected to his wife even in his loss: "He spoke about her constantly ... his reference to her was as if she was just in the next room... It felt like we met her, but she wasn't there."[16]

In the wake of Ramona's death, two major aspects of Bill's personality changed. The first: he developed something of a hoarding disorder. Without Ramona to make it a home, his house became "a place to sleep and a place to live ... a place to pray and get stuff done."[17] He did not entertain others there often, and his mind was occupied with many matters. As such, he paid less attention to the neatness of his space. However, unlike hoarders who buy things just to own them, it appears that Bill's "capital 'C' cluttered" belongings consisted mainly of papers.[18] Though the problem was never professionally diagnosed, anyone who went to his house in Kensington could see the piles of documents on every flat surface. The halls were made even narrower by boxes and boxes of paperwork and saint videos for children that he was donating to schools. When Sr. Joan and some fellow "media nuns" visited Bill's home for lunch one day, she confessed she did not know where they would eat: "There was no kitchen table. The counter was covered ... there was a dining room table, but it was filled—I mean, literally *filled*—with piles of papers."[19] Luckily, Bill pulled out TV tray tables and they ate lunch upon those. She continued on to say, "We got the sense that [Ramona] was the one who kept the house clean, and since she wasn't there, it was not clean."[20]

"He was a voracious reader," Dr. Timothy O'Donnell of Christendom College said, "and he was a packrat. He had his magazines and books all over his apartment there. You could tell he was very well read and deeply knowledgeable."[21] He even had historical artifacts stacked around his home. It showed that Bill "cared more about people than things."[22]

Fr. Michael Sliney, L.C., who visited Bill's house several times, noted that the collection of items was more than just hoarding. It was not rotting junk items, trash that he refused to throw out due to mental illness, or knick-knacks purchased only for the momentary pleasure of buying and owning. Instead, he suggested that the apparently disordered state of Bill's home was actually surprisingly *well*-ordered, a sign of his intelligence.[23] After thrusting his hand into a chaotic pile of "every paper document ... he owned on the kitchen table," Bill produced precisely what he sought: a document and, a moment later, a pad of stamps. Fr. Sliney was amazed, but Bill simply said, "I know where everything is."[24]

The second change: Bill developed a strong dislike of hospitals. Forced to watch his beloved wife receive hospice care where she was "treated in an impersonal way by the majority of the medical and nursing staff," dismayed to see the spiritual element of love so soundly ignored, he grew callous.[25] He stated bitterly, "[Ramona's suffering] would not have occurred if she had been in Padre Pio's Home for the Relief of Suffering."[26]

This fear and distrust clashed painfully with his stubborn independence. "Never go to the hospital," Bill told his neighbor, the President/CEO of SPC Financial, Edward Geoff Sella. "You die there."[27] Geoff knew Bill's views better than most; he had been on the receiving end of it. In a downpour of freezing rain one day, Bill slipped on his front stairs and fell. Struggling to help Bill, Geoff told him he needed to be treated at a hospital— he had broken bones (ribs or a hip, depending on who recalls it) and could not get up.[28] Yet Bill refused, repeating, "Just bring me inside [the house]."[29] Evidently, after much argument, Geoff succeeded in convincing Bill to receive professional care. "He just always wanted to take care of himself," Geoff suggested. "He never seemed to me like he blamed the hospital for [Ramona's] death. He just wasn't going to go there. These are not his words, but I think he viewed hospitals as God's waiting room, and he didn't want to be there."[30]

∽

THE ATTACK

As Bill entered his nineties, his fragility and vulnerability reached a peak, but he grew used to living on his own and taking care of himself. His fierce independence became ever more evident: he refused to give up his driver's license. Despite his age, he drove himself to daily Mass in all kinds of weather. Upon learning that his friend, John Kuhn, had contracted cancer and could not drive, "Bill ... would stop every day to pick him up and bring him to Mass."[31] W. Shepherdson Abell, who walked to Holy Redeemer for Mass, would in bad weather think, "no ninety-three-year-old man is going to get here this morning," only to see "a familiar vehicle pulling up, and out would step the intrepid Mr. Carrigan."[32] Nobody, his family joked, wanted to know what happened during those drives from Bill's home to the parish!

Until he was about ninety-four years old, Bill managed his affairs by himself, which became increasingly dangerous for him. As his mind declined, greedy people sought his money. They inserted themselves into his life, taking advantage of his age and infirmity and generosity. One woman, for instance, played "the Catholic card" and lived on Bill's land for free.[33] "Renting implies that some form of compensation is being extended," Steve Critzer explained, but that tenant stayed on Bill's property in Washington, Virginia, for "nine years and never paid the first month's rent."[34] As more people—increasingly powerful people—attempted to prey on Bill in frightening ways, his extended family realized that he needed help. But the elderly Mr. Carrigan did not want help. It was not until an almost deadly incident in June of 1996 that he finally recognized that he could no longer manage entirely on his own. In his own words, he was "nearly killed."[35]

Around midnight on June 12, 1996, two days after his nine-ty-fourth birthday, Bill returned to his Kensington home. He had been in Rappahannock County, Virginia, discussing insurance matters regarding the Fourth of July parties at Avon Hall.[36] He parked his car in his sloping driveway and pushed himself out. He leaned on his cane and locked his vehicle. As he ascended the short flight of stairs, surrounded by bushes, which led to his front door, someone struck him from the left. The blow to his head knocked him down.

Early the next morning—June 13, 1996—one of Bill's neigh-bors up the street left his home to walk his small, gray dog. When passing Bill's house, the dog began to sniff the ground wildly, tugging on the leash. It led the owner to Bill's house, where blood splattered the porch and the front door stood ajar. The neighbor did not go inside and, despite looking for Bill on the property, could not find him anywhere.

Between five and five-thirty that morning, Geoff Sella left his house to play racquetball. His car was parked right in front of Bill's house, as it usually was. As he approached his car to leave, he heard something. Confused, Geoff went to the front door, saw the blood, and immediately called an ambulance. Despite EMS helping him search, they could not find Bill anywhere. The ambulance left, but not a moment later, Geoff heard moans from a bush on the next-door neighbor's property. He called 9-1-1 again; the EMTs made a quick about-face.[37]

Bill Carrigan had spent the night outside, exposed to the elements. Desperate for help, he had dragged himself across the street. A smear of blood just beneath Geoff Sella's doorbell suggested Bill had tried, unsuccessfully, to reach for the buzzer, then inched back across the street to try another home.[38]

When the first responders returned, they were initially unable to check Bill's eyes because his head and face were covered in so much dried blood and outdoor debris. A physical exam at Suburban Hospital nearby showed bruising on the left side of his torso, fractured ribs, bruising to his upper left arm, and awful lacerations on his scalp. He had severe ecchymosis—bleeding under the skin due to blunt force trauma— around his left eye.[39] "They said he would have bled out," Geoff noted, "except he was wearing a hat of some type."[40] The hospital's intake paperwork noted that, for an unknown stretch of time, he most likely lost consciousness. For eight days after the attack, he suffered memory loss and confusion.[41] He was lucky to be alive.

On the third or fourth day of Bill's recovery in the hospital, while friends and family visited, Tom Cunningham dropped in. A recipient of Mr. Carrigan's charity, Tom wanted to make sure his friend would be alright. While there, Bill related an incredible experience—a dream or a vision that occurred during the night of the attack. "Tom," Bill said, "I saw the light and I traveled toward the light ... and then Padre Pio grabbed my arm."[42] Alongside Padre Pio, he continued to move forward until he said to the saint, "Padre, there are some things I have to do first."[43] Then he woke up, safe in the hospital. Assuming that the vision was real, that Bill had really been dying at that moment, the fact that Padre Pio personally came to fetch him to heaven is a powerful witness. Yet he was not ready to go; his mission on Earth was not complete.

⚬⚬

Once Bill was out of immediate danger, the minds of his friends and family turned to finding the perpetrator. There was not much to go on. Even though Bill was interviewed in October 1996 on the Channel 4 evening news in Washington, and authorities asked for witnesses or informants to come forth, nothing came of the search.[44] It could have been a man or a woman; someone who knew him personally, or someone he had only met in passing; young or old. The motives were unknown. Based on the type of wounds Bill sustained, his assailant may have used a bat or a similar object to beat Bill across the head.[45] The broken ribs and bruising on the arm may have been due to a second hit, or perhaps from Bill falling on the stairs. Upon their investigation, police discovered cigarette butts scattered and smashed down in a corner of Bill's porch.[46] This indicated to them that the attacker had lain in wait for some time. Unfortunately, DNA tests on the discarded cigarettes yielded no results.

This attack was not the first time that neighbors witnessed suspicious activity around Bill's home. Geoff Sella recounted an episode where, one evening, Bill had been approached by two men who "knocked on his door ... telling him he needed his house painted."[47] To Geoff, this was highly unusual. Bill's Kensington home was made mostly of stone, and the painted parts could hardly be seen from the street, even in the daytime. Why would anyone—at night, no less—claim that they had seen the need for fresh paint? "I don't think that they had legitimate reasons to be talking to him about it," Geoff said.[48] Though never officially connected to the attack Bill suffered, the strange activity indicated that someone may have been casing his home. Similarly, Steve Critzer implied that police thought the perpetrator may have worked on Bill's house before.

Another lead soon presented itself: a potential money trail. Bill's annual Fourth of July party was undergoing some changes. The firework display was in the process of being turned over to the Rappahannock County fire department, and some insurance money was involved in that change. Steve Critzer recalled that, not long after the attack, "three homicide investigators from the county up there came [to Washington, Virginia]. And one of their biggest questions [was] 'Who gets the money from Fourth of July?'"[49] The investigators even questioned a woman living in Rappahannock County, apparently considering her a suspect. But like the rest of the case, it was a dead end.

Since the attacker was never found and brought to justice, the motivations behind the attack remain hidden to all but the perpetrator and God. This did not stop friends and family from speculating. Why would anyone want to hurt an elderly gentleman who had done so much good in his life? Geoff Sella suggested that Bill's business dealings may have garnered him some enemies. Some suspect that his car may have been the intended target, and that Bill threw his keys into the bushes around the driveway to prevent the attacker from stealing the car. Others think that the attacker may have been a debtor to Bill and had intended to threaten him into forgiving the debt, to force him to keep the money flowing, or to rob his home. Still others propose that, because Bill was outspokenly pro-life and firmly supportive of the Catholic Church, an enemy who felt differently may have wanted to silence him or intimidate him into backing down. Another speculation is that some renters considered Bill an absentee landlord and had wanted to punish him for this.

Whatever the reason, the mugging attempt did not seem to damage Bill's outlook on life. Those who visited in the days after his hospitalization noticed that he did not seem to hold any grudge against his attacker. John Ciskanik, who visited Bill from Christendom College, said, "I saw no vindictiveness ... [it] was another moment of revelation about this man—that there was no anger in his heart over the attack and [he] didn't talk much about it."[50] The assault did not impact his charity either, for he continued to give to schools, the Church, and individuals who needed a leg up.

❧

Guardianship

In 1997, in light of the attempt on Bill's life and the greed of others, Bill's nephew Chuck Furr made a significant personal decision: he wanted to become his uncle's legal guardian. Chuck and his wife Marylin saw that Bill could no longer manage his own affairs. "We knew he was a good person," Chuck said, "and he had that wonderful relationship with Padre Pio, but it was evident that he was suffering from dementia."[51] Plus, Bill had done "a tremendous amount" for Chuck and the Furr family over the years, so much so that Chuck's daughter Janet suggested that the guardianship was "their way of giving back to him."[52]

And that was true. Bill had stepped in when Loretta Marie, Chuck's mother, passed away. He consistently challenged Chuck to greater virtue; he once scolded his nephew for using the phrase *horse's ass*. "If you hold a line, you hold the line," Bill declared.[53] And of course, through Bill, Padre Pio became the patron saint of the Furr family.[54] With this meaningful generational impact in mind, Chuck visited Bill in Washington, D.C., from Oahu, Hawaii—not a short trip!—to support the man who had done so much to support others.

Bill, however, did not want a guardian. His Irish pride, as Chuck called it, made accepting help extremely unpalatable. He rejected the idea for quite some time. Yet one day, while Chuck and his wife Marylin visited him, Bill abruptly changed his mind. Mass at Holy Redeemer parish had just finished, and as the two men were leaving the church, Bill beckoned his nephew over. They stood outside the three arched parish doors in silence for a moment. Suddenly, Bill began to weep. An usher brought a chair and Bill sat down. In front of the great brick church, he finally admitted that he could no longer manage his affairs alone. With humility, he accepted Chuck's offer of guardianship. "It was a very emotional moment," Chuck recalled. "I felt elated. It was a real breakthrough."[55]

Touched, Chuck knelt down, took Bill's two hands in his own, asked Bill to look into his eyes, and said, "Uncle Bill, you are looking into the mirror, and Marylin and I are here to see that what you want done will be done. I want you to trust us."[56] Bill responded, quiet but firm, "I know that, and I understand I cannot handle my affairs myself. *I will not be the problem.*"[57] In 1997, Chuck Furr legally became the guardian of William Maurice Carrigan.

Chuck and Marilyn made a total of twelve trips between Hawaii and Washington, D.C., to manage Bill Carrigan's estate. It made an impact on the Furrs; Marilyn, who had only packed for a three-day trip, decided she was not going to leave her husband to sort through all Bill's paperwork alone, so she called the hospital she worked at and "ended a forty-year nursing career over the telephone."[58] There was much to do. Chuck needed to take over all fiduciary responsibilities, including tracking down the people who owed money to Bill and his estate. But since the documents necessary for such a venture were scattered through Bill's home, Chuck, along with Marilyn and a lawyer friend, were forced to organize every single piece of paper in Bill's cluttered home "so that they could appropriately manage it."[59] It took them five days just to clear Bill's kitchen table and the space beneath it. Despite the excessive task at hand, the Furrs knew it was the only way. If law firm interns—or anybody who did not truly have Bill's welfare at heart—had taken over, valuable articles would have ended up in trash bags on the curb. Chuck firmly believed that Padre Pio guided their efforts; Marylin once pulled from the enormous pile of papers "a stock certificate worth $80,000" and Chuck discovered the letter from Padre Pio expressing his sympathy and prayers for the deceased Loretta Marie.[60]

Eventually, Chuck and Marylin needed to return to Hawaii. To ensure that Uncle Bill received consistent help in their absence, they hired a full-time, live-in caregiver—a wonderful Spanish woman named Pilar Nombela. She proved to be a great help and became a close friend. With Bill in good hands, Chuck and Marilyn went home sixty-three days later. Remarking on the dedication of the Furrs in helping Bill, Shep Abell noted, "Everybody should have someone who cares that much about them ... when they're in need."[61]

Bill's charitable activities slowly came to a close in the late 1990s, but he never stopped promoting Padre Pio. Many visitors to his home in Kensington claimed that he kept the statue of the great saint given by Dr. Timothy O'Donnell from Christendom College next to his favorite armchair. He had given hundreds of talks, commissioned art and photographs, handed out countless blessed rosaries and medals, distributed over one million holy cards, spoken on EWTN about Padre Pio, interviewed for and supported books on the mystic, and opened many channels of grace for the Western world by connecting them with the saint in Foggia. When his age prevented him from doing these things, he talked for hours with anyone who would listen about his experiences meeting Padre Pio.

THE CONCLUSION OF BILL'S MINISTRY

After over fifty years sharing Padre Pio's sanctity across the United States, Bill finally witnessed the culmination of his efforts. Fr. Michael Sliney, L.C., testified that Bill's whole focus after Ramona's death was Padre Pio.[62] "His life revolved around Padre Pio, probably even more so after Ramona died, and when I knew him, that was his one-hundred percent focus," Fr. Sliney stated.[63] He even suggested that Bill had "some sort of mystical connection with Padre Pio... There was a union there that was very powerful."[64]

In late April of 1999, with an entourage of Chuck, Marilyn, the caregiver Pilar, five other Furr siblings and their spouses, and Sr. Philip Joseph Davis, O.P. from Mount de Sales Academy, Bill made his final pilgrimage to Italy. Padre Pio's beatification was scheduled for May 2, 1999; Chuck and Marilyn thought Bill deserved to see his old friend move one step closer to canonization. After sending several letters to the Vatican that cited Bill's unwavering dedication to Padre Pio and his personal ministry as a sufficient cause for free tickets, they were awarded such.[65] Even James Cardinal Hickey, a close colleague of Bill's and a fellow philanthropist, put in a good word.[66]

Bill's dementia had increased significantly by this point. It became harder and harder for him to keep track of where he was and what was going on. The change in location, routine, and time zone made keeping up even harder for him. While on the plane to Rome, he suddenly unfastened his seatbelt and stood. Sr. Philip Joseph, seated beside him, asked where he was going. "I am getting off this train," he said.[67] When Sr. Philip

Joseph informed him that he was, in fact, on an airplane "40,000 feet in the air," he collapsed back into his seat in shock.[68]

"Due to his dementia," Chuck said, "it was difficult to read, really, how Uncle Bill understood that, but I do think he knew his good friend was being recognized by the Catholic Church."[69] But even though he was "very old and very sick," the Furrs made certain that he would be able to honor his saintly friend.[70]

On the day of Padre Pio's beatification, Chuck led Bill's group into Vatican City. They joined more than 300,000 people from all over the world who flocked to St. Peter's Square to witness Pope John Paul II recognize the Italian mystic's progression in the canonization process. Since Bill was elderly and wheelchair-bound, he and Chuck received special assistance, front-row seats. The rest of the group watched the Mass and ceremony from a nearby building, the Pope's residence itself. As Bill and Chuck worked their way toward their seats, Bill encouraged his nephew to hand out Padre Pio holy cards. Chuck had a stack in his front pocket. "They don't belong in there," Bill insisted.[71]

After the beatification ceremony, the group went to lunch. They were not certain if Bill even knew what had just occurred, as Sr. Philip Joseph claimed: "We actually thought he was not aware, until after the Beatification when we all went to lunch together and were seated. He said out loud, 'Well, we finally have a saint.' Everybody at the table almost dropped their forks in amazement."[72]

The group spent a brief time in Rome, then traveled six hours via double-decker bus to San Giovanni Rotondo. For the final time, Bill visited the places where he had walked with and talked with his great friend over half a century earlier. Bill did not once, in fifty-five years of knowing him, doubt that Padre Pio was a saint. He knew it all the way back in late 1943 when he attended those first Masses and brought those first groups of soldiers to the monastery.

∽

BILL'S PASSING

A year and seven months after returning from Padre Pio's beatification, at ninety-eight years old, William Maurice Carrigan died in his home of a heart attack on November 20, 2000.[73] Though his family knew he was approaching the end of his earthly life, it was a heavy blow indeed. Those who loved him hope that he was walked into heaven by his dear friend Padre Pio and enjoys eternal rest with Ramona in the light of God's all-satisfying love.

Bill Carrigan's funeral and burial were held on November 30, 2000, at Holy Redeemer parish in Kensington, Maryland. Dozens of people attended the funeral Mass and wake: representatives of Catholic causes, food banks, schools, "Jewish people, secular people," and more.[74] Everyone wanted to respect Bill Carrigan. His family and close friends took intimate parts in the funeral service. Bill's nephews and grandnephews served as pallbearers. The president of Mount de Sales Academy's Board of Trustees, Fr. Michael J.P. Roach, concelebrated the Mass. Friends and family participated in the Liturgy of the Word. Chuck read the Prayers of the Faithful. "In grateful thanksgiving for the beautiful reunion of Bill Carrigan with his beloved wife,

Ramona, and that great friend and spiritual mentor, Blessed Padre Pio—that their reunion in heaven is full of the joy and peace that Uncle Bill so richly deserves," he said as he led the congregation in prayer.[75] He continued: "For the continued success of the many projects, foundations, charities, and schools that Mr. Carrigan supported... In thanksgiving for the intense stewardship commitment that drove Mr. Carrigan, that by his example we will leave this service challenged and more determined to become better stewards of our time, talent, and treasure, by giving back to the Lord as Mr. C has taught us... Let us pray to the Lord."[76]

Alongside Bill's family, W. Shepherdson Abell, Bill's lawyer friend, and Elizabeth Connolly, class president of Mount De Sales Academy for the year 2000, gave eulogies. "For so long as there are Mount de Sales girls," Elizabeth declared, "Mr. William Carrigan will never have to worry about prayers!"[77]

Shep Abell added, "The Gospel tells us to give to everyone who begs from you. As much as any man I ever knew, Bill Carrigan seems to have done exactly that... He was known and loved by doctors, lawyers, cardinals, schoolchildren, janitors, bank tellers. As someone once said of the Catholic Church, 'Here comes everybody!' Bill loved that. He seemed to have time for them all."[78] And indeed, his large extended family, his community which encompassed so many people brought him great joy.

His incredible charity was no doubt inspired by the Gospels he heard daily at Mass. Shep speculated that Bill may have "attended ten thousand Masses" at Holy Redeemer parish. When he could no longer drive himself, Sr. Philip Joseph brought him daily Communion.[79] This devotion to Mass and his willingness to help others get there too showed the culmination of his life-long advancement in holiness; the older he got, the more his love for Christ, the Church, and Padre Pio seemed to grow. One monsignor half-joked to Chuck that "Mr. Carrigan had to go to heaven to make [Padre Pio's canonization in 2002] happen."[80]

Shep concluded his eulogy by calling the funeral attendees to action: "[Bill] was a man of virtue—of many virtues, really. Perhaps his final gift to us is the challenge to try to imitate those virtues."[81]

Truly, Bill's entire life was a testimony to the loving guidance of God, to strength of character and of will, to service to others and an admirable marriage, to a life of virtue, to what it means to authentically live the Gospel. He fulfilled his destiny with Padre Pio, becoming one point of contact in the passage of grace from God to Padre Pio, and onwards to countless others.

Bill's challenge extends to each person who wishes to live well. As Bill told a high school group in 1945, less than a month after returning to the United States from Foggia, "You are it. The men who fought this war say you are it... Your time for the play is fast coming up."[82] Understanding that his audience wanted a chance at greatness, and knowing that true greatness consists of continually striving for virtue, he issued a challenge: "Will you be able to take this olive branch of peace and make something of it?"[83]

"I dare you."

Appendix

War Poetry

Bill Carrigan was, among many other things, an amateur poet. Some of his favorite reading material—before, during, and after the war—included *The Hound of Heaven* by Francis Thompson and the *Rubaiyat of Omar Khayyam* by Omar Khayyam, an ancient Persian poet, mathematician, and philosopher. Bill considered these poems profound, believing that they were "the two great philosophies of life struggling, each in its own way, to bring man to an answer to his life's problem... And the Christian always finds the answer for the question in the [*Rubaiyat*] in *The Hound of Heaven*."[1] When Bill put his own pen to paper, his poems revolved around topics of war and Catholicism. Replicated here with minor spelling corrections, his verses give testament to what he considered most important.

The first poem Bill wrote on September 19, 1943—not long after the Invasion of Sicily began. It is partially metered and partially spoken word. He had strong feelings about this piece; "I wouldn't show this thing to anyone. I thought a long time before I decided to show you," he told Ramona.[2]

On Giving a Rosary

Soldier!
Take this Rosary—just for today.
Maybe—it will help you pray.
For tomorrow, Soldier!
You may not be.

Take the Rosary, Pray!
For when the soul from
The body part—
By bullet through the heart,
Or shell burst
Scatter your poor body
O'er the field
This Rosary, plus the prayers
You say—
May help you in that
Awful day.[3]

Bill's second poem is longer and is written as a man might speak, once again giving the impression that drew upon his own war experience. The date for his second was March 10, 1944, after he met Padre Pio. The priest mentioned in the poem does not appear to be Padre Pio himself, though, for the saint did not enter the war zone the way Bill describes.

GOD WILL BE WORSHIPED

'Round the cliff there
In the deeper cave.
Keep a watch, fellow
They're dropping close.
Wait, Soldier! Don't go yet,
Hit the ditch! There's an eighty-eight!

Hi! Fellows, this way,
'Round the cliff there
In the deeper cave.
You'll have time
The Padre will wait.
Yes, Colonel! Holy Mass.
Padre found a place
'Round the cliff there
In the deeper cave.
A bit crowded, but there'll be room.
There will be a hundred soon.
Confessions 'till ten, then Mass.
Come on, fellow, you're a little lame!
Corporal, a hand here, the trail is rough
Quick! Around that ledge—duck!
They fly low when they want their man.
Ten more coming, pass the word along.
Get along, men, confessions 'till ten,

General Absolution if you can't get in.

Just around the cliff,

In the deeper cave—

All here now, no more in sight.

Ok, Padre, I'll light the lights.

The altar? On the rock back there.

Dark! Your flash, sir. Thanks!

Someone to serve? Sergeant? Good!

How many for Communion? Hands, men.

"*Introibo ad Altare Dei.*

Ad Deum qui laetificat iuventutem meam."

What was that?

A bomb hit out front—

Dusty—yes, but all ok.

"*Iudica me, Deus,*

Et discerne causam meam de gente non sancta,"

God was worshiped at the front that day![4]

It seems highly likely that, as a field director, Bill did actually help gather soldiers for Mass and Confession in the middle of a bombing at the front lines. The poem shows his incredible devotion to the Mass, as well as the dedication of those around him. Notable also is his use of prayers from the very beginning of the Extraordinary Rite Latin Mass, which translates as follows: *I will go unto the altar of God. To God, Who gives joy to my youth. / Judge me, O God, and distinguish my cause from the unholy nation.*

The fact that he uses these words in the poem paints a picture of the soldiers' desire for the Eucharist; not even falling bombs could prevent the priest and soldiers from having Holy Mass. Bill really viewed the Mass as a plea for peace and deliverance from the enemy, both spiritually and culturally. In addition, it is not difficult to imagine what unholy nation the poem might be referencing.

Acknowledgments

Chuck Furr

This project was envisioned by Our Lord and Saint Padre Pio decades before I knew that I would become the catalyst of this remarkable story of two very holy and spiritual men and what they accomplished together to aid mankind in so many ways.

This began during the time I was the guardian of my uncle William M. Carrigan in the years 1997 through 2000. My wife Marilyn and I made twelve trips from our home in Hawaii to the Washington D.C. area where my uncle resided. It became our obligation as Bill's guardians to determine which of over five hundred thousand papers contained information of value enough to save. A total of seven boxes containing information of significance dealt with the many charitable endeavors my uncle contributed to. These materials were stored in my home for twenty-two years before I decided to use the information they contained to write a book.

God entered the scene when I told my friend Susan Duffy that I intended to write this book. She told me that her daughter, Makena, was a film producer, and her friend, Ava, was a recent graduate of Franciscan University of Steubenville, Ohio. These young ladies were not yet born when Marilyn and I were saving these materials, and Our Lord and Padre Pio knew that I was not an author so, by divine providence, these scholars entered my life. Each of these professionals took this challenge, likened to unleavened bread into which they mixed yeast and created a remarkably better story—which seems to be a miracle!

～

AVA R. MONTES

Significant research went into the creation of this biography, and it would severely lack important details if not for the interviews of a set of truly wonderful individuals: Chuck Furr, Janet Johnson, W. Shepherdson Abell, Sister Joan Paula Arruda, F.S.P., Dr. Timothy O'Donnell, Edward Geoff Sella, Mark Eggert, Fr. Michael Sliney, L.C., John Ciskanik, Steve Critzer, Mark and Clare Cohagan, Victoria Sheffield, Richard Viguerie, Sister Philip Joseph Davis, O.P., Tom Cunningham, and Gerry Early. I am in your debt; thank you for sharing your wealth of memories about Bill and Ramona Carrigan. If your name is not listed here, know that Padre Pio knows how you helped bring Bill's story to life.

To Chuck especially I owe deep gratitude. His dream of having a book about Bill and Padre Pio made my dream of writing a book possible. In 2022, more than two years before Chuck's unexpected passing into eternal life, I wrote him an email that, for some reason now forgotten, I did not send. I will leave it here as a belated expression of my feelings about the opportunity he gave me.

Dear Chuck, I've been reflecting recently on my post-graduation life, and I wanted to send you this note to thank you.

The more I think about it, the more I realize that working on the Carrigan Project is my dream job. It is everything I had hoped for and more. I get to serve the Church with my God-given talents by researching and writing about a worthy topic. It is so interesting. Carrigan and his life are intriguing. This is to say that there's nothing boring about the work, even if some parts are tedious. I have the privilege of handling priceless historical documents. I even get to expand my skill set by conducting interviews and networking with people from various walks of life. I'm challenged intellectually and spiritually in a positive way by the work—it's not mindless stuff. I've even been touched on several occasions by Bill and Ramona's spirituality, which is, I think, improving a few areas of my life. In all, it is fulfilling, meaningful, eventful, and fascinating work.

As I said, I could not have dreamed up a better post-graduation job than this. I am truly, truly indebted to God, Padre Pio, and you for the honor of getting to work with you and Makena (and everyone else!) on this project.

Thank you, thank you, thank you.

God bless,

Ava

The Carrigan Project, as we so affectionately called it, really did change my life.

My acknowledgements would be incomplete if I did not mention Makena Duffy, for her unwavering prayer, listening ear, and enjoyable personality. My deepest love and gratitude I give to Mom, Dad, Sofia, Stella, and all my extended family, who supported me and the project, bolstering me when I was low and celebrating with me when I was excited. My sincere thanks also to Mya Riley and Isabella Hein, for beta-reading and being awesome writer buddies, and to St. Padre Pio, St. Anthony of Padua, and Bill and Ramona Carrigan, without whom this book would not exist. Thank you.

The Flow of Grace Made This Book Possible

St. Pio of Pietrelcina

William M. Carrigan

Chuck Furr

Makena Duffy

Ava R. Montes

Author Bio

Ava Montes is a Catholic author and teacher from Melbourne, Florida. She holds a bachelor's degree in English/Writing from the Franciscan University of Steubenville and spent three years delving deep into William M. Carrigan's remarkable life. As a kid, she wanted to be a paleontologist, a detective, and an author ... writing this biography combined all three careers into one. When she is not educating chaotic but good-hearted middle school students, she spends her time catering to her needy, diabetic cat and thanking St. Anthony of Padua for helping her find all the things she loses, especially citations.

END NOTES

Introduction

1. Carrigan, William M. "Speech to Mount de Sales Academy." Speech, Mount de Sales Academy, Catonsville, Maryland, November 20, 1986. Carrigan Project Archives.

2. Carrigan, William M. "Private Note: Recollection of First Meeting Padre Pio," September 6, 1985. Carrigan Project Archives.

3. As this was pre-Vatican II, the Mass was celebrated *ad orientem*— facing away from the congregation.

4. Carrigan, William M. "Private Note: Recollection of First Meeting Padre Pio," September 6, 1985. Carrigan Project Archives.

5. Carrigan, William M. "An Introduction to Padre Pio." EWTN, c 1996. *https://www. ewtn.com/catholicism/library/ introduction-to-padre-pio-5765.*

6. Abell, W. Shepherdson. "Eulogy – William M. Carrigan." Padrepio.net, November 30, 2000. *https://www. padrepio.net/eulogy.html.*

7. Duffy, Makena, and Ava Montes. Interview with W. Shepherdson Abell. Film, May 2022. Carrigan Project Archives.

8. Montes, Ava. Interview with Chuck Furr. In-person Meeting, August 11, 2020. Carrigan Project Archives.

9. "Letter to William M. Carrigan." Personal Correspondence; Convento del Min Cappuccini, July 14, 1948. Carrigan Project Archives.

10. Carrigan, William M. Personal Correspondence. "Letter to Ramona." Personal Correspondence, February 5, 1945. Carrigan Project Archives. (Emphasis added)

11. Abell, W. Shepherdson. "Eulogy – William M. Carrigan." Padrepio. net, November 30, 2000. *https:// www.padrepio.net/eulogy.html.*

12. Duffy, Makena, and Ava Montes. Interview with W. Shepherdson Abell. Film, May 2022. Carrigan Project Archives.

13. Makena Duffy and Ava Montes, Interview with the Cohagans. Film, May 2022. Carrigan Project Archives.

Chapter One:
A Family History and Bill's Early Life

1. A note about spelling: Sometimes "Hanora" is spelled "Hanna" and "Maguire" is spelled "McGuire," likely due to foreign names changing during immigration and definite misspellings on official documents. Despite this, the other relevant information, such as names and number of children, match, indicating that the same person is referenced.

2. Furr, Charles E. Interview with William M. Carrigan. Cassette Tape, May 14, 1982. Carrigan Project Archives.

3. "William Carrigan: St. Paul Person of the Year." Unknown, c 1992. Carrigan Project Archives.

4. Carrigan, William M. "Private Notes: Notes for Recounting Family History," February 26, 1977. Carrigan Project Archives.

5. Carrigan, William M. "Private Notes: Notes for Recounting Family History," February 26, 1977. Carrigan Project Archives.

6. Bill's paternal uncle, Bernard Jacob Carrigan; not to be confused with Bill's older brother, Bernard Joseph Carrigan.

7. Furr, Charles E. Interview with William M. Carrigan. Cassette Tape, May 14, 1982. Carrigan Project Archives.

8. Ibid.

9. Ibid.

10. Ibid.

11. Carrigan, William M. "Private Notes: Notes for Recounting Family History," February 26, 1977. Carrigan Project Archives.

12. USA Facts. "Climate in Palo Alto County, Iowa," n.d. *https://usafacts. org/issues/climate/state/iowa/county/ palo-alto-county?endDate=1910-10- 17&startDate=1902-02-01#climate.*

13. Furr, Charles E. Interview with William M. Carrigan. Cassette Tape, August 15, 1990. Carrigan Project Archives.

14. Duffy, Makena, and Ava Montes. Interview with Fr. Michael Sliney, L.C. Film, May 2022. Carrigan Project Archives.

15. Furr, Charles E. Interview with William M. Carrigan. Cassette Tape, August 15, 1990. Carrigan Project Archives.

16. Ibid.

17. *Evening times - Republican*. "Jury Awards One-Third of Sum Asked In Carrigan Case." December 10, 1913. State Historical Society of Iowa.

18. Ibid.

19. *The Emmetsburg Democrat*. "Mrs. Carrigan Wins Verdict for $5,000." December 10, 1913, Vol. XXX edition, sec. Number 50. Newspaper Archives.

20. Ibid.

21. *Evening times - Republican*. "Jury Awards One-Third of Sum Asked In Carrigan Case." December 10, 1913. State Historical Society of Iowa.

It is important to note that other news articles published the same day state that Bill's mother sued for $10,000, not $15,000. It is difficult to determine which sum is the correct one.

22. *The Emmetsburg Democrat*. "Mrs. Carrigan Wins Verdict for $5,000." December 10, 1913, Vol. XXX edition, sec. Number 50. Newspaper Archives.

23. Ibid.

24. Ibid.

25. Duffy, Makena, and Ava Montes. Interview with Fr. Michael Sliney, L.C. Film, May 2022. Carrigan Project Archives.

26. Ibid.

27. Ibid.

28. Duffy, Makena, and Ava Montes. Interview with the Cohagans, May 2022. Carrigan Project Archives.

29. Ibid.

Chapter Two: Bill's Adventures as a Rancher

1. Furr, Charles E. Interview with William M. Carrigan. Audio Recording, November 10, 1983. Carrigan Project Archives.

2. Ibid.

3. Ibid.

4. Ibid.

5. Ibid.

6. Ibid.

7. Ibid.

8. Furr, Charles E. Interview with William M. Carrigan. Cassette Tape, May 14, 1982. Carrigan Project Archives.

9. Furr, Charles E. Interview with William M. Carrigan. Audio Recording, November 10, 1983. Carrigan Project Archives.

10. Ibid.

11. Ibid.

12. Ibid.

13. Ibid.

14. Ibid.

15. Ibid.

16. Ibid.

17. Ibid.

18. Ibid.

19. Furr, Charles E. Interview with William M. Carrigan. Cassette Tape, May 14, 1982. Carrigan Project Archives.

20. Ibid.

21. Ibid.

22. Furr, Charles E. Interview with William M. Carrigan. Audio Recording, November 10, 1983. Carrigan Project Archives.

23. Ibid.

24. Ibid.

25. Ibid.

26. Ibid.

27. Furr, Charles E. Interview with William M. Carrigan. Cassette Tape, May 14, 1982. Carrigan Project Archives.

28. Ibid.

29. Ibid.

30. Ibid.

31. Ibid.

32. Ibid.

33. Ibid.

34. Ibid.

35. Ibid.

36. Furr, Charles E. Interview with William M. Carrigan. Audio Recording, November 10, 1983. Carrigan Project Archives.

37. Furr, Charles E. Interview with William M. Carrigan. Cassette Tape, May 14, 1982. Carrigan Project Archives.

38. Ibid.

39. Ibid.

40. Ibid.

41. Ibid.

42. *Ruthven Free Press.* "Local and Personal." January 1, 1919. *http://www.celticcousins.net/paloalto/1919ruthven.htm.*

43. *Ruthven Free Press.* "Local and Personal." January 7, 1920. *http://www.celticcousins.net/paloalto/news_1920.htm.*

44. Furr, Charles E. Interview with William M. Carrigan. Cassette Tape, May 14, 1982. Carrigan Project Archives.

45. Ibid.

46. Ibid.

47. Ibid.

48. Ibid.

49. Ibid.

50. Ibid.

51. "William Carrigan: St. Paul Man of the Year," unknown author, date, publisher

Chapter Three:
Discernment and Business Affairs

1. Furr, Charles E. Interview with William M. Carrigan. Cassette Tape, May 14, 1982. Carrigan Project Archives.

2. Ibid.

3. Ibid.

4. Ibid.

5. Ibid.

6. Ibid.

7. Ibid.

8. "William Carrigan Donates Property to CCLC." Unknown, c. 1980s. Carrigan Project Archives.

9. Carrigan, William M. "Notes for a Speech to Mt. de Sales Academy Seniors." Speech, Mount de Sales Academy, Catonsville, Maryland, May 5, 1993.

10. Dwyer, Thomas F. "The Quiet Ways of William Carrigan." *Senior Living*, May 23, 1993. Carrigan Project Archives.

11. Carrigan, William M. "Notes for a Speech to Mt. de Sales Academy Seniors." Speech, Mount de Sales Academy, Catonsville, Maryland, May 5, 1993.

12. Ibid.

13. "William Carrigan: St. Paul Person of the Year." Unknown, c 1992. Carrigan Project Archives.

14. Carrigan, William M. "Notes for a Speech to Mt. de Sales Academy Seniors." Speech, Mount de Sales Academy, Catonsville, Maryland, May 5, 1993.

15. Though it is not certain, Bill may have attended here because he was a fairly new Catholic who required extra formation in the teachings of the Church.

16. Hawton, Howard J. "Letter to William M. Carrigan." Personal Correspondence, December 17, 1926. Carrigan Project Archives.

17. Ibid.

18. Unknown Paulist Priest. "Letter to William M. Carrigan." Personal Correspondence, August 14, 1927. Carrigan Project Archives.

19. CUA. "Catholic University of America Commencement Ceremony: The School of the Sacred Sciences - Seminary Division, Bachelor of Arts." The Catholic University of America, 1931. Catholic University of America Archives.

20. Society of St. Sulpice. "Theological College." Blog, n.d. *http://sulpicians.org/seminaries/theological-college/*.

21. Society of St. Sulpice. "The Society of the Priests of Saint Sulpice: Who We Are." Blog, n.d. *http://sulpicians.org/who-we-are/*.

22. Aarney, Fr. John B. "Letter to William M. Carrigan." Personal Correspondence, June 28, 1933. Carrigan Project Archives.

23. Aarney, Fr. John B. "Letter to William M. Carrigan." Personal Correspondence, September 23, 1933. Carrigan Project Archives.

24. "N.C.W.C. (National Catholic Welfare Council News Service)." August 7, 1933. Carrigan Project Archives.

25. "William Carrigan: St. Paul Person of the Year." Unknown, c 1992. Carrigan Project Archives.

26. *The Evening Star.* "Orphans Delight in Outdoor Pool: St. Vincent's Achievement, Result of Initiative of W. M. Carrigan of Catholic U." August 17, 1933. Library of Congress.

27. "Sidelights of Washington." N.C.W.C. News Service, August 7, 1933. Carrigan Project Archives.

28. "N.C.W.C. (National Catholic Welfare Council News Service)." August 7, 1933. Carrigan Project Archives.

29. "William Carrigan: St. Paul Person of the Year." Unknown, c 1992. Carrigan Project Archives.

30. "N.C.W.C. (National Catholic Welfare Council News Service)." August 7, 1933. Carrigan Project Archives.

31. "William Carrigan: St. Paul Person of the Year." Unknown, c 1992. Carrigan Project Archives.

32. "N.C.W.C. (National Catholic Welfare Council News Service)."

August 7, 1933. Carrigan Project Archives.

The monetary amount of the donations differs between publications. Whether it was $700 or $750, what matters is that the money continued to assist the orphanage beyond what was originally desired.

33. "William Carrigan: St. Paul Person of the Year." Unknown, c 1992. Carrigan Project Archives.

34. *The Evening Star.* "Orphans Delight in Outdoor Pool: St. Vincent's Achievement, Result of Initiative of W. M. Carrigan of Catholic U." August 17, 1933. Library of Congress.

35. *The Evening Star.* "Dedication of Pool Planned on Fourth." July 3, 1935. Library of Congress.

36. *The Washington Post.* "As New Swimming Pool Was Dedicated." July 8, 1935. Carrigan Project Archives.

37. Chuck Furr preserved a cut-out the news article "As New Swimming Pool Was Dedicated." *The Washington Post,* July 8, 1935. On it, Chuck wrote the following note: "Uncle Bill spoke of this many times. He was very proud of this," giving evidence to how important Bill considered the orphans' pools.

38. Abell, D.M., Kathryn. "Nonagenarian Knight Keeps Schedule of Non-Stop Civic, Volunteer Activities." *Federal Malta Review,* July 1997. Carrigan Project Archives.

39. *The Washington Times.* "Boy Guidance to Be Topic." March 1, 1938. Library of Congress.

40. Ibid.

41. Abell, D.M., Kathryn. "Nonagenarian Knight Keeps Schedule of Non-Stop Civic, Volunteer Activities." *Federal Malta Review,* July 1997. Carrigan Project Archives.

42. Ibid.

43. Ibid.

44. *The Washington Times.* "Carroll Auxiliary Session Tonight." March 8, 1938.

45. *The Evening Star.* "Family Lectures to Begin March 14: Boys' Guidance Association to Sponsor Speakers of Prominence." March 1, 1938. Library of Congress.

46. Carrigan, William M. "Letter to Ramona." Personal Correspondence, March 2, 1945. Carrigan Project Archives.

Chapter Four:
Ramona Newman: Love of Bill's Life

1. Spelling differs. In some news sources, *Anna* is spelled *Anne*, but Mrs. Newman's personal letters indicate that her name is, in fact, spelled with an *e*.

2. *The Evening Journal.* "Rehoboth Beach." April 20, 1912.

3. Spielway, Amos E. "Fourteenth Census of the United States: 1920 – Population." United States Department of Commerce, Bureau of the Census, January 8, 1920. *https://www.familysearch.org/ark:/61903/3:1:33SQ-GRNX-C43?view=index&action=view.*

4. *The Smyrna Times.* "Coming Federation of Women's Clubs, Rehoboth." May 3, 1911.

5. *The Evening Journal.* "Rehoboth Gets Many Visitors: Cottages at Seaside Resort Filling Up as Summer Draws Near." June 17, 1911.

6. *The Middletown Transcript.* "St. Anne's Church: Parent-Teacher Meeting." October 14, 1916.

7. *The Evening Journal.* "Churce Auxiliary Names New Officers." April 24, 1915.

Junior Auxiliary groups are part of the larger American Legion Auxiliary. Local JA chapters provided volunteer experiences for young girls 0-17 years old in areas like charities, nonprofits, and education centers.

8. *The Middletown Transcript.* "Eloquent Address: Dr. Mitchell Witty and Pleasing as Guest of Century Club - In the High School Room." December 12, 1914, Vol. 47, No. 50 edition.

9. American Red Cross. "The American Red Cross and the First Christmas Seals," December 20, 2016. *https://www.redcross.org/about-us/news-and-events/news/Early-Christmas-Seals-Join-the-Fight-Against-Tuberculosis.html#:~:text=In%20 1907%2C%20the%20Christmas%20 Seal,)%20hospital%20in%20 Wilmington%2C%20Delaware.*

10. *The Washington Times.* "Obituarites: Ramona Carrigan, Local Philanthropist." May 11, 1989. The Washington Times Archive.

11. *The Washington Times.* "Soloists at Y.M.C.A." January 28, 1921, Final edition.

12. *The Washington Times.* "Among Musicians: Y.M.C.A. Concert." February 3, 1921, Final edition. Library of Congress.

13. *The Evening Star.* "Today on the Radio: WJSV." April 8, 1931. Library of Congress.

14. *The Evening Star.* "Calvary Church Wedding Attended by Many Guests." September 20, 1923. Library of Congress.

15. *The Evening Star.* "Diplomas Awarded Normal Graduates." January 31, 1924. Library of Congress.

16. CUA. "Catholic University of America Commencement Ceremony: The Graduate School of Arts and Sciences - Bachelor of Arts in Education." The Catholic University of America, 1936. Catholic University of America Archives.

17. *The Washington Post.* "Henry Kaiser, 77, D.C. Labor Lawyer, Dies: Obituaries - Ramona Carrigan." May 11, 1989. The Washington Post Archive. *https://www.washingtonpost.com/archive/local/1989/05/12/henry-kaiser-77-dc-labor-lawyer-dies/6e997cef-68f0-4040-a096-47f77200bf15/.*

18. *The Washington Times.* "Obituarites: Ramona Carrigan, Local Philanthropist." May 11, 1989. The Washington Times Archive.

19. *The Evening Star.* "Mrs. Roper Ranks at Officers' Dinner." October 27, 1935. Library of Congress.

20. *The Washington Post.* "Henry Kaiser, 77, D.C. Labor Lawyer, Dies: Obituaries - Ramona Carrigan." May 11, 1989. The Washington Post Archive. *https://www.washingtonpost.com/archive/local/1989/05/12/henry-kaiser-77-dc-labor-lawyer-dies/6e997cef-68f0-4040-a096-47f77200bf15/.*

21. *The Washington Times.* "Obituarites: Ramona Carrigan, Local Philanthropist." May 11, 1989. The Washington Times Archive.

22. *The Washington Times.* "Obituarites: Ramona Carrigan, Local Philanthropist." May 11, 1989. The Washington Times Archive.

23. Carrigan, Ramona. "V-Mail to Bill." Personal Correspondence, August 26, 1943. Carrigan Project Archives.

Carrigan, Ramona. "Letter to Bill." Personal Correspondence, November 18, 1943. Carrigan Project Archives.

24. *The Evening Star.* "Family Lectures to Begin March 14: Boys' Guidance Association to Sponsor Speakers of Prominence." March 1, 1938. Library of Congress.

25. Carrigan, Ramona. "V-Mail to Bill." Personal Correspondence, August 10, 1943. Carrigan Project Archives.

26. Carrigan, William M. "Letter to Ramona." Personal Correspondence, December 3, 1943. Carrigan Project Archives.

27. Carrigan, Ramona. "Letter to Bill." Personal Correspondence, September 23, 1943. Carrigan Project Archives.

28. Carrigan, Ramona. "V-Mail to Bill." Personal Correspondence, December 25, 1943. Carrigan Project Archives.

29. Carrigan, Ramona. "V-Mail to Bill." Personal Correspondence, December 31, 1943. Carrigan Project Archives.

30. Carrigan, William M. "Letter to Ramona." Personal Correspondence, December 29, 1944. Carrigan Project Archives.

31. Carrigan, William M. "Letter to Ramona." Personal Correspondence, June 8, 1945. Carrigan Project Archives.

32. Carrigan, Ramona. "Letter to Bill." Personal Correspondence, August 3, 1938. Carrigan Project Archives.

33. Carrigan, Ramona. "Letter to Bill." Personal Correspondence, August 1938. Carrigan Project Archives.

34. *The Evening Star.* "Miss Newman Wed to Mr. Carrigan Today." September 3, 1938. Library of Congress.

35. Ibid.

36. Ibid.

37. Carrigan, Ramona. "Letter to Bill." Personal Correspondence, August 30, 1943. Carrigan Project Archives.

38. Carrigan, Ramona. "Letter to Bill." Personal Correspondence, September 3, 1943. Carrigan Project Archives.

39. Carrigan, Ramona. "Letter to Bill." Personal Correspondence, September 10, 1943. Carrigan Project Archives.

40. Carrigan, Ramona. "Letter to Bill." Personal Correspondence, January 30, 1944. Carrigan Project Archives.

41. Carrigan, William M. "Letter to Ramona." Personal Correspondence, July 8, 1943. Carrigan Project Archives.

42. Carrigan, William M. "Letter to Ramona." Personal Correspondence, August 19, 1943. Carrigan Project Archives.

43. Carrigan, William M. "Letter to Ramona." Personal Correspondence, July 16, 1944. Carrigan Project Archives.

44. Carrigan, William M. "Letter to Ramona." Personal Correspondence, November 11, 1944. Carrigan Project Archives.

45. Carrigan, William M. "Letter to Ramona." Personal Correspondence, November 20, 1944. Carrigan Project Archives.

46. Carrigan, William M. "Letter to Ramona." Personal Correspondence, March 7, 1945. Carrigan Project Archives.

47. Carrigan, Ramona. "Letter to Bill." Personal Correspondence, August 7, 1943. Carrigan Project Archives.

48. Carrigan, William M. "Letter to Ramona." Personal Correspondence, March 28, 1944. Carrigan Project Archives.

Chapter Five: WWII: Bill Begins His Service

1. This information can be found on William M. Carrigan's draft papers.

2. Carrigan, William M. "Letter to Ramona." Personal Correspondence, June 19, 1945. Carrigan Project Archives.

Bill sent this letter exactly two years after leaving America.

3. Unknown name. This is how Bill spelled it, but it is unclear if this ship actually existed or if Bill made an error. It may have been "Mariposa."

4. Carrigan, William M. "Talk for Roosevelt High School Assembly." Speech, Roosevelt High School, Washington, D.C., December 7, 1945.

5. Ibid.

6. Ibid.

7. Ibid.

8. Ibid.

9. Carrigan, William M. "Letter to Ramona." Personal Correspondence, July 15, 1943. Carrigan Project Archives.

10. Carrigan, William M. "Letter to Ramona." Personal Correspondence,

July 24, 1943. Carrigan Project Archives.

11. Carrigan, William M. "Letter to Ramona." Personal Correspondence, November 25, 1943. Carrigan Project Archives.

12. Carrigan, William M. "Letter to Ramona." Personal Correspondence, November 13, 1943. Carrigan Project Archives.

13. Carrigan, William M. "Letter to Ramona." Personal Correspondence, August 2, 1943. Carrigan Project Archives.

14. Ibid.

15. Carrigan, William M. "Letter to Ramona." Personal Correspondence, August 22, 1943. Carrigan Project Archives.

16. Ibid.

17. Carrigan, William M. "Letter to Ramona." Personal Correspondence, November 13, 1943. Carrigan Project Archives.

18. Carrigan, William M. "Letter to Ramona." Personal Correspondence, December 4, 1943. Carrigan Project Archives.

19. Carrigan, William M. "Letter to Ramona." Personal Correspondence, November 13, 1943. Carrigan Project Archives.

20. Carrigan, William M. "Letter to Ramona." Personal Correspondence, August 14, 1943. Carrigan Project Archives.

21. Ibid.

22. Carrigan, William M. "Talk for Roosevelt High School Assembly." Speech, Roosevelt High School, Washington, D.C., December 7, 1945.

23. Carrigan, William M. "Letter to Ramona." Personal Correspondence, July 9, 1943. Carrigan Project Archives.

24. Carrigan, William M. "Letter to Ramona." Personal Correspondence, July 14, 1943. Carrigan Project Archives.

25. Ibid.

26. Ibid.

27. Carrigan, William M. "Talk for Roosevelt High School Assembly." Speech, Roosevelt High School, Washington, D.C., December 7, 1945.

28. Ibid.

29. Ibid.

30. Ibid.

31. Ibid.

32. LST stands for Landing Ship, Tank. LCI stands for Landing Craft

Infantry. Both were ships designed to bring troops, supplies, and sometimes vehicles onto enemy beaches.

33. Carrigan, William M. "Talk for Roosevelt High School Assembly." Speech, Roosevelt High School, Washington, D.C., December 7, 1945.

34. Ibid.

35. Carrigan, William M. "Letter to Ramona." Personal Correspondence, July 19, 1943. Carrigan Project Archives.

36. Carrigan, William M. "Talk for Roosevelt High School Assembly." Speech, Roosevelt High School, Washington, D.C., December 7, 1945.

37. Ibid.

38. Ibid.

39. Ibid.

40. Ibid.

41. Ibid.

42. Ibid.

43. William "Bill" Stevenson was an Olympic gold medalist-turned-ARC commanding officer. "He and his wife organized and administered *American Red Cross* operations in *Great Britain*, northern Africa, *Sicily*, and *Italy*," according to Wikipedia.

44. Carrigan, William M. "Talk for Roosevelt High School Assembly." Speech, Roosevelt High School, Washington, D.C., December 7, 1945.

45. Charles, Emily. "99th Bomb Group." American Air Museum in Britain, June 7, 2021. *https://www. americanairmuseum.com/archive/ unit/99th-bomb-group.*

The strategic bombing missions flown by the 99th included "oil refineries, marshaling yards, aircraft factories, and steel plants in Italy, France, Germany, Poland, Czechoslovakia, Austria" and more. Their missions disrupted a significant portion of Nazi productions.

46. Lauer III, Ford J. "History of the 99th Bombardment Group." 99th Bomb Group Historical Society, n.d. *https://www.99bombgroup.org/history. php.*

47. Abandoned, Forgotten & Little-Known Airfields in Europe. "Tortorella," February 2, 2013. *https://www.forgottenairfields.com/ airfield-tortorella-571.html.*

Chapter Six:
WWII: Destiny Encountered
and Ministry to Soldiers

1. This is the most unclear, disputable part of Bill's life, as several unique sources give different information about *when* he first encountered Padre Pio. Discrepancy exists between Bill's recollections and other documented sources.

C. Bernard Ruffin's book *Padre Pio: The True Story*, as well as Frank Rega's *Padre Pio and America* which drew from Ruffin, suggest that Bill took twenty soldiers with him to San Giovanni Rotondo on that first trip. However, Bill's written testimonies, as well as those from Bill's nephew Chuck Furr, state that only two men, the original pair who asked for transportation, accompanied Bill to the monastery on that first trip.

Additionally, it does not appear that Bill was the first uniformed American to meet Padre Pio, though Bill and Padre Pio both reportedly said he was. Author Frank Rega indicates that two G.I.s, Joe De Santis and Ray Ewen of the 484th Bombardment Group, were the first soldiers to speak with Padre Pio. The exact timeline is unclear. Rega simply suggests that De Santis

and Ewen may have met Padre Pio first, and then propagated the stories which Bill apparently heard. This corroborates with Bill's memory, in which he states that two soldiers came to him with tales from their friends. They most likely refer to De Santis, who had been hunting for fresh food, had met Mary Pyle, and then had brought the story of Padre Pio back to his friends, including Ray Ewen. Unfortunately, the full truth is lost to time, and one can only speculate whether Frank Rega's G.I. interviewees spoke of the same Mass as Bill remembered. Most importantly, the discrepancy means that Bill Carrigan likely was not the *first* uniformed American to meet Padre Pio, though he certainly was *one of* the earliest American guests at San Giovanni Rotondo. (Frank Rega, *Padre Pio and America*, p.119-120)

2. Ruffin, C. Bernard. *Padre Pio: The True Story*. First. Huntington, Indiana: Our Sunday Visitor, 1982. 229.

3. Carrigan, William M. "Private Note: G.I.s Discovered Padre Pio 50 Years Ago," c. 1980s-1990s. Carrigan Project Archives.

4. Ruffin, C. Bernard. *Padre Pio: The True Story*. First. Huntington, Indiana: Our Sunday Visitor, 1982. 229.

5. Carrigan, William M. "An Introduction to Padre Pio." EWTN, c 1996. *https://www.ewtn.com/catholicism/library/introduction-to-padre-pio-5765.*

6. Ruffin, C. Bernard. *Padre Pio: The True Story*. First. Huntington, Indiana: Our Sunday Visitor, 1982. 229.

7. Ruffin 230.

8. Carrigan, William M. "Private Note: G.I.s Discovered Padre Pio 50 Years Ago," c. 1980s-1990s. Carrigan Project Archives.

9. Carrigan, William M. "Speech Notes for a Talk at Mount de Sales Academy," September 23, 1994. Carrigan Project Archives.

10. Carrigan, William M. "Private Note: Recollection of First Meeting Padre Pio," September 6, 1985. Carrigan Project Archives.

11. Carrigan, William M. "Padre Pio–His First 100 Years," c. 1990s. Carrigan Project Archives.

12. Carrigan, William M. "Speech to Mount de Sales Academy." Speech, Mount de Sales Academy, Catonsville, Maryland, November 20, 1986.

The phrase in Italian typed in the speech notes is more than likely a mistranslation of the Italian language, which Bill did not speak.

13. Ibid.

14. Ibid.

15. Ibid.

16. Carrigan, William M. "Padre Pio–His First 100 Years," c. 1990s. Carrigan Project Archives.

17. Carrigan, William M. "Private Note: Padre Pio Review," July 18, 1984. Carrigan Project Archives.

18. Carrigan, Ramona. "Letter to Bill." Personal Correspondence, February 3, 1944. Carrigan Project Archives.

19. Carrigan, William M. "Private Note: Padre Pio Review," July 18, 1984. Carrigan Project Archives.

20. Ibid.

21. Ruffin, C. Bernard. *Padre Pio: The True Story*. First. Huntington, Indiana: Our Sunday Visitor, 1982. 228.

22. Ruffin 231.

23. Carrigan, William M. "Speech Notes for a Talk at Mount de Sales Academy," September 23, 1994. Carrigan Project Archives.

24. Carrigan, William M. "Letter to Ramona." Personal Correspondence, February 26, 1944. Carrigan Project Archives.

25. Carrigan, William M. "U.S. Soldiers Attend Padre Pio's Masses." News article draft; letter to Colonel John F. Laboon, Sr. Italy, May 18, 1944.

26. Carrigan, William M. "Letter to Ramona." Personal Correspondence, February 26, 1944. Carrigan Project Archives.

27. Carrigan, William M. "The American and British Soldier Seek Spiritual Values." News article draft. Italy, April 2, 1944. Carrigan Project Archives.

28. Ibid.

29. This truth of his statement was hard to verify; most historical sources assert that Col. LaBoon was not the military governor at the time. Bill was likely incorrect in this piece of information.

30. Carrigan, William M. "U.S. Soldiers Attend Padre Pio's Masses." News article draft; letter to Colonel John F. Laboon, Sr. Italy, May 18, 1944. Carrigan Project Archives. Emphasis added.

31. Carrigan, William M. "Speech to Mount de Sales Academy."

Speech, Mount de Sales Academy, Catonsville, Maryland, November 20, 1986.

32. Carrigan, William M. "Letter to Ramona." Personal Correspondence, May 4, 1944. Carrigan Project Archives.

33. Carrigan, William M. "Speech to Mount de Sales Academy." Speech, Mount de Sales Academy, Catonsville, Maryland, November 20, 1986.

34. LaBoon, Sr., John. "Letters to William M. Carrigan." Personal Correspondence, July 17, 1974. Carrigan Project Archives.

35. Caccioppoli. "1943-5: The 'Flying Friar' and American Aviators." Blog. Padre Pio, n.d. *https://www.caccioppoli.com/"%20 %2015%20Vita%20Il%20frate%20 volante%20e%20gli%20aviatori%20 americani.html.*

36. Carrigan, William M. "U.S. Soldiers Attend Padre Pio's Masses." News article draft; letter to Colonel John F. Laboon, Sr. Italy, May 18, 1944. Carrigan Project Archives.

Chapter Seven:
Who Was Padre Pio?

1. Padre Pio Foundation. "St. Pio of Pietrelcina (Padre Pio)," n.d. *https://www.padrepiofoundation.com/Padre_Pio_path_pietrelcina.htm.*

2. Ibid.

3. Ibid.

4. Saint Pio Foundation. "Saint Pio's Biography," n.d. *https://saintpiofoundation.org/saint-pios-biography.*

5. Carrigan, William M. "An Assessment of Padre Pio, Capuchin, of San Giovanni Rotondo, Foggia, Italy," c. 1990s. Carrigan Project Archives.

6. Testa, Mirko. "The Secret Story of Padre Pio's Stigmata." Zenit; reprinted by EWTN, September 22, 2008. *https://www.ewtn.com/catholicism/library/secret-story-of-padre-pios-stigmata-6002.*

7. Carrigan, William M. "Padre Pio, Capuchin Stigmatic." Speech, Dumont Midday Chapel, April 7, 1954.

8. Parente, S.T.D., Ph.D., J.C.B., Pascal P. *Padre Pio: A City on a Mountain.* Washington, New Jersey: Ave Maria Institute, 1968. 90.

9. Caccioppoli. "1943-5: The 'Flying Friar' and American Aviators." Blog. Padre Pio, n.d. *https://www.caccioppoli.com/"%20%2015%20Vita%20Il%20frate%20volante%20e%20gli%20aviatori%20americani.html.*

10. Kosloski, Philip. "How Padre Pio Stopped Allied Forces from Bombing His Monastery During WWII." Aleteia, September 23, 2019. *https://aleteia.org/2019/09/23/how-padre-pio-stopped-allied-forces-from-bombing-his-monastery-during-wwii.*

11. Stelluto, Elia. "The Story of the Flying Monk: A Myth, a Legend or a Reality?" Blog. Italian Tribune, n.d. *https://italiantribune.com/the-story-of-the-flying-monk-a-myth-a-legend-or-reality/.*

12. Parente, S.T.D., Ph.D., J.C.B., Pascal P. *Padre Pio: A City on a Mountain.* Washington, New Jersey: Ave Maria Institute, 1968. 91.

13. Padre Pio Foundation. "Padre Pio's Healing," n.d. *http://www.padrepiofoundation.com/healing.htm.*

14. Amorth, Fr. Gabriel. *Padre Pio: Stories and Memories of My Mentor and Friend.* Translated by Matthew Sherry. San Francisco: Ignatius Press, 2021. Pages 14-15.

15. Padre Pio Foundation. "Padre Pio," n.d. *http://www. padrepiofoundation.com/devil.htm.*

16. Campanella, Stefano. *Mercy in Padre Pio.* Translated by Edmund C. Lane. English. Staten Island, New York: The Society of St. Paul, 2017. 12.

17. Campanella 126.

18. This Psychosomatic Principle was printed on holy cards which were among Bill Carrigan's belongings.

19. Campanella, Stefano. *Mercy in Padre Pio.* Translated by Edmund C. Lane. English. Staten Island, New York: The Society of St. Paul, 2017. Pages 142-147

20. Ibid.

21. Campanella, Stefano. *Mercy in Padre Pio.* Translated by Edmund C. Lane. English. Staten Island, New York: The Society of St. Paul, 2017. Pages 142-152

22. Ibid,

23. Pope John Paul II. "Canonization of St. Pio of Pietrelcina, Capuchin Priest." The Holy See, June 16, 2002. *https:// www.vatican.va/content/john-paul-ii/ en/homilies/2002/documents/hf_jp-ii_ hom_20020616_padre-pio.html.*

Chapter Eight:
WWII: Bill as Field Director

1. Carrigan, William M. "Letter to Ramona." Personal Correspondence, March 2, 1945. Carrigan Project Archives.

2. Ibid.

3. Carrigan, William M. "Letter to Ramona." Personal Correspondence, February 27, 1945. Carrigan Project Archives.

In fact, as he accustomed himself to the role of field director, Bill almost immediately had to deal with some kind of corruption or underhanded dealings within the Red Cross in Foggia. Though his letters home never gave any specifics, he did note that, "I at first worried because I did not know what was behind it. I've got something to go on now, and I believe I can prepare for any further attacks—I really enjoy it, because life is full of this sort of thing and one ought to know how to deal with it." This situation gave Bill, a contemplative man, the chance to grow; he admitted that acting quickly and decisively in tandem posed a difficulty for him. He could do both, but the latter much better than the former.

4. Carrigan, William M. "Letter to Ramona." Personal Correspondence, October 28, 1944. Carrigan Project Archives.

5. Ibid.

6. Carrigan, William M. "Letter to Ramona." Personal Correspondence, June 1, 1944. Carrigan Project Archives.

7. Carrigan, William M. "Letter to Ramona." Personal Correspondence, September 9, 1943. Carrigan Project Archives.

8. Carrigan, William M. "Letter to Ramona." Personal Correspondence, June 24, 1945. Carrigan Project Archives.

9. Carrigan, William M. "Letter to Ramona." Personal Correspondence, March 24, 1944. Carrigan Project Archives.

10. Ibid.

In a letter dated March 28, 1944, Bill mentioned the Hollywood troupe again and stated that he "... took Jean Darling to church on the mountain," possibly referring to Padre Pio's monastery in San Giovanni Rotondo.

11. Carrigan, William M. "Talk for Roosevelt High School Assembly." Speech, Roosevelt High School, Washington, D.C., December 7, 1945.

12. Demonstrated in several letters, including letters to Ramona on October 15, 1944, and October 28, 1944

13. Carrigan, William M. "Letter to Ramona." Personal Correspondence, October 15, 1944. Carrigan Project Archives.

14. Carrigan, William M. "Letter to Ramona." Personal Correspondence, December 18, 1944. Carrigan Project Archives.

15. Carrigan, William M. "An Assessment of Padre Pio, Capuchin, of San Giovanni Rotondo, Foggia, Italy," c. 1990s. Carrigan Project Archives.

16. Carrigan, William M. "U.S. Soldiers Attend Padre Pio's Masses." News article draft; letter to Colonel John F. Laboon, Sr. Italy, May 18, 1944. Carrigan Project Archives.

17. Carrigan, William M. "Letter to Ramona." Personal Correspondence, December 10, 1944. Carrigan Project Archives.

18. Carrigan, William M. "Letter to Ramona." Personal Correspondence, November 20, 1944. Carrigan Project Archives.

19. Ibid.

20. Ruffin, C. Bernard. *Padre Pio: The True Story*. First. Huntington, Indiana: Our Sunday Visitor, 1982. 231.

21. Ibid.

22. Ruffin 232.

23. Letter to Ramona, December 23, 1944

24. Carrigan, William M. "Letter to Ramona." Personal Correspondence, November 20, 1944. Carrigan Project Archives; first letter on this day.

25. Ibid.

26. Carrigan, William M. "Letter to Ramona." Personal Correspondence, November 20, 1944. Carrigan Project Archives; second letter on this day.

27. Carrigan, William M. "Letter to Ramona." Personal Correspondence, December 10, 1944. Carrigan Project Archives.

28. Ibid.

29. Carrigan, William M. "Letter to Ramona." Personal Correspondence, July 4, 1945. Carrigan Project Archives.

30. Unknown. "Venereal Disease and Treatment during WW2." WW2 US Medical Research Centre, n.d. *https://www.med-dept.com/articles/venereal-disease-and-treatment-during-ww2/*.

31. Carrigan, William M. "Letter to Ramona." Personal Correspondence, July 4, 1945. Carrigan Project Archives.

32. Ibid.

33. Carrigan, William M. "Letter to Ramona." Personal Correspondence, December 18, 1944. Carrigan Project Archives.

34. Carrigan, Ramona. "Letter to Bill." Personal Correspondence, December 16, 1943. Carrigan Project Archives.

35. Carrigan, William M. "Letter to Ramona." Personal Correspondence, May 4, 1945. Carrigan Project Archives.

36. Carrigan, William M. "Letter to Ramona." Personal Correspondence, January 8, 1945. Carrigan Project Archives.

37. Carrigan, William M. "Letter to Ramona." Personal Correspondence, March 2, 1945. Carrigan Project Archives.

38. Carrigan, William M. "Letter to Ramona." Personal Correspondence, March 24, 1945. Carrigan Project Archives.

39. Carrigan, William M. "Letter to Ramona." Personal Correspondence, December 4, 1943. Carrigan Project Archives.

40. Carrigan, William M. "Letter to Ramona." Personal Correspondence, May 5, 1945. Carrigan Project Archives.

41. Ibid.

42. Carrigan, William M. "Letter to Ramona." Personal Correspondence, March 24, 1945. Carrigan Project Archives.

43. Carrigan, William M. "Letter to Ramona." Personal Correspondence, June 14, 1945. Carrigan Project Archives.

44. Duffy, Makena, and Ava Montes. Interview with Fr. Michael Sliney, L.C. Film, May 2022. Carrigan Project Archives.

45. Carrigan, William M. "Talk for Roosevelt High School Assembly." Speech, Roosevelt High School, Washington, D.C., December 7, 1945.

46. Ibid.

47. Ibid.

48. Ibid.

49. Carrigan, William M. "Letter to Ramona." Personal Correspondence, April 2, 1944. Carrigan Project Archives.

50. Ibid.

51. Duffy, Makena, and Ava Montes. Interview with Fr. Michael Sliney, L.C. Film, May 2022. Carrigan Project Archives.

52. Carrigan, William M. "Letter to Ramona." Personal Correspondence, March 2, 1945. Carrigan Project Archives.

53. Ibid.

54. Carrigan, William M. "Letter to Ramona." Personal Correspondence, June 19, 1945. Carrigan Project Archives.

55. Duffy, Makena, and Ava Montes. Interview with Fr. Michael Sliney, L.C. Film, May 2022. Carrigan Project Archives.

56. Ibid.

57. Ibid.

58. Carrigan, William M. "Letter to Ramona." Personal Correspondence, July 19, 1943. Carrigan Project Archives.

59. Carrigan, William M. "Letter to Ramona." Personal Correspondence, March 12, 1944. Carrigan Project Archives.

60. Carrigan, William M. "Letter to Ramona." Personal Correspondence, November 14, 1943. Carrigan Project Archives.

61. Carrigan, William M. "Letter to Ramona." Personal Correspondence, November 30, 1943. Carrigan Project Archives.

62. Carrigan, William M. "Letter to Ramona." Personal Correspondence, May 4, 1944. Carrigan Project Archives. Emphasis added.

63. Carrigan, William M. "Letter to Ramona." Personal Correspondence, May 4, 1944. Carrigan Project Archives. Emphasis added.

64. Carrigan, William M. "Letter to Ramona." Personal Correspondence, October 28, 1944. Carrigan Project Archives.

Chapter Nine:
Bill's Personal Experiences with Padre Pio

1. Carrigan, William M. "Speech to Mount de Sales Academy." Speech, Mount de Sales Academy, Catonsville, Maryland, November 20, 1986.

2. Carrigan, William M. "Padre Pio, Capuchin Stigmatic." Speech, Dumont Midday Chapel, April 7, 1954.

Carrigan, William M. "Letter to Ramona." Personal Correspondence, February 5, 1945. Carrigan Project Archives.

3. Carrigan, William M. "Letter to Ramona." Personal Correspondence, June 30, 1945. Carrigan Project Archives.

4. Carrigan, William M. "Private Note: Thoughts on Padre Pio," January 20, 1986. Carrigan Project Archives.

5. "Letter to William M. Carrigan." Personal Correspondence; Convento del Min Cappuccini, July 14, 1948. Carrigan Project Archives.

6. Carrigan, William M. "An Assessment of Padre Pio, Capuchin, of San Giovanni Rotondo, Foggia, Italy," c. 1990s. Carrigan Project Archives.

7. Ruffin, C. Bernard. Padre Pio: The True Story. First. Huntington, Indiana: Our Sunday Visitor, 1982. 253.

8. Ibid.

9. Carrigan, William M. "Padre Pio and Holy Week." The Catholic Standard, April 11, 1974.

10. Ruffin, C. Bernard. *Padre Pio: The True Story*. First. Huntington, Indiana: Our Sunday Visitor, 1982. 263.

11. Ruffin 270.

12. Ibid.

13. Ibid.

14. Carrigan, William M. "Letter to Ramona." Personal Correspondence, March 26, 1944. Carrigan Project Archives.

15. Carrigan, William M. "Letter to Ramona." Personal Correspondence, December 12, 1944. Carrigan Project Archives.

16. Carrigan, William M. "Speech to Mount de Sales Academy." Speech, Mount de Sales Academy, Catonsville, Maryland, November 20, 1986.

17. Ibid.

18. Ibid.

19. Carrigan, William M. "Letter to Ramona." Personal Correspondence, December 18, 1944. Carrigan Project Archives.

20. Carrigan, William M. "Speech to Mount de Sales Academy." Speech, Mount de Sales Academy, Catonsville, Maryland, November 20, 1986.

21. Ibid.

22. Ibid.

23. Ibid.

24. Ibid.

25. Ibid.

26. Ibid.

27. Ibid.

28. Ibid.

29. Bill may be referring to the wife of Frank Abresch, the German photographer with whom Bill worked to capture the pictures of Padre Pio which later graced thousands of holy cards; perhaps the Abresch couple were visiting with Bill in order to shoot film when this health incident occurred. However, it is inconclusive from Bill's recollection whether this Mrs. Abresch was related to Frank in any way.

30. Carrigan, William M. "Speech to Mount de Sales Academy." Speech, Mount de Sales Academy, Catonsville, Maryland, November 20, 1986.

31. Ibid.

32. Ibid.

33. Ibid.

34. Ibid.

35. Ibid.

36. Carrigan, William M. "Letter to Ramona." Personal Correspondence, June 30, 1945. Carrigan Project Archives.

37. Carrigan, William M. "Letter to Ramona." Personal Correspondence, July 2, 1945. Carrigan Project Archives.

38. Carrigan, William M. "Speech to Mount de Sales Academy." Speech, Mount de Sales Academy, Catonsville, Maryland, November 20, 1986.

39. Carrigan, William M. "Letter to Ramona." Personal Correspondence, July 2, 1945. Carrigan Project Archives.

40. Ibid.

41. Carrigan, William M. "Speech to Mount de Sales Academy." Speech, Mount de Sales Academy, Catonsville, Maryland, November 20, 1986.

42. Carrigan, William M. "Letter to Ramona." Personal Correspondence, July 2, 1945. Carrigan Project Archives.

43. Carrigan, William M. "Letter to Ramona." Personal Correspondence, February 2, 1945. Carrigan Project Archives.

44. Ibid.

45. Father Superior. "Letter to Ramona." Personal Correspondence; Convento del Min Cappuccini, September 22, 1950. Carrigan Project Archives.

46. Father Superior. "Letter to William M. Carrigan." Personal Correspondence; Convento del Min Cappuccini, July 14, 1947. Carrigan Project Archives.

47. Carrigan, William M. "Padre Pio and Holy Week." *The Catholic Standard*, April 11, 1974. Carrigan Project Archives.

48. Carrigan, William M. "Letter to Ramona." Personal Correspondence, February 2, 1945. Carrigan Project Archives.

49. Father Superior. "Letter to Ramona." Personal Correspondence; Convento del Min Cappuccini, September 22, 1950. Carrigan Project Archives.

Chapter Ten:
WWII: Married Life During Wartime

1. Carrigan, William M. "Letter to Ramona." Personal Correspondence, July 23, 1943. Carrigan Project Archives.

2. Carrigan, Ramona. "Fifth Anniversary Letter to Bill." Personal Correspondence, September 3, 1943. Carrigan Project Archives.

3. Ibid.

4. Carrigan, William M. "Letter to Ramona." Personal Correspondence, July 8, 1943. Carrigan Project Archives.

5. Carrigan, Ramona. "Letter to Bill." Personal Correspondence, July 30, 1943. Carrigan Project Archives.

6. Carrigan, Ramona. "Letter to Bill." Personal Correspondence, August 2, 1943. Carrigan Project Archives.

7. Carrigan, Ramona. "Letter to Bill." Personal Correspondence, July 30, 1943. Carrigan Project Archives.

Carrigan, Ramona. "Letter to Bill." Personal Correspondence, September 20, 1943. Carrigan Project Archives.

8. Carrigan, Ramona. "Letter to Bill." Personal Correspondence, October 16, 1943. Carrigan Project Archives.

9. Carrigan, Ramona. "Letter to Bill." Personal Correspondence, January 1, 1944. Carrigan Project Archives.

10. Carrigan, William M. "Letter to Ramona." Personal Correspondence, July 15, 1944. Carrigan Project Archives.

11. Carrigan, William M. "Letter to Ramona." Personal Correspondence, December 26, 1944. Carrigan Project Archives.

12. Carrigan, Ramona. "Letter to Bill." Personal Correspondence, June 26, 1944. Carrigan Project Archives.

13. Carrigan, William M. "Letter to Ramona." Personal Correspondence, February 2, 1945. Carrigan Project Archives.

14. Carrigan, Ramona. "Letter to Bill." Personal Correspondence, April 11, 1944. Carrigan Project Archives.

15. Carrigan, Ramona. "Letter to Bill." Personal Correspondence, June 26, 1944. Carrigan Project Archives.

16. Carrigan, William M. "Letter to Ramona." Personal Correspondence, September 26, 1943. Carrigan Project Archives.

17. Carrigan, William M. "Letter to Ramona." Personal Correspondence, January 6, 1945. Carrigan Project Archives.

18. Carrigan, William M. "Letter to Ramona." Personal Correspondence, October 15, 1944. Carrigan Project Archives.

19. Ibid.

20. Carrigan, William M. "Letter to Ramona." Personal Correspondence, December 1943. Carrigan Project Archives.

21. Carrigan, Ramona. "Letter to Bill." Personal Correspondence, September 24, 1943. Carrigan Project Archives.

22. Carrigan, William M. "V-Mail to Ramona." Personal Correspondence, September 21, 1943. Carrigan Project Archives. Emphasis added.

23. Carrigan, Ramona. "V-Mail to Bill." Personal Correspondence, September 8, 1943. Carrigan Project Archives.

24. Carrigan, William M. "Letter to Ramona." Personal Correspondence, September 20, 1943. Carrigan Project Archives.

25. Ibid.

26. Carrigan, Ramona. "V-Mail to Bill: The First on This Date." Personal Correspondence, September 7, 1943. Carrigan Project Archives.

What Ramona did not know, but which history recorded, was that the accident had occurred due to excessive friction which caused a fire beneath one of the train's cars. An axle snapped, throwing the seventh car into the air. The eighth car slammed into a signal gantry, and the remaining six passenger cars derailed completely. Bodies littered the tracks. The dead numbered 79, with Catherine Saunders among them, and 117 wounded. It became known as the Frankford Junction wreck. *https:// en.wikipedia.org/wiki/1943_Frankford_ Junction_train_wreck*

27. Carrigan, Ramona. "V-Mail to Bill: The Second on This Date." Personal Correspondence, September 7, 1943. Carrigan Project Archives.

28. Ibid.

29. Carrigan, William M. "Letter to Ramona." Personal Correspondence, September 22, 1943. Carrigan Project Archives.

30. Ibid.

31. Carrigan, William M. "Letter to Ramona." Personal Correspondence, December 17, 1943. Carrigan Project Archives.

32. Carrigan, William M. "Letter to Ramona." Personal Correspondence, January 8, 1945. Carrigan Project Archives.

33. Carrigan, William M. "Letter to Ramona." Personal Correspondence,

July 19, 1943. Carrigan Project Archives.

34. Carrigan, William M. "Letter to Ramona." Personal Correspondence, July 19, 1943. Carrigan Project Archives.

"I can see now that we have been living only half a life," Bill wrote.

35. Carrigan, William M. "Letter to Ramona." Personal Correspondence, December 5, 1943. Carrigan Project Archives.

36. Carrigan, William M. "Letter to Ramona." Personal Correspondence, July 19, 1943. Carrigan Project Archives.

37. Carrigan, Ramona. "Letter to Bill." Personal Correspondence, August 2, 1943. Carrigan Project Archives.

38. Carrigan, Ramona. "Letter to Bill." Personal Correspondence, August 3, 1943. Carrigan Project Archives.

39. Carrigan, William M. "Letter to Ramona." Personal Correspondence, August 30, 1943. Carrigan Project Archives.

40. Ibid.

41. Carrigan, William M. "Letter to Ramona." Personal Correspondence, August 31, 1943. Carrigan Project Archives.

42. Carrigan, William M. "Letter to Ramona." Personal Correspondence, April 15, 1945. Carrigan Project Archives.

43. Carrigan, William M. "Letter to Ramona." Personal Correspondence, March 5, 1944. Carrigan Project Archives.

44. Duffy, Makena, and Ava Montes. Interview with Steve Critzer. Film, May 2022. Carrigan Project Archives.

45. Ibid.

46. Carrigan, William M. "Letter to Ramona." Personal Correspondence, March 24, 1945. Carrigan Project Archives.

47. Ibid.

Chapter Eleven: Bill's Ministry Reaches America

1. Carrigan, William M. "Letter to Ramona." Personal Correspondence, November 19, 1944. Carrigan Project Archives.

2. Ibid.

3. Carrigan, William M. "Letter to Ramona." Personal Correspondence, November 1, 1944. Carrigan Project Archives.

4. Carrigan, William M. "Speech Notes for a Talk at Mount de Sales Academy," September 23, 1994. Carrigan Project Archives.

Interestingly, in the novel, Crusoe mentions that he and his subordinate, Friday, had a relationship that mimicked both master and servant *and* father and son. It seems poignant that Bill would choose that story and those characters to describe his and Padre Pio's connection.

5. Carrigan, William M. "Letter to Ramona." Personal Correspondence, July 7, 1945. Carrigan Project Archives.

6. Carrigan, William M. "Letter to Ramona." Personal Correspondence, November 8, 1945. Carrigan Project Archives.

7. Carrigan, William M. "An Introduction to Padre Pio." EWTN, c 1996. *https://www. ewtn.com/catholicism/library/ introduction-to-padre-pio-5765.*

8. Abell, W. Shepherdson. "Eulogy - William M. Carrigan." PadrePio.net, November 30, 2000. *https://www. padrepio.net/eulogy.html.*

9. Furr, Charles E. Interview with William M. Carrigan. Cassette Tape, January 21, 1983. Carrigan Project Archives.

10. Ibid.

11. Ibid.

12. Ibid.

13. Ibid.

14. Montes, Ava. Interview with Sr. Philip Joseph Davis, O.P. E-mail Conversation, April 2022. Carrigan Project Archives.

15. Ibid.

16. Zimmerman, Mark. "Witness to a Saint." *The Catholic Standard*, April 29, 1999. Carrigan Project Archives.

17. Furr, Charles E. Interview with William M. Carrigan. Cassette Tape, January 21, 1983. Carrigan Project Archives.

18. Though not every impact can be detailed in this biography, no doubt remains that the messages Bill circulated affected others.

19. Furr, Charles E. Interview with William M. Carrigan. Cassette Tape, January 21, 1983. Carrigan Project Archives.

20. Ibid.

21. Ibid.

22. Bill kept this unknown young girl's letter for many years; it is retained in the Carrigan Project Archives.

23. Furr, Charles E. Interview with William M. Carrigan. Cassette Tape, January 21, 1983. Carrigan Project Archives.

24. Montes, Ava. Interview with Chuck Furr. Phone Call, March 27, 2023. Carrigan Project Archives.

25. Ibid.

26. Chuck Furr related further that the burns were so significant that the funeral home placed white gloves on her hands so that her family did not see extensive damage while at the funeral service.

27. Furr, Charles E. Interview with William M. Carrigan. Cassette Tape, January 21, 1983. Carrigan Project Archives.

28. Ibid.

29. Furr, Charles E. Interview with William M. Carrigan. Audio Recording, November 10, 1983. Carrigan Project Archives.

30. Father Superior. "Letter to William M. Carrigan from the Father Superior of the Conv. Dei Min. Cappuccini." Personal Correspondence, October 10, 1949. Carrigan Project Archives.

31. Carrigan, William M. "Speech to Mount de Sales Academy." Speech, Mount de Sales Academy, Catonsville, Maryland, November 20, 1986.

32. Ibid

33. Ibid.

34. Ibid.

35. Ibid.

36. Montes, Ava. Interview with Sr. Philip Joseph Davis, O.P. E-mail Conversation, April 2022. Carrigan Project Archives.

37. Carrigan, William M. "Speech to Mount de Sales Academy." Speech, Mount de Sales Academy, Catonsville, Maryland, November 20, 1986.

38. Ibid.

39. Ibid.

40. Ibid.

41. Ibid.

42. Ibid.

43. Ibid.

44. Ibid.

45. Ibid.

46. Ibid.

47. Ibid.

48. Ibid.

Chapter Twelve:
An Important Assortment of Charities

1. "William Carrigan Donates Property to CCLC." Unknown, c. 1980s. Carrigan Project Archives.

2. Duffy, Makena. Interview with Chuck Furr. Film, November 2022. Carrigan Project Archive.

3. Chuck Furr stated this in passing; the humorous detail provided a striking example of Bill's personal frugality.

4. Duffy, Makena, and Ava Montes. Interview with Fr. Michael Sliney, L.C. Film, May 2022. Carrigan Project Archives.

5. Duffy, Makena, and Ava Montes. Interview with the Cohagans, May 2022. Carrigan Project Archives.

6. Abell, W. Shepherdson. "Eulogy - William M. Carrigan." PadrePio.net, November 30, 2000. https://www.padrepio.net/eulogy.html.

7. Ibid.

8. Montes, Ava. Interview with Tom Cunningham. Zoom Web Conference, April 19, 2022. Carrigan Project Archives.

9. Ibid.

10. Ibid.

11. Ibid.

12. Carrigan, William M. "Address to Senior Graduating Class." Speech, Mount de Sales Academy, Catonsville, Maryland, May 18, 1990.

13. Ibid.

14. Montes, Ava. Interview with Victoria Sheffield. Phone Call, September 19, 2020. Carrigan Project Archives.

15. "William Carrigan: St. Paul Person of the Year." Unknown, c 1992. Carrigan Project Archives.

16. Montes, Ava. Interview with Victoria Sheffield. Phone Call, September 19, 2020. Carrigan Project Archives.

17. Ibid.

18. Ibid.

19. International Eye Foundation. "Our History," n.d. https://www.iefusa.org/our_history.

20. Ibid.

21. Montes, Ava. Interview with Victoria Sheffield. Phone Call, September 19, 2020. Carrigan Project Archives.

22. Duffy, Makena, and Ava Montes. Interview with Fr. Michael Sliney, L.C. Film, May 2022. Carrigan Project Archives.

23. Ibid.

24. Groff, Chalmers F. "Land Deed: 1939023924." Office of Tax and Revenue Recorder of Deeds, August 14, 1939. Office of Tax and Revenue Archives. *https://countyfusion4.kofiletech.us/countyweb/disclaimer.do.*

25. Montes, Ava. Interview with Tom Cunningham. Zoom Web Conference, April 19, 2022. Carrigan Project Archives.

26. Holy Family Catholic Church. "History of Holy Family Church," n.d. *https://holyfamilyparishmd.org/history-of-place.*

27. Ibid.

28. Ibid.

29. Andriote, John-Manuel. "'Magi' Group Will Seek to Rejuvenate Sacred Arts." *The Register,* January 5, 1986. Carrigan Project Archives.

30. Carrigan, William M. "The William M. and Ramona N. Carrigan Magi Endowment Fund: For the Support of the Liturgical Arts." Catholic University of America, December 16, 1980. Carrigan Project Archives.

31. Ibid.

32. Ibid.

33. Ibid.

34. Ibid.

35. CARA. "About CARA," n.d. *https://cara.georgetown.edu/about-us.*

36. Ibid.

37. *North County Catholic.* "Study to Probe Marian Devotion." October 12, 1977. NYS Historic Newspapers.

38. Ibid.

39. Montes, Ava. Interview with Gerry Early. E-mail Conversation, April 13, 2023. Carrigan Project Archives.

40. "William Carrigan: St. Paul Person of the Year." Unknown, c 1992. Carrigan Project Archives.

41. Abell, W. Shepherdson. "Eulogy - William M. Carrigan." PadrePio.net, November 30, 2000. *https://www.padrepio.net/eulogy.html.*

42. Furr, Charles E. Interview with William M. Carrigan. Cassette Tape, January 21, 1983. Carrigan Project Archives.

43. Duffy, Makena, and Ava Montes. Interview with Sr. Joan Paula Arruda. Film, July 2021. Carrigan Project Archives.

44. Ibid.

45. "William Carrigan: St. Paul Person of the Year." Unknown, c 1992. Carrigan Project Archives.

46. Father Superior. "Letter to William M. Carrigan." Personal Correspondence; Convento del Min Cappuccini, March 29, 1953. Carrigan Project Archives.

47. Eggert, Mark. "E-Mail Conversation with Mark Eggert, Chuck Furr, and Ava Montes," July 20, 2021.

48. Eggert, Mark W. Business Correspondence. "Legal Letter to Dr. Richard Belleville." Business Correspondence, December 31, 2008. Carrigan Project Archives.

49. Cizik, Fr. Ladis J. Business Correspondence. "Letter to Mark W. Eggert." Business Correspondence, July 16, 2001. Carrigan Project Archives.

50. Chuck Furr related this while speaking with the author.

51. Roman Catholic Church in the State of Hawaii: Diocese of Honolulu. "Serra Club of Honolulu," n.d. *https://www.catholichawaii.org/catholic-living/associations/serra-club-of-honolulu/#:~:text=Founded%20in%201970%2C%20the%20Serra,diaconate%2C%20and%20vowed%20religious%20life*.

52. Montes, Ava. Interview with Gerry Early. E-mail Conversation,

April 13, 2023. Carrigan Project Archives.

53. Duffy, Makena, and Ava Montes. Interview with John Ciskanik. Film, May 2022. Carrigan Project Archives.

Chapter Thirteen:
How Bill Impacted
Rappahannock County,
Virginia

1. Staff Writer. "Town of Washington Rolls out the Welcome Mat for Saturday's Garden Tour." *Rappahannock News*, April 27, 2017. *https://www.rappnews.com/features/town-of-washington-rolls-out-the-welcome-mat-for-saturday-s-garden-tour/article_1e75449b-b52a-53a8-8b30-f79e82e55e11.html*.

2. Audette, Don. "1918 – 1919: Franklin Clyde Baggarly, Bureau of Investigation Agent." *Rappahannock News*, January 5, 2017. *https://www.rappnews.com/features/history/1918-1919-franklin-clyde-baggarly-bureau-of-investigation-agent/article_44f8ca2a-813a-5e23-8586-25d1c0e10bf4.html*.

3. Staff Writer. "Town of Washington Rolls out the Welcome Mat for Saturday's Garden Tour."

Rappahannock News, April 27, 2017. *https://www.rappnews.com/features/ town-of-washington-rolls-out-the-welcome-mat-for-saturday-s-garden-tour/ article_1e75449b-b52a-53a8-8b30-f79e82e55e11.html.*

4. Clatterbuck, Jan. "Down Memory Lane for Jan. 24." Rappahannock News, January 23, 2019. *https:// www.rappnews.com/features/ downmemorylane/down-memory-lane-for-jan-24/article_caa27df7-43d2-5c72-b861-4c1bbc8239bb.html.*

5. Clatterbuck, Jan. "Down Memory Lane for Jan. 24." Rappahannock News, January 23, 2019. *https:// www.rappnews.com/features/ downmemorylane/down-memory-lane-for-jan-24/article_caa27df7-43d2-5c72-b861-4c1bbc8239bb.html.*

6. Clatterbuck, Jan. "Down Memory Lane for Oct. 6." Rappahannock News, October 6, 2016. *https:// www.rappnews.com/features/ downmemorylane/down-memory-lane-for-oct-6/article_0c92268c-8e82-5196-aef7-b3cb44ac53b5.html.*

7. Clatterbuck, Jan. "Down Memory Lane for Oct. 6." Rappahannock News, October 6, 2016. *https:// www.rappnews.com/features/ downmemorylane/down-memory-lane-for-oct-6/article_0c92268c-8e82-5196-aef7-b3cb44ac53b5.html.*

8. Duffy, Makena, and Ava Montes. Interview with Steve Critzer. Film, May 2022. Carrigan Project Archives.

9. Ibid.

10. Clatterbuck, Jan. "Down Memory Lane for Jan. 24." Rappahannock News, January 23, 2019. *https://www.rappnews.com/ features/downmemorylane/down-memory-lane-for-jan-24/article_caa27df7-43d2-5c72-b861-4c1bbc8239bb.html.*

11. Duffy, Makena, and Ava Montes. Interview with Steve Critzer. Film, May 2022. Carrigan Project Archives.

12. McCaslin, John. "The Free State of Rappahannock." Rappahannock News, June 30, 2017. *https://www. rappnews.com/opinion/columnists/ the-free-state-of-rappahannock/ article_8e813ae9-9737-5b01-9fe7-73f157feb76c.html.*

13. Duffy, Makena, and Ava Montes. Interview with the Cohagans, May 2022. Carrigan Project Archives.

14. McCaslin, John. "The Free State of Rappahannock." Rappahannock News, June 30, 2017. *https://www. rappnews.com/opinion/columnists/ the-free-state-of-rappahannock/ article_8e813ae9-9737-5b01-9fe7-73f157feb76c.html.*

15. Duffy, Makena, and Ava Montes. Interview with the Cohagans, May 2022. Carrigan Project Archives.

16. Ibid.

17. Ibid.

18. Ibid.

19. Carrigan, William M. "Speech Notes for Farewell Talk," July 4, 1991. Carrigan Project Archives.

20. Willis, J. Stewart. Legal Letter. "Use of Avon Hall Grounds for Independence Day Celebration in the Town of Washington." Legal Letter, July 30, 1997. Carrigan Project Archives.

21. Duffy, Makena, and Ava Montes. Interview with the Cohagans, May 2022. Carrigan Project Archives.

22. Duffy, Makena, and Ava Montes. Interview with Steve Critzer. Film, May 2022. Carrigan Project Archives.

23. Lynn, Pamela. "A Brief History of St. Peter's Catholic Church," c. 1980s-1990s. St. Peter's Catholic Church Records. Kindly provided by Kathryn Reinboldt.

24. Hutchinson, Daphne. "Catholic Masses Begin." *Rappahannock News*, August 23, 1979. St. Peter's Catholic Church Records.

25. Montes, Ava. Interview with Richard Viguerie. Phone Call, Fall 2022. Carrigan Project Archives.

26. Ibid.

27. Ibid.

28. Lynn, Pamela. "A Brief History of St. Peter's Catholic Church," c. 1980s-1990s. St. Peter's Catholic Church Records. Kindly provided by Kathryn Reinboldt.

29. Ibid.

30. Castillon, Fr. Maurice du. Business Correspondence. "Letter to Most Reverend Thomas J. Welsh, Bishop of Arlington." Business Correspondence, September 17, 1981. Carrigan Project Archives.

31. "St. Peter's Catholic Church: First Parish Meeting Minutes," September 6, 1981. St. Peter's Catholic Church Records.

32. Ibid.

33. Ibid.

34. Duffy, Makena, and Ava Montes. Interview with Steve Critzer. Film, May 2022. Carrigan Project Archives.

35. Clatterbuck, Jan. "Down Memory Lane for Dec. 18." Rappahannock News, December 18, 2014. *https://www.rappnews. com/features/downmemorylane/*

down-memory-lane-for-dec-18/
article_7b120da0-f143-5c07-97e9-
f99d02d1282c.html.

36. "William Carrigan Donates Property to CCLC." Unknown, c. 1980s. Carrigan Project Archives.

37. Staff Writer. "Citizens of the Year, 1978-2014." Rappahannock News, November 25, 2015. *https://www.rappnews.com/features/citizens-of-the-year-1978-2014/*article_ff2a1958-bb7d-5b15-aa68-6f1cfb66e448.html.

38. Clatterbuck, Jan. "Down Memory Lane for Dec. 7." Rappahannock News, December 7, 2017. *https://www.rappnews.com/features/downmemorylane/down-memory-lane-for-dec-7/article_ea89574d-34f8-5cc1-8c11-fbb01890f3e6.html.*

39. Ibid.

Chapter Fourteen:
Saving Christendom College and Resurrecting Mount de Sales Academy

1. Carrigan, William M. "Talk for Roosevelt High School Assembly." Speech, Roosevelt High School, Washington, D.C., December 7, 1945.

2. Ibid.

3. Abell, W. Shepherdson. "Eulogy - William M. Carrigan." PadrePio.net, November 30, 2000. *https://www.padrepio.net/eulogy.html.*

4. Ibid.

5. Gossin, Laura S. *One Man Perched on a Rock: A Biography of Dr. Warren H. Carroll.* First. Front Royal, Virginia: Christendom Press, 2018. 217.

6. Duffy, Makena, and Ava Montes. Interview with Dr. Timothy O'Donnell. Film, May 2022. Carrigan Project Archives.

7. 5. Gossin, Laura S. *One Man Perched on a Rock: A Biography of Dr. Warren H. Carroll.* First. Front Royal, Virginia: Christendom Press, 2018. Page 217.

8. Gossin 218.

9. Ibid.

10. Ibid.

11. McFadden, Jr., Thomas L. *Restoring All Things in Christ: A History of the Founding of Christendom College.* 35th Anniversary Commemorative Book. Christendom College, 2013. 11. *https://issuu.com/christendomcollege/docs/35th.*

12. Duffy, Makena, and Ava Montes. Interview with Dr. Timothy

O'Donnell. Film, May 2022. Carrigan Project Archives.

13. Ibid.

14. Ibid.

15. Ibid.

16. Gossin, Laura S. *One Man Perched on a Rock: A Biography of Dr. Warren H. Carroll*. First. Front Royal, Virginia: Christendom Press, 2018. Page 218-219.

17. Gossin 219.

18. Duffy, Makena, and Ava Montes. Interview with John Ciskanik. Film, May 2022. Carrigan Project Archives.

19. Ibid.

20. Ibid.

21. Ibid.

22. Ibid.

23. Gossin, Laura S. *One Man Perched on a Rock: A Biography of Dr. Warren H. Carroll*. First. Front Royal, Virginia: Christendom Press, 2018. Page 219.

24. Duffy, Makena, and Ava Montes. Interview with the Cohagans, May 2022. Carrigan Project Archives.

25. Montes, Ava. Interview with Sr. Philip Joseph Davis, O.P. E-mail Conversation, April 2022. Carrigan Project Archives.

26. Ibid.

27. Ibid.

28. Ibid.

29. Ibid.

30. Ibid.

31. Ibid.

32. Ibid.

33. Ibid.

34. Ibid.

35. Ibid.

36. Duffy, Makena, and Ava Montes. Interview with the Cohagans, May 2022. Carrigan Project Archives.

37. Ibid.

38. Ibid.

39. Ibid.

40. The art center was finally completed in 2021 and now serves as a beautiful place for artists to learn and practice their various mediums.

41. Duffy, Makena, and Ava Montes. Interview with the Cohagans, May 2022. Carrigan Project Archives.

42. Ibid.

43. Montes, Ava. Interview with Sr. Philip Joseph Davis, O.P. E-mail Conversation, April 2022. Carrigan Project Archives.

44. Ibid.

45. Ibid.

46. Ibid.

47. Duffy, Makena, and Ava Montes. Interview with the Cohagans, May 2022. Carrigan Project Archives.

48. Ibid.

49. Ibid.

50. Montes, Ava. Interview with Sr. Philip Joseph Davis, O.P. E-mail Conversation, April 2022. Carrigan Project Archives.

51. Ibid.

52. Ibid.

53. Ibid.

54. Ibid.

55. Ibid.

56. Carrigan, William M. "Address to Senior Graduating Class." Speech, Mount de Sales Academy, Catonsville, Maryland, May 18, 1990.

Chapter Fifteen:
The Final Years

1. Hickey, James Cardinal. Professional Correspondence. "Letter to His Excellency, Most Reverend Cardinal James Harvey, Archpriest of the Papal Basilica of St. Paul Outside-the-Walls." Professional Correspondence, April 13, 1999. Carrigan Project Archives.

2. Carrigan, William M. "Speech to Mount de Sales Academy." Speech, Mount de Sales Academy, Catonsville, Maryland, November 20, 1986.

3. Duffy, Makena, and Ava Montes. Interview with Fr. Michael Sliney, L.C. Film, May 2022. Carrigan Project Archives.

4. Carrigan, William M. "Letter to Ramona." Personal Correspondence, April 25, 1945. Carrigan Project Archives.

5. Ibid.

6. *The Washington Post*. "Henry Kaiser, 77, D.C. Labor Lawyer, Dies: Obituaries - Ramona Carrigan." May 11, 1989. The Washington Post Archive. *https:// www.washingtonpost.com/archive/ local/1989/05/12/henry-kaiser-77-dc-labor-lawyer-dies/6e997cef-68f0-4040-a096-47f77200bf15/.*

7. Carrigan, William M. "Personal Note: Six Days after Ramona's Death," May 15, 1989. Carrigan Project Archives.

"The spiritual grace when it touches us lifts us up—even in great tragedy and suffering, spiritual grace is often present, and tends to inspire action and...joy on a much higher plane. than we commonly understand," Bill continued in his private note.

Duffy, Makena, and Ava Montes. Interview with the Cohagans, May 2022. Carrigan Project Archives.

8. As she aged, Ramona's ability to drive her car decreased. For her own safety, as well as the safety of others, Bill had to take away her keys. This infuriated her. While Chuck chauffeured her one day, she expressed her anger: "Your uncle makes me so mad." She paused for a moment, then blurted out, "Your uncle makes me so damn mad! There, I said it!" This Chuck recalled with a chuckle.

9. Duffy, Makena, and Ava Montes. Interview with the Cohagans, May 2022. Carrigan Project Archives.

10. Montes, Ava. Interview with Sr. Philip Joseph Davis, O.P. E-mail Conversation, April 2022. Carrigan Project Archives.

11. Albacete, Msgr. Lorenzo. "The Ramona Carrigan Science Center Closing Remarks." Speech, Mount de Sales Academy, Catonsville, Maryland, September 29, 1989.

12. Carrigan, William M. "Address to Senior Graduating Class." Speech, Mount de Sales Academy, Catonsville, Maryland, May 18, 1990.

13. Ibid.

14. Duffy, Makena, and Ava Montes. Interview with Fr. Michael Sliney, L.C. Film, May 2022. Carrigan Project Archives.

15. This note, made most likely in the 1990s, was found on the envelope of a letter from Ramona to Bill, November 11, 1943. He wrote it after Ramona passed away.

16. Duffy, Makena, and Ava Montes. Interview with Sr. Joan Paula Arruda. Film, July 2021. Carrigan Project Archives.

17. Duffy, Makena, and Ava Montes. Interview with Fr. Michael Sliney, L.C. Film, May 2022. Carrigan Project Archives.

18. Duffy, Makena, and Ava Montes. Interview with Sr. Joan Paula Arruda. Film, July 2021. Carrigan Project Archives.

19. Ibid.

20. Ibid.

21. Duffy, Makena, and Ava Montes. Interview with Dr. Timothy

O'Donnell. Film, May 2022. Carrigan Project Archives.

22. Duffy, Makena, and Ava Montes. Interview with W. Shepherdson Abell. Film, May 2022. Carrigan Project Archives.

23. Duffy, Makena, and Ava Montes. Interview with Fr. Michael Sliney. Film, May 2022. Carrigan Project Archives.

24. Ibid.

25. "Fifty Years Ago the Group Leader Was a Military Man and Met Padre Pio." Unknown, c. 1980s. Carrigan Project Archives.

26. Albacete, Msgr. Lorenzo. "A Trip to Meet Padre Pio." Unknown, c. 1980s. Carrigan Project Archives.

27. Duffy, Makena, and Ava Montes. Interview with Edward Geoff Sella. Audio Recording, May 2022. Carrigan Project Archives.

28. Ibid.

29. Ibid.

30. Ibid.

31. Abell, W. Shepherdson. "Eulogy - William M. Carrigan." PadrePio.net, November 30, 2000. *https://www.padrepio.net/eulogy.html.*

32. Ibid.

33. Duffy, Makena, and Ava Montes. Interview with Steve Critzer. Film, May 2022. Carrigan Project Archives.

34. Ibid.

35. This quotation was found on the back of Bill's Avon Hall Guest List, October 6 or 7, 1996. It appears to be Bill's notes.

36. Duffy, Makena, and Ava Montes. Interview with Steve Critzer. Film, May 2022. Carrigan Project Archives.

37. Duffy, Makena, and Ava Montes. Interview with Edward Geoff Sella. Audio Recording, May 2022. Carrigan Project Archives.

38. Ibid.

39. This information came from Bill's medical paperwork, collected upon medical evaluation and preserved by Chuck Furr.

40. Duffy, Makena, and Ava Montes. Interview with Edward Geoff Sella. Audio Recording, May 2022. Carrigan Project Archives.

41. Ibid.

42. Montes, Ava. Interview with Tom Cunningham. Zoom Web Conference, April 19, 2022. Carrigan Project Archives.

43. Ibid.

44. Ibid.

45. This information came from Bill's medical paperwork, collected upon medical evaluation and preserved by Chuck Furr.

46. Duffy, Makena, and Ava Montes. Interview with Steve Critzer. Film, May 2022. Carrigan Project Archives.

47. Duffy, Makena, and Ava Montes. Interview with Edward Geoff Sella. Audio Recording, May 2022. Carrigan Project Archives.

48. Ibid.

49. Duffy, Makena, and Ava Montes. Interview with Steve Critzer. Film, May 2022. Carrigan Project Archives.

50. Duffy, Makena, and Ava Montes. Interview with John Ciskanik. Film, May 2022. Carrigan Project Archives.

51. Montes, Ava. Interview with Chuck Furr. Phone Call, July 7, 2024. Carrigan Project Archives.

52. Duffy, Makena. Interview with Janet Johnson. Film, September 2021. Carrigan Project Archives.

53. Chuck Furr told this story in late 2020 during a conversation with the author.

54. Duffy, Makena. Interview with Janet Johnson. Film, September 2021. Carrigan Project Archives.

55. Montes, Ava. Interview with Chuck Furr. Phone Call, July 7, 2024. Carrigan Project Archives.

56. Furr, Charles E. "Family Letter: Uncle Bill Carrigan's Moment of Acceptance," June 1997. Carrigan Project Archives.

57. Ibid.

58. Duffy, Makena. Interview with Chuck Furr. Film, November 2022. Carrigan Project Archives.

59. Duffy, Makena. Interview with Janet Johnson. Film, September 2021. Carrigan Project Archives.

60. Duffy, Makena. Interview with Chuck Furr. Film, June 2020. Carrigan Project Archives.

61. Duffy, Makena, and Ava Montes. Interview with W. Shepherdson Abell. Film, May 2022. Carrigan Project Archives.

62. Duffy, Makena, and Ava Montes. Interview with Fr. Michael Sliney, L.C. Film, May 2022. Carrigan Project Archives.

63. Ibid.

64. Ibid.

65. Hickey, James Cardinal. Professional Correspondence. "Letter to His Excellency, Most Revered Cardinal James Harvey, Archpriest of the Papal Basilica of St. Paul Outside-the-Walls." Professional Correspondence, April 13, 1999. Carrigan Project Archives.

66. Ibid.

67. Montes, Ava. Interview with Sr. Philip Joseph Davis, O.P. E-mail Conversation, April 2022. Carrigan Project Archives.

68. Ibid.

69. Duffy, Makena. Interview with Chuck Furr. Film, November 2022. Carrigan Project Archives.

70. Ibid.

71. Chuck mentioned this to the author during a personal conversation.

72. Montes, Ava. Interview with Sr. Philip Joseph Davis, O.P. E-mail Conversation, April 2022. Carrigan Project Archives.

73. The Washington Post. "Obituaries: William M. Carrigan, Real Estate Investor," November 22, 2000. *https://www.washingtonpost. com/archive/local/2000/11/23/ obituaries/980fb786-231d-46c7-8d86-15ef1d4e2a3f/.*

74. Montes, Ava. Interview with Tom Cunningham. Zoom Web Conference, April 19, 2022. Carrigan Project Archives.

75. This document, possibly the exact papers Chuck Furr used at Bill's funeral, include the prayers of the faithful. Chuck Furr archived these papers in 2000.

76. Ibid.

77. Connolly, Elizabth. "Mr. William Carrigan: Our Hero–A Man Who Believed in Miracles." Mount de Sales Academy, Catonsville, Maryland, November 30, 2000.

78. Abell, W. Shepherdson. "Eulogy - William M. Carrigan." PadrePio.net, November 30, 2000. *https://www. padrepio.net/eulogy.html.*

79. Montes, Ava. Interview with Sr. Philip Joseph Davis, O.P. E-mail Conversation, April 2022. Carrigan Project Archives.

80. Duffy, Makena. Interview with Chuck Furr. Film, June 2020. Carrigan Project Archives.

81. Abell, W. Shepherdson. "Eulogy - William M. Carrigan." PadrePio.net, November 30, 2000. *https://www. padrepio.net/eulogy.html.*

82. Carrigan, William M. "Talk for Roosevelt High School Assembly."

Speech, Roosevelt High School,
Washington, D.C., December 7,
1945.

83. Ibid.

Appendix I

1. Carrigan, William M. "Letter to
Ramona." Personal Correspondence,
November 13, 1943. Carrigan
Project Archives.

2. Carrigan, William M. "Letter to
Ramona." Personal Correspondence,
September 19, 1943. Carrigan Project
Archives.

3. Ibid.

4. Carrigan, William M. "Letter to
Ramona." Personal Correspondence,
March 10, 1944. Carrigan Project
Archives.